OUT OF PLACE

Social Exclusion and Mennonite Migrants in Canada

The flow of migrants from south to north and east to west carries with it growing concerns about the economic integration, political incorporation, and social inclusion of newcomers and their children. But what happens when a group of people deliberately excludes itself from mainstream society? How can social policies, human services, and communities best understand and respond to them?

In *Out of Place*, Luann Good Gingrich explores social inclusion and exclusion in relation to the approximately 60,000 Low German–speaking Mennonites who have migrated from traditionally self-sufficient and agrarian colonies in Latin America to rural areas of Canada. By examining the free-market principles that organize the human services industry the author exposes the inherent conflict that arises when this "market logic" is imposed on a group that does not embrace these ideals. The author's innovative approach to social policy and human services, which emphasizes the relationship between dominant and subordinate cultures, encourages us to find new ways to authentically engage with difference and bridge the gaps that divide us.

LUANN GOOD GINGRICH is an associate professor in the School of Social Work at York University.

LUANN GOOD GINGRICH

Out of Place

Social Exclusion and Mennonite Migrants in Canada

UNIVERSITY OF TORONTO PRESS
Toronto   Buffalo   London

© University of Toronto Press 2016
Toronto Buffalo London
www.utppublishing.com

ISBN 978-1-4875-0042-9 (cloth)   ISBN 978-1-4875-2029-8 (paper)

Library and Archives Canada Cataloguing in Publication

Good Gingrich, Luann, 1960–, author
Out of place : social exclusion and Mennonite migrants in Canada / Luann Good
Gingrich.

Includes bibliographical references and index.
ISBN 978-1-4875-0042-9 (cloth).—ISBN 978-1-4875-2029-8 (paper)

1. Mennonites—Canada—Social conditions.   2. Mennonites—Canada—Economic
conditions.   3. Mennonites—Services for—Canada.   4. Mennonites—Latin
America.   5. Immigrants—Canada—Social conditions.   6. Immigrants—
Canada—Economic conditions.   7. Social isolation—Canada.   8. Canada—Social
policy.   9. Canada—Rural conditions.   I. Title.

BX8118.5.G65 2016   305.6'89771   C2016-902512-8

This book has been published with the help of a grant from the Federation for the
Humanities and Social Sciences, through the Awards to Scholarly Publications Program,
using funds provided by the Social Sciences and Humanities Research Council of Canada.

University of Toronto Press acknowledges the financial assistance to its publishing
program of the Canada Council for the Arts and the Ontario Arts Council, an agency of
the Government of Ontario.

Canada Council   Conseil des Arts
for the Arts   du Canada

ONTARIO ARTS COUNCIL
CONSEIL DES ARTS DE L'ONTARIO
an Ontario government agency
un organisme du gouvernement de l'Ontario

Funded by the   Financé par le
Government   gouvernement
of Canada   du Canada

Canadä

Contents

Preface

I begin with a story of an inherited life interrupted – a cherished heritage that has been uprooted, taken out of place and on the move.

MARGARETHA: Where do you like it better?

SUSANA: We liked it in Mexico better.

MARGARETHA: Was there not enough work there, or why did you come here [Canada]?

SUSANA: We couldn't make a living there anymore. In Mexico, there was enough work, but it seemed like it was so hard. That's why we left.[1]

MARGARETHA: And in Bolivia there wasn't enough work?

SUSANA: No, there it was like that too. It seemed like the work was there, but you weren't supposed to work for income,[2] and that's why we left. We wanted a better living.

MARGARETHA: What about your children, how did they feel that they first had to move from Bolivia to Mexico and then from Mexico to here?

SUSANA: Oh, they were happy to go to Mexico, and they had settled there. And to come here, they were happy too, but not so much as from Bolivia to Mexico.

MARGARETHA: I wonder how come?

SUSANA: Then they had never moved. They didn't know what it was. Then they were all excited.

MARGARETHA: Now they know it isn't all fun?

SUSANA: It isn't all fun, so they're not so excited.

MARGARETHA: Had they made a lot of friends in Mexico?

SUSANA: Oh, they have good friends in Mexico.

MARGARETHA: Oh, that must have been hard, back and forth.

SUSANA: Yes, that was hard for them.

Susana and Margaretha met on a warm, humid day in August. At the time of the interview, Susana was a thirty-eight-year-old married woman living in rural Ontario. She had given birth to ten children; two had died.

> SUSANA: We have eight children and buried two. Altogether there are ten. The oldest is eighteen and the youngest is five, and the others are in between.
> MARGARETHA: Why did you have to bury the two?
> SUSANA: The one got sick and died and the other was dead [stillborn].
> MARGARETHA: How old was the first that died?
> SUSANA: A year and two and a half months.
> MARGARETHA: That was in …
> SUSANA: … a boy …
> MARGARETHA: … Mexico?
> SUSANA: Bolivia.
> MARGARETHA: Oh, in Bolivia. That must have been hard.
> SUSANA: Oh yeah, it was very hard.

Margaretha, the interviewer, had recently graduated from high school and was living and working in her parents' home, helping her mother tend the household and eight younger siblings. Although Margaretha was then a single woman almost twenty years younger and with many more years of formal education than Susana, they were both Old Colony women who shared the experience of emigration from a Mennonite colony in Latin America. Margaretha moved from Mexico to Canada with her parents and siblings when she was five years old. Even though her parents wished to return to the colony, they settled in Canada because the family could not afford the mounting medical bills required to treat her father's ailing health in Mexico. A few weeks prior to the interview, Margaretha had accepted an offer of admission into a highly competitive dental hygiene program at a local community college and was preparing to move into her own apartment in a nearby city. This transition would mark a second emigration of sorts for Margaretha, as to leave her parent's home before she was married and to enter higher education was to go against the cultural and religious norms of her people.

Susana was still a relative newcomer, as she and her family had then lived in Canada for only a few years and she was still not *Tus*, or "home," in Canada. In *Plautdietsch*, or Low German, the language of Mennonite colonists, *Tus* or "home" is more pragmatic than sentimental, as to be "at home" is to have "papers" documenting legal residency in the place one lives. Despite her intention to settle in Canada, Susana's ties to the colony and old way of life were quite evident. She wore a simple traditional Mennonite dress, and her black head covering (*Düak*) fastened over her long uncut hair indicated that she was a married (and subordinate) woman. Yet suggesting some measure of distance from her heritage, Susana also wore a plain gold wedding band, which contradicts traditional Mennonite practice.

Initially, Susana was hesitant to do the interview because she did not want to be discussed in the Mennonite community. She was especially fearful that her brother-in-law might find out that she had participated in the study. She explained to Margaretha that her brother-in-law was not a nice person. He believed that her husband (his brother) should maintain tighter control over Susana. She noted that even though her husband gave his approval for her to do the interview, her brother-in-law would never allow his own wife to participate in this or any other research study.

At Susana's request, the interview was conducted in Margaretha's truck parked in the driveway of Susana's rural home. Despite her initial misgivings, she talked freely with Margaretha. She agreed to the interview being audio recorded, yet after about one hour of conversation, she figured that she had said enough for us on record. However, she sat and talked to Margaretha for another hour or more.

As is typical of *Dietsche*[3] women, Susana was a woman of few words, resulting in a somewhat mechanical style of conversation. She seemed uncomfortable talking about herself, as if this was an indulgence for which she would later be reprimanded. Nonetheless, she was careful to respond to each question, sometimes appearing to provide the answers she thought would meet the interviewer's approval. The interview was conducted in Plautdietsch, since Susana's English-language skills were quite limited. Margaretha then simultaneously translated and transcribed the dialogue, adding her own analytical notes and observations. Excerpts of the transcription are reconstructed here to provide a glimpse into Susana's life.

To the reader

There are multiple ways to regard Susana's migration story. How you, the reader, take up Susana's narrative matters. The vantage point you and I adopt makes all the difference in how we evaluate and judge the circumstances of her life. My point of view has everything to do with who I know myself to be – or wish to be – in relation to the person or group that is in my line of vision. In many ways, this is the gist of the entire book – how we encounter and relate to *difference*.

So I invite you to move alongside Susana, even if this may not be your inclination: to resist assuming a place far away or above or beneath, but to accompany her for a time. I also invite you to move alongside the social workers, teachers, employment counsellors, truancy officers, nurses, doctors, and other human service professionals who work to make a positive difference for Mennonite migrants in Canada. To feel the world from disparate social positions and identities and to turn towards the Other without efforts to control or change or even to give – to turn alongside in "interhuman relationship" (Levinas, 2006) – is to interrupt the forces of social exclusion that divide us between and within.

Susana's story

Susana was born in a Mennonite village in the Mexican state of Chihuahua. When she was a few months old, her family moved to a colony in Bolivia, where she grew up and was married at the age of nineteen. As for generations past, hers is a story of migration. But Susana's life has taken a different turn, as the Mennonite migratory heritage was always only within or between the religious colonies of her people.

MARGARETHA: When did you move from Bolivia to Mexico?
SUSANA: That was on September 29, 1999.
MARGARETHA: And when was the first time you came to Canada?
SUSANA: It was on December 22 in 2005.
MARGARETHA: 2005. Are you going back and forth from here or are you staying here?
SUSANA: No, we want to stay here.
MARGARETHA: Have you ever driven back and forth?
SUSANA: No, not myself. But my husband has done it several times, just for a month that he was there.
MARGARETHA: Does he go back to Bolivia or where does he go?
SUSANA: No, back to Mexico.
MARGARETHA: Do you still have family in Mexico?
SUSANA: No, our children are all here. I don't have anything there. Just cousins and uncles and aunts.

MARGARETHA: Do you have land there?

SUSANA: No, in Mexico, no. We have never had land there. We always lived in rented [houses]. In Bolivia, we had a farm. We just did milking. We had some cows, we had some pigs, and horses. I had to do the milking morning and evening and further work with the children.

MARGARETHA: There, where you lived in Bolivia and Mexico, did they have electricity there yet?

SUSANA: In Bolivia no, but in Mexico yes.

MARGARETHA: Then you still had to wash [do laundry] with your hands and everything?

SUSANA: Uh-hmm, with the hands in Bolivia, yes. It was a lot of work, and the children were all small. It was very busy.

To leave behind an impoverished and traditional colony life would seem the obvious choice to get ahead. Yet the losses associated with doing so are significant and difficult to fully appreciate from the outside.

SUSANA: I got my land from home [from her parents]. And that we always owned as long as we were there [in Bolivia]. And when we wanted to leave, then my parents took it back.

MARGARETHA: They took it back?

SUSANA: Yeah, then they took it back. They didn't want it sold to someone else. Then they just paid for it.

MARGARETHA: Do you still have a lot of family in Bolivia?

SUSANA: Oh, yes. I have my parents and relatives there. All except two sisters. Two sisters are in Paraguay and the others are all in Bolivia.

MARGARETHA: How did they feel when you moved here?

SUSANA: Oh, they were disappointed that we moved away from there, but you can't stay when you don't have anything to eat.

MARGARETHA: Do you sometimes talk with your family in Bolivia and Mexico?

SUSANA: No, not now.

MARGARETHA: Do you ever send money there to your relatives?

SUSANA: No, nothing. We would like to sometimes but the money doesn't stretch that far yet.

Transgressing the boundaries of the colony is not only costly in terms of relationships with family and friends; it is expensive in dollars and cents. As a result, emigration from the colonies in Latin America is not an option for families who lack the necessary material resources. Furthermore, most who migrate to Canada have a claim to Canadian citizenship.[4]

> MARGARETHA: Is anyone in your family a Canadian citizen?
> SUSANA: No not yet, but we should hear something any day. But not yet.
> MARGARETHA: How could you come here then?
> SUSANA: We did with a passport. We all have passports. We have Mexican passports.
> MARGARETHA: Who helped you get your passports?
> SUSANA: Oh, that we did ourselves. We had borrowed money from a farmer and with borrowed money we came here. We still owe a lot. We have to earn it here yet and pay it back.
> MARGARETHA: Was it very costly?
> SUSANA: Yeah. It cost $15,000 before we were all the way here, with driving here, and the papers and everything.[5]

The cost of migration does not end when Dietsche families find a home and work in Canada. For many, realizing their claim to Canadian citizenship is both expensive and complicated. Citizenship is a necessity for most families who migrate with less than nothing, as having "papers" is the ticket to important social supports, such as healthcare, social assistance, the Child Tax Benefit, and even education.

> MARGARETHA: Who is helping you here now, with getting your Canadian citizenship?
> SUSANA: Henry Bueckert [pseudonym] here from Vienna [small town].
> MARGARETHA: Do you have to pay him too?
> SUSANA: Yes, we had to pay him. We had filed it once, and then it went broke [fell through], and then he took it on and now he is going with it further. And for paying, we had to pay $70 apiece or something, and now later when he took it on, we had to pay another $100.
> MARGARETHA: Why did it fall through the first time?
> SUSANA: I don't know. It was sent off to Leamington by Abe [her brother-in-law]. He had depended on someone else, and he broke it [it fell through], and now this man took it on.
> MARGARETHA: So then you have had a lot of trouble with making it.
> SUSANA: Yeah. We have had a lot of trouble with it. I think it is three years from April that they had sent it off.

MARGARETHA: And you still don't have them.

SUSANA: We still don't have them.

MARGARETHA: If you don't have those papers, can you have health cards and social insurance?

SUSANA: No. No, we can't start with any of that.

MARGARETHA: So, how do you do it then, if you have to go to the doctor or something?

SUSANA: Then we just have to pay for it.

MARGARETHA: Is it very expensive?

SUSANA: It is very expensive, yes. We were at the doctor last Thursday and once everything was said and done, it was over $200.

MARGARETHA: For how many people?

SUSANA: Just for me.

MARGARETHA: Was it just for a check-up, or for what was it?

SUSANA: Uh-hmm, for a check-up. I had filed for a new [landed immigrant] permit. My permit was run out because I'm not a citizen. I had filed for one year, and because I hadn't been to the doctor's I only got it for six months. I had to have been to the doctor's within sixty days and if not, then they wouldn't give me a permit anymore. And it was just a check-up, and it cost a little over $200.

MARGARETHA: You don't have your driver's licence here then either, right? Or do you?

SUSANA: Yeah, beginners I have already.

MARGARETHA: Who helped you with it?

SUSANA: Maria Reimer [pseudonym] from St Thomas did it.

MARGARETHA: You had to pay her too?

SUSANA: Yeah, we had to give Maria $125, and there where you take the eye test, there we had to pay $125 as well.

MARGARETHA: It becomes expensive if you don't know the English language, right?

SUSANA: Yeah. But everyone has to do it like that, right, when you can't speak it. Yeah, then she teaches you for an hour before you fill it out. Then she explains how it is and what they are going to ask and what this sign and that sign is. And then in there, she just asks the questions and then you mark which answer you think is right. Just mark it. You have to do it all by yourself because we don't know the language. She translates to [Low] German, and then you have to think of which answer you think is right and mark it yourself. With that you have to do it on your own. She just translates to German so you can understand it. So you can think of which answer sounds right.

MARGARETHA: Did it come easy for you?

SUSANA: Yes, I just had to do it once. My husband had to do it three times, I think. He did it first in Spanish and he didn't make it. And then he did it in English, and he didn't make it. And then for the third time, I think he did it with Maria Reimer and he made it right away, when he did it with her.[6] And I did too.

Mennonite colonists are commonly described as an ignorant people who do not value education. Parents are often criticized (and sometimes reprimanded) for not ensuring that their children regularly attend school. Yet the barriers to education for Dietsche children can be significant.

MARGARETHA: Do all the children work, or are there some that are too young?

SUSANA: Yes, our youngest is five. She doesn't work. She always stays home with me.

MARGARETHA: Then you just clean the house and play with and take care of the child?

SUSANA: Yes. And then I have school or I have to help her. We have school at home then, when I'm not busy, in between, or like that.

MARGARETHA: How do you do it in the winter, with the school?

SUSANA: Oh, I don't know how we are going to do it this winter, but last winter, we went to the [public] school close to Leamington. And then they said we couldn't. We had to first have a citizenship and a health card for them. So then I just taught them at home in [Low] German so they wouldn't forget everything. And to get English, they couldn't go then yet. I don't know if they will be able to this winter.

MARGARETHA: So you haven't enrolled them?

SUSANA: No, we haven't yet because when we lived there, they said we couldn't ahead of time [before they have documentation]. And now we didn't try here. It would maybe be the same here.

MARGARETHA: I didn't know that they couldn't go to school if they weren't a citizen.

The rules of eligibility and terms of entitlement for human services and citizenship in Canada are sometimes elusive and change without explanation or warning.

MARGARETHA: If you don't have your citizen papers, then you don't get the child tax,[7] right?

SUSANA: No. Like the family cheque, do you mean? No we can't file for that yet.

MARGARETHA: But as soon as you are citizens, then you can. Right?

SUSANA: Yes. Yeah, it's supposed to work then, but if you can't become a citizen, then isn't it something that runs on my name? That family cheque?

MARGARETHA: I can't say for sure, but I think it should work anyway if your husband is a citizen.

SUSANA: Then I have to do something else. I don't know quite how they say it. I don't know how to repeat it, but ... At MCC,[8] we went there for my new permit. They have helped us with it and looked over everything because I couldn't read what it said on the letter that came back. And they read it to me, about having a check-up and all that in order to get a permit. They read it all to me. For us they have been a lot of help. It worked very well. I have gotten my permit again for six months and now I have been to the doctor. And they said the next time if I needed it again then I would get it for a year. Now I have to do it every six months. But then we asked if we needed to do it for everyone, make a new permit. And then they said for them that the citizenship was filed, it would be an unneeded cost.

MARGARETHA: They are filing for citizenship and you can't?

SUSANA: They say I have never had anybody look at it that is familiar with it. I really wouldn't be able to. I've just heard it here from people that I couldn't.

MARGARETHA: Why are they saying you can't?

SUSANA: They say I don't have the right.

Some Mennonite migrants report having to leave their colony in Latin America because of a health crisis in the family, as was the case for Margaretha's family. In recent years, newcomers with medical needs – whether they are refugees, labour migrants, or family class immigrants – have been targeted by Canadian politicians who claim that Canada's publicly funded healthcare system ought to be reserved for tax-paying citizens. Indeed, public health care in Canada is not accessible for everyone, as the criteria for inclusion shift regularly, causing confusion among patients and health professionals alike.[9] Yet not all migrants consider Canada's health care system to be superior, or even more affordable.

MARGARETHA: You said you had all your children in Bolivia?

SUSANA: Just not two.

MARGARETHA: Oh, those you had in Mexico?

SUSANA: Uh-huh. But we have made them home (*Tus*); they are all home in Mexico. We have made it so we are all home in Mexico.[10]

MARGARETHA: Have you ever had friends that have had babies here? Have you ever seen how it is here?

SUSANA: Yes, our grandchild was born here ... in the hospital. I was there [at the hospital] only once, just to look a little bit.

MARGARETHA: Does it look comfortable to you here?

SUSANA: Yes, just it is so very expensive.

MARGARETHA: Did your daughter-in-law have the health card?

SUSANA: No, she doesn't either. She doesn't have her citizen either.

MARGARETHA: Do you know how expensive it was?

SUSANA: It was 4,100 and some dollars, but I don't know exactly how much. But over $4,000.

MARGARETHA: Oh, and they had to pay all that right away?

SUSANA: No, with a little over $400 they could go home. Our church paid it then, so that she could go home. And the rest is in payments. They pay $50 a month. And it was an operation. I said if it had gone without an operation, then it maybe wouldn't have been so expensive. She had to stay [in hospital] from Tuesday evening that she had the baby until Thursday morning. She was there two days, or almost two days.

MARGARETHA: Does she like the way the doctors did things?

SUSANA: Oh, she was very satisfied. She said she got very good treatment when she couldn't speak the language.

MARGARETHA: Who helped her with it?

SUSANA: Our son, who is her husband, he can almost speak enough English that he can get by with the doctor or like that. And then I have a niece in Leamington who helped them until it was all through. Before the baby was born, she always went to the doctor with her and talked for her. And now when it was time for the birth, then our son could almost talk enough that he could get by. But my niece was there anyway. If there was something he couldn't understand, she helped them.

MARGARETHA: Where do you like to deal with the doctors better? In Mexico or here?

SUSANA: We have been to the doctor here just this one time, and I thought it was good enough. But I said it didn't feel like a Mexican doctor. He said he was Mexican, and he spoke Spanish, but it felt different. I don't know how I should say it, like he didn't give feedback. Very good care – that was all good, but it was like he wasn't as willing for everything as the Mexican doctors. Maybe it wasn't like that, but it felt like it to me a little.

MARGARETHA: Oh. When you have to pay a lot of money, then you want good service, right?

SUSANA: Yeah, that's just as I thought. But this was just for a check-up. I don't know how it would be if you actually needed help. That I don't know how it would be.

MARGARETHA: Were you always satisfied with how it was in Mexico or Bolivia with the doctors?

SUSANA: No. It wasn't always exactly right, then. And when you had given a lot of money and it didn't work accordingly, then it was disappointing.

MARGARETHA: Did you always have to pay every time at the doctor's there?

SUSANA: No, in Mexico, no. There we have had what they call Seguro.[11] For years, it was for free, if we had to go to a doctor. We have had two children operated on there, there in the Seguro hospital. We can just say thank you and walk out. All the medicine and all the operations are all for free.

MARGARETHA: Do you have to pay something for it every year there [in Mexico]?

SUSANA: We have to pay ourselves every year for each child, like we did at the beginning of this year. We have bought for all of us. It was $102 [CAD] for one, I think that we had to pay then. They say if we want to keep it, we have to come in before the date of last year with the same amount of money and pay it again for a year. I kept saying I would like it if we couldn't have a health card here [in Canada], then if we kept it open there [in Mexico] and we all of a sudden needed something, then we had a route to go. But I don't think we will do it. Maybe we can get the health cards here and then we wouldn't need that.

MARGARETHA: Yeah, because it would be costly to go back and forth for doctoring.

SUSANA: Yeah, that would be very costly, but a lot of people do that when they need a big operation and you can have a big operation there without paying any more than a little over $100 a year.

In Canada, as in the colony, life is work and work is life. To make a living on the land is not only about providing the necessities of life, it is cultural and religious survival.

MARGARETHA: Now I want to talk a little about what you have worked here, in Canada.

SUSANA: Oh, I just work here at home and my husband and the children work on the field. First they picked cucumbers and then later hoed cucumbers and picked peppers, and now they're supposed to pick cucumbers again.

MARGARETHA: Do they get paid well?

SUSANA: I think it is good enough. For hoeing and picking peppers, they got $8 an hour, and the cucumbers it was half.

MARGARETHA: Does it usually bring a lot a year?

SUSANA: No, it doesn't. With picking cucumbers? Well, they picked for three weeks and one day and that was a little over $5,000 that it made. And earlier they cut asparagus and with that they had done very good. Then they got $8 an hour.

MARGARETHA: Do you get benefits, that they pay for checking eyes and teeth all that?

SUSANA: No, we pay. And if you need doctoring, then we have to pay ourselves.

MARGARETHA: Is the work here different for your boys and girls than it was in Mexico or Bolivia?

SUSANA: Oh yes. They have done different work in Mexico and in Bolivia. They were all still small there. They couldn't work yet. But in Mexico, they did different work than here. Our daughter, she worked on the field first when she was too young to work in a restaurant, and then in the last while, she worked in the restaurant and our oldest worked in a shop. And my husband worked in a shop. And the second son, he worked in … it was also like a shop, but in a tractor repair shop.

MARGARETHA: What do they do here?

SUSANA: Here they just work on the field, the children that are still home [not married].

MARGARETHA: What about in the winter, last winter?

SUSANA: Then they worked on a cow farm.

MARGARETHA: And this year, they haven't found anything for this winter?

SUSANA: No, for this winter we haven't found anything. Last winter we lived … well, we came here half-way through winter or the beginning of winter. Then they worked on a cow farm, my husband with three children. But only my husband and the oldest daughter got paid. The other two had to work for free, and then it was so very hard. And we told the boss we would move to this side [Aylmer area], where there was field work. Maybe it would be easier. Making a start with only a couple of hundred dollars, it is just very hard.

MARGARETHA: How come only two got paid?

SUSANA: He said he didn't have work for the other two, but he sent them out for the whole day.

MARGARETHA: That isn't right.

SUSANA: That wasn't right, but he did it like that.

MARGARETHA: Is it harder for your girls to work here?

SUSANA: Yes, it is hard for them. It's hard for all of the children when they have to work on the field, but they'd much rather do that than be at home with no work. They don't like it when they just have to sit around. They want to work, and they work hard.

The Dietsche preference for seasonal farm work, requiring some to rely on social assistance in the winter months, is sometimes judged to be "milking the system." For Susana, it is simply fact that fieldwork runs out in the fall and acceptable winter work is hard to find, so the family may be without a source of income for a season.

MARGARETHA: What do you do in the winter if you don't get money from the government?

SUSANA: Well, we don't have work yet for the winter. I don't know yet what we are going to do.

Housing and employment are often tied, as is common for agricultural migrant workers in Canada. The laws and protections usually afforded most Canadians or even temporary foreign workers are not necessarily available to Dietsche families. A yielding disposition is apparent in Susana's reluctance to claim (or even know) her rights:

MARGARETHA: Now I just want to talk a little about how you have it here in Canada now.

SUSANA: When my husband and the children go to work on the field, then we have to get up at six in the morning.

MARGARETHA: And what do you do at home?

SUSANA: I do the work at home then, cleaning and making food, washing. What a woman's job is. But if I can do the washing, a lot of times we are here with no water. I can't even do the washing, and then I have to wait until he is home from work, and then we have to go to the laundromat with all the wash.

MARGARETHA: Don't you have water in the house?

SUSANA: Not all the time. This well is a very bothersome well. There is no water again right now. It's very hard, when you have so much work and you can't clean. You can't wash anything, can't make food.

MARGARETHA: Do you have to pay rent here?

SUSANA: Yes, $600 a month we have to pay here, and then when they let water in, we have to pay for that besides. It costs $80 to let the well fill once.

MARGARETHA: And the landowner doesn't pay it?

SUSANA: The water is not [included] with the rent. When the well gets empty we have to deal with it.

MARGARETHA: How often does the well get empty?

SUSANA: It is almost every day that it goes empty, and then the water and everything has to be transported.

MARGARETHA: So you have to fill it up every day, and then every day give eighty dollars?

SUSANA: No, we don't do it every day. We just leave the well and then we transport the water, so it's not so costly for us.

MARGARETHA: From where do you transport the water?

SUSANA: It's from the boss who we work for on the field. We can have it for free from there.

MARGARETHA: Doesn't your boss there have a house for you to live in?

SUSANA: No, he doesn't.

MARGARETHA: And he doesn't help you to pay the rent?

SUSANA: Yes, he always pays the rent. When it's time to pay the rent he does it for us, then we pay him for it later.

MARGARETHA: How do they pay you when working with cucumbers? Do they just pay it at the end, once you are done?

SUSANA: Yes. We get a cheque every fifteen days. But now the farmers didn't get paid very well. Now it didn't come out with every fifteen days from one cheque to another. Now it was longer.

MARGARETHA: Is that why your boss pays the rent first?

SUSANA: Yes, that's why. Because a lot of times we don't have the money when it's time to pay the rent, and then he pays and later when they calculate it, it just comes off [our cheque].

MARGARETHA: He's a very nice boss then, right?

SUSANA: Yes, he is a very nice boss. We are very satisfied with him, and he lets us have all the water for free. We can take all the water we need. We just have to use small containers, but we can take it.

MARGARETHA: That's good then. How do you like it here in Canada?

SUSANA: Oh, now that we are living here [in a rural area], now we like it here. But in town, to live there, we didn't really like it, because in town, we don't have the mindset to live there. We lived in town for the first four months. We came here on December 22 and then the first four months we lived in the town of Wheatley. And there we were really tight for space, a very small house, and it was very bad. The room there was very bad, and we have a lot of children, and they're not used to living in town. It was a very hard time.

MARGARETHA: Do all your children still live at home with you?

SUSANA: We have one that is married and doesn't live at home, but those that are not married all live at home with us.

Later in the interview, Susana and Margaretha returned to the topic of housing. Susana was reluctant to complain, but with a little encouragement, she told more about the conditions in which she was trying to make a home for her family:

MARGARETHA: Can you talk a little about where you're living now? You said you were renting a house for $600, that there was not even good water there. Is there anything else in the house that isn't very good?

SUSANA: Oh, it is very drafty. Mice in the walls, and they get into everything.

MARGARETHA: Does it have heating and everything in it?

SUSANA: No, it doesn't have heating. It's not ready for the winter. The windows and everything are way too broken. Can't cool it or heat it.

MARGARETHA: Oh, my. That's not good. How do you do it with bathing if there isn't always water?

SUSANA: Then we just heat water on the stove that we have transported, and then we can bathe ourselves like that.

MARGARETHA: Oh, then it's almost like you had to do it in Bolivia, right?

SUSANA: Yeah. [Laughter] Get water everywhere so that you have a big mess.

MARGARETHA: Oh, that's too bad. You don't ever tell anyone that it needs to be fixed up?

SUSANA: Yes, we said … or I said to our boss the other day that I wasn't satisfied with the house, that he was supposed to fix it up. And we wanted to have water here if we already pay such high rent for such an old house, then we wanted to have water here. Then he just said I shouldn't make such good food, then the mice wouldn't come in.

MARGARETHA: Oh, my! Then he just joked over it.

SUSANA: Yes.

MARGARETHA: Oh, that's not good. Have you ever thought about telling other people about him, that he rents such a house?

SUSANA: No, that we haven't and we don't want to have trouble. But otherwise, you get discouraged when you can't clean, can't make food. You know, your husband and children come home hungry and tired and there's no clean clothes or food ready. That is hard.

MARGARETHA: I would believe that. You would think if you had to pay so much you would get something good out of it.

SUSANA: Yes, and I would think if it was so expensive, I could handle it if it was a nice house. But such an old house that is chewed through, that smells so strongly like mice and everything, then you're disappointed. And then not even water that you can clean properly.

MARGARETHA: How many bedrooms does the house have?

SUSANA: Four.

MARGARETHA: Is it enough room for the children?

SUSANA: Oh, yes. Enough room it is. Just it is bad.

MARGARETHA: That's too bad. Do you live here with other people, or do you live here alone?

SUSANA: No, we live here alone. Just with our family.

MARGARETHA: What kind of people live around you, like your neighbours?

SUSANA: Those there [pointing], I don't know what kind of neighbours they are. And these here beside us, is Willy, the owner of this house.

MARGARETHA: Is he a Mennonite?

SUSANA: No, he is one that is born in Canada.

MARGARETHA: Do you like your neighbours here?

SUSANA: Oh yes. We have peace from the neighbours. There is nothing. We are totally at peace with that. It is the owner that is our neighbour, and he is very strict. He doesn't like it if there's anything lying around on the yard that shouldn't be. But that's okay if he wants to keep it nice.

Susana explained that she and her family still did not know many people in the rural Mennonite community in which they lived, and it seemed to Margaretha that Susana and other members of her family were often lonely. Social life in Canada is very different for all members of Susana's family, but especially her teenage children. In the colonies of Latin America, young people gather on Sunday afternoons in the village streets to socialize and find their future spouse. In Canada, far from the close community of the colony and familiar social traditions, young people can face boredom and isolation.

MARGARETHA: Do you have friends in town that you sometimes go and visit?

SUSANA: Yeah, we have our pastor couple. And we have friends too. On Sunday, we more often go to church first, and later if we want to, we go to Aylmer again to visit our friends. We have some friends here already.

MARGARETHA: Have your children found a lot of friends here?

SUSANA: No, they don't have any friends here yet. They know some, but not enough to visit with. For that they don't know anyone well enough. Then the Sunday seems so long for them.

MARGARETHA: How do they want to do it then? Do they want to go away and try to get some friends?

SUSANA: Well, they haven't really yet tried too hard to find friends here. Our oldest does sometimes go with another family to see where she can find friends, but it's like she doesn't altogether know how ... or how I should say it? It's like it's strange or unfamiliar.

MARGARETHA: It would be hard to if she can't speak the language, right?

SUSANA: Yeah, the language.

MARGARETHA: Are they happy that they are here?

SUSANA: One day yes, and one day no. It depends on how busy they are. If they are working, then they are encouraged. And when they don't have anything to do, then it is like it is with a person; then they're not encouraged.

MARGARETHA: Now I just want to ask you a little bit, if there is anything that has happened to you in Canada that has been very hard for you?

SUSANA: No, not yet. We have been quite well off since we have been here. In the family we have not lost anyone. That part is all good.

MARGARETHA: Some people say that when you come to Canada, they can almost pick money from a tree. They think it's very easy.

SUSANA: Oh, yeah.

MARGARETHA: Do you still think it is that easy?

SUSANA: Oh, no. It isn't that easy all the time.

MARGARETHA: Would you want to give them some advice, or what would
you say?

SUSANA: Oh, I would tell them that you have to earn the money here just
like elsewhere.

When asked about personal aspirations or hopes for their children, it
is typical for colony Mennonites to have little to say beyond the desire
to "make a living." The ideal is to carry the past into the future. This
is accomplished by attending to the basic practicalities of daily life in
the present. In mainstream Canadian culture, guided by the values and
ideals of capitalism, this submission to the necessities of life is commonly interpreted to indicate a lack of ambition, which borders on
immorality.

MARGARETHA: Are you still encouraged?

SUSANA: It seems to me, I would just as well live in Mexico as well as here.

MARGARETHA: Now you are home here, too?

SUSANA: Yes, we are. We have come here in the hopes to make it our home
and work here.

MARGARETHA: Then if you look on it good, it works a bit better, right?

SUSANA: Yes, it works better then. Here it is better. Like this, now in the
summer, we have had better opportunity to make money than we did in
Mexico.

MARGARETHA: What do you want for your children? And later, once they
are a little older?

SUSANA: I would like if they could have their own bed and dresser, or like
all that. When they could have their own. And that they could have a
good beginning. That I would like.[12]

MARGARETHA: Would you like it if they finished school here, or if they just
always worked here on the farms?

SUSANA: In that, I leave it up to them. They can figure out what would
interest them.

MARGARETHA: You would be okay with it if they went to school?

SUSANA: It would be okay with me. What they decide to do, it will be okay.
It's up to them if they would like it and want to, and there is a way, then
it would be okay. But if they don't want school, and would rather work,
that would be okay too. That I leave to them to decide.

MARGARETHA: Oh, you're just happy for them if they are happy.

SUSANA: Yes, I am just thankful for the good family, and that's what I
can do.

Although there is great diversity among Mennonite migrants from Latin America, Susana is rather typical of this population in a number of important ways, and her life experiences exemplify several key themes that are explored in the chapters that follow. Specifically her migration account makes reference to four forms of social exclusion (economic, spatial, sociopolitical, and subjective); self-imposed hardship; classification and symbolic violence; and conflict and double binds. These are defining features of the social processes that are set in motion when this traditional and distinct migrant population encounters Canada's human service system.

Introduction to the book

The book is organized in such a way as to encourage the reader to look beneath the surface. I begin, in the Preface, with Susana's story, to situate the theory that follows. Chapter one introduces the questions that frame the research and the people whose narratives tell the story. Returning to the idea of point of view that was introduced in the Preface, chapter two considers the "common sense" of "official" accounts of Dietsche (im)migrant needs and human service responses. Chapters three and four examine the outcomes and processes of social exclusion as they are made visible among Dietsche in Canada's market-state social field. Keeping our attention on everyday practices made necessary in social relations and exchanges, chapter five considers the confrontation, contradiction, and conflict that arise when the Dietsche traditional and anti-capitalist world view encounters Canada's market-based human services. Chapter six takes a rather deep look at the double binds and internal splits of social exclusion and symbolic violence, and the necessity for self-imposed social exclusion in the in-between spaces of migration. To conclude, chapter seven considers lessons learned through the examination of the official procedures and everyday practices of social exclusion and begins to imagine ideas and practices of social inclusion.

Acknowledgments

The act of writing cannot begin until one overcomes, for at least a time, the inclination to recede into invisibility, silence. Writing is always commitment. To write as a Mennonite woman is to write from a place and language of "otherness" in relation to dominant western culture (Brandt, 1993, 18). Yet I also write as a scholar – a position of some influence – in the public language of social science research. I cannot dismiss or escape from either place. I have learned to be (at least) two very different people at once. On the surface, it may appear that preserving clear separation and distance between such incompatible worlds, or social fields, is simply a matter of pragmatics. But it takes inordinate "energy and clear thinking" to remain split, divided from one's self, living with heart and soul "somewhere halfway between sixteenth-century northern Europe and the Old Testament," and mind and body, "at least some part of them," in twenty-first-century Canada (Brandt, 1996, 33). And it is this "split-ness" that has made this work possible.

For the courage to write, to forge this space in-between, I have many to thank. I am grateful to Ernie, who made the absurd suggestion that perhaps it was acceptable – even necessary – for me to acknowledge and embrace the contradictions of identities within me, and to Adrienne, who patiently holds my worlds – me – together. I owe much to Suzanne and Karen and their no-nonsense approach to combatting my impulse to put it away, unfinished, forever. My children, Caleb and Rachel, cheered me on through their growing-up years and have become wise, inspiring, and caring confidants. And I am honoured to share my life with Dennis, whose steadfastness, insight, and unfailing belief in me give me a solid place in this life.

Much credit for this work is due to Dr Kerry Fast, my knowledge-able co-researcher, skilled editor, careful Plautdietsch interpreter and language consultant, and trusted friend. She diligently worked her way through at least two complete versions of this manuscript. I am quite certain that this book would not be without her encouragement, constructive criticism, and company along the way. I am indebted to the three anonymous reviewers – one of whom has stuck with me since the early days when this project was something quite different – whose careful engagement with my manuscript and supportive dialogue with me over the years drew from me courage for and confidence in this work. The publication of this writing is owed to the time, expertise, and dedication of many others, including Doug Hildebrand, University of Toronto Press, who patiently waited for the work to take its final shape and directed me through each step of the process; Kristine Culp, who read through the entire manuscript to remind me what it's about; and Catherine Frost, whose meticulous yet gentle copy editing greatly improved the quality of my writing. The research on which this work is based was generously funded by the Social Sciences and Humanities Research Council (SSHRC) of Canada and the Delbert F. Plett Foundation.

Above all, I am deeply grateful to those who shared their stories with me. The research process was the beginning of many friendships and working relationships that endure and enrich my life immeasurably.

Because this is not my story, what does it mean to "write" someone else, to bring someone else into being? To translate from the mother('s)-tongue of silence into the codified, brazen language we call "scholarship"? Am I not forcing exposure, *being*, on all those lives I write? This is the only reconciliation I have to offer: I am writing a story of social exclusion. It is the story that we (the participants, the interpreters, and I) uncovered together. It is a shared meaning to which we came. Any "life" that is written must be my own. The limits of my responsibility in this project were made clear by two Mennonite immigrant practitioners:

> CORNELIUS: We're not portrayed properly to the world, because we haven't told our own story. If we don't tell our own story, somebody else will. So we need to tell our own story.
> LUANN: So that raises a question that I hadn't intended to ask, but has certainly been on my mind. I have been fully aware, from the very beginning, that this is not my story. Is it possible for me to tell any story,

or several stories, as an outsider? How do I do that in a way that is respectful and is not taking your story from you?

CORNELIUS: Or telling a story that isn't even ours?

TINA: Absolutely.

LUANN: My hope was, if it's possible, to give opportunity for you to tell your stories, and that I might be sort of a channel or a vessel for that. And maybe that's just way too grandiose of me. But that was my hope. Now, what do I do with the gifts that I have been given – the gifts of these stories?

CORNELIUS: I think a good preamble, and a good conclusion to something like that could be that you have seen a little piece of us. Sometimes it's portrayed as, "I've been there, and I know all about them." And that's what hurts. You know, if people think that they know all about us, and you read into it for just a little, you see that that person doesn't really know us at all. And it's portrayed as if they know everything. And I think a good preamble is to say that, "I've studied into it just a little bit, and I have a little glimpse of who these people are."

TINA: That is so true. I'm not sure that I'll be able to bring my point across. But just about two weeks ago I got called in the middle of the night to a hospital. And it was a mom with a sick baby, and she spoke no English. And when I walked in, she looked so, so Mennonite, with her flowered dress and *Dÿak*. And such an old jacket. And we sat there for eight hours while they were doing testing. And so we got to know each other. We started talking. And to hear her story, and to hear what she's gone through to make it to Canada, and her desire to go to school. And when I got to know her, I just absolutely loved that woman. The desire that she had to learn. And the love that she had for her children. And I thought, "You are an example for me, and I hope that I can be to other people what you are to me." But I'm sure she didn't think of that, that she was being an example for me. The doctors and nurses that walked by, they just look at her as if to say, "There's another Mennonite mom there." They do not know that every person has a story to tell. I'm not sure if I'm making sense here. [*Chuckles nervously in exasperation.*] I adore her for her courage, and for her …

LUANN: Well, I think I do understand you, because I have also met women and men who have impressed me in that way. Some stories should not remain untold.

CORNELIUS: That's true.

OUT OF PLACE

Social Exclusion and Mennonite Migrants in Canada

Chapter One

Social Exclusion in a World on the Move

Len leaned forward and spoke in a hushed voice, indicating that what he had to say to me was important, yet off the record. He described how his mother, a young widow with no material possessions, had emigrated from Russia with several children in tow. He spoke of her triumph over unimaginable suffering and adversity. Evidence of her (and his) success was presented with a motion of his arm, signalling his spacious office. He turned his attention to the population with whom he works, the people about whom I had come to enquire. Like him, they are descendants of Mennonites who emigrated from Russia, although their migration story was set in a different time and followed different routes. More important, most Mennonites migrating to Canada from Mexico have not achieved the prosperity and status he enjoys. Yet he insisted, "These people are not – what was the word you used? – vulnerable. These people are not vulnerable in Canadian society. And I wouldn't say they live in poverty." Len was emphatic in his assertion that the visibly impoverished conditions of their lives were not markers of exclusion, but manifestations of their own foolish choices. "They are comfortable and familiar with a vagabond and gypsy way of life. They've never known anything else. Any barriers to a better life are all self-imposed. They have only their culture and legalistic religion to blame." One argument mingled with others: their apparent material lack does not constitute poverty; they prefer their lives of scarcity; any hardship they may suffer they have brought on themselves; they deserve unpleasant, low-paying jobs because they refuse to make themselves more competitive in the labour market; and their desire for separation and a distinct culture negates their right to the benefits of a life in Canada.[1]

My interest was social exclusion. Surely this was something different. Academic experts on the topic note that "Indeed, some marginal or deviant individuals may not want to be included; they can deliberately choose to be social drop-outs" (Silver, 1994, 545). If so, how do we make sense of such seemingly self-defeating behaviour? Is social exclusion self-imposed and necessary when a people resist the norms and values of the dominant culture, and is social inclusion available only to those who are willing to conform? What do we do with people who seem to prefer the margins and refuse to fit in? Is integration an appropriate or useful goal? What does meaningful inclusion look like for groups who live in contemporary "western" societies yet wish to preserve their cultural distinctiveness in daily life practices – such as some First Nations peoples, groups adhering to traditional Islam, or Orthodox Jews? Are such instances of exclusion-by-choice best treated as private community and family matters, of little or no concern to the social welfare system and society at large?

The subject of this book is social exclusion, with emphasis on its self-imposed expressions. Through the life experiences of migrant men and women who participate in Canada's human services, I offer here an account of the workings of social exclusion and inclusion in and through everyday and ordinary practices. I aim to develop conceptual understandings of the *ideas* of social inclusion and exclusion and to investigate the material and social *realities* that may be represented by these concepts. Through this particular Canadian case example, I focus on the everyday practices and official procedures by which distance – and all associated social dynamics, such as classification, subject-formation, alienation, and shame – is necessarily produced and reinforced in many contemporary social welfare systems and human services, particularly in encounters with (im)migrant and culturally distinct populations. My overall objective is to move towards a meaningful understanding of social inclusion in increasingly diverse societies and to inform a working model for policies and practices within human services.

At the centre of this examination of Canada's human services are people such as Susana and Margaretha – members of various ethno-religious and traditional communities of Mennonite migrants from Latin America who have settled, to varying degrees, in rural regions of Canada. Yet, this book is not an ethnographic study of Mennonite (im)migrants in Canada. Rather, the object of study is the policies and practices of Canada's social welfare system. Thus, social service workers and health professionals, such as Len, also are important to the story. Even more broadly, my research is focused on the logic of the market – or market fundamentalism, as the exaggerated and irrational blind faith in markets has come to be identified[2] – as it is played out in a particular case example of human services. I give attention to the practices of main actors in this social field, including a specific "client" group (Mennonite [im]migrants) and practitioners, to analyse market principles as they function in this social space. Thus, this work is in keeping with an economic anthropology (Bourdieu, 2005).

Why Mennonite (im)migrants?

Mennonite (im)migrants in Canada are illustrative in this study of social exclusion. This population is easily recognized as "Mexican Mennonite" in specific rural towns in Canada, primarily owing to the traditional dress and practices that are maintained by the most recent and/or most conservative[3] (im)migrants, although many are quick to make adaptation. For example, typical attire for women and girls consists of dresses cut from brightly coloured floral fabric with pleated, calf-length skirts; long, gathered sleeves; and aprons tied tightly at the waist. Their long, parted hair, firmly secured at the back of their heads, is covered with a black kerchief (*Düak*) or, in the summer, a broad-brimmed straw sun hat. It is common in winter and summer alike for women to wear dark ankle socks over bare legs with running shoes. For everyday wear men and boys typically dress in jeans, denim work pants, overalls or coveralls, western-style plaid shirts (snaps, front and back yokes, large collars), and often cowboy boots. The women usually sew clothes for the entire family in order to save money and to conform to their customs. Fabric, clothing, and food imported from Mexican suppliers can be purchased in Mennonite stores that have been established in rural towns where the population is most concentrated.

Mennonite (im)migrant homes are often distinguishable by the lace curtains hanging in the windows, brightly coloured and carefully tended flower beds lining the front of the house, and at least one large and well-worn van sitting in the laneway. On sunny laundry days, summer or winter, traditional Mennonite dresses and trousers hang to dry in the breeze, pinned neatly to the clothesline near the house.

Moving well beyond dress and cultural practices, issues such as drug trafficking, alcoholism, incest, and sexual violence among colony Mennonites have become the subject of newspaper and magazine articles, films, documentaries, popular books, and Internet websites. These graphic portrayals of colony life in Mexico and Bolivia depict a "peculiar and colourful people, who in many respects seem stuck in a bygone age" (Quiring, 2004, 85). The reasons for their curious practices are rarely explored. While their lives in Canada receive relatively little attention, representations of Mennonite (im)migrants and citizens usually emphasize the material, social, or moral failings of a few.[4]

Despite such unbalanced portrayals of a people (as is characteristic of popular media), external markers of material deprivation – including inadequate housing, un- and under-employment, illiteracy, substance abuse, and poor physical and mental health – are readily visible among some Mennonite (im)migrant families in rural Canada. These social "symptoms" indicate some degree of social exclusion as it is most commonly recognized. However, as some are quick to point out, the tenacious Mennonite commitment to a distinctive way of life – a culture that is intensely traditional, religious, agrarian, and patriarchal – and a disposition for endless migration suggest that their social exclusion is collectively self-imposed and, furthermore, voluntary.

Mennonite families who migrate to Canada from Latin America carry with them a distinct heritage and cyclical history of displacement, migration, settlement, and displacement. Yet this rather peculiar group of people is not peculiar at all, as stories like theirs abound. They are among the ceaseless flow of economic migrants who make their way to Canada and the United States from the Global South, where the divides of social exclusion are extraordinarily profound.[5] More and more people are engaged in various official and unofficial versions of migratory livelihoods.[6] This is the "people river, as it were" that flows "toward jobs and hope," "away from suffering and violence" (Lederach, 2014, 24). The United Nations reports that the absolute number of women, men and children on the move has increased dramatically in response to changing economic and environmental conditions. It is estimated that there are currently 244 million international migrants in the world, an increase of 41 per cent since 2000 (UNDESA, 2016). The Organisation for Economic Co-operation and Development (OECD) notes that one in ten people living in its thirty-four member countries was born abroad, totalling approximately 115 million immigrants. Whereas some research claims that the proportion of the world's population represented by international migrants has remained at a relatively stable 2.5 to 3 per cent for the past half-century, others report steady increases in the absolute numbers of migrants that far outstrip population growth, especially in the past fifteen years.[7] Looking ahead, "large and persistent economic and demographic asymmetries between countries" (UNDESA, 2015, 7), as well as uneven climate change impacts, are likely to remain powerful generators of international migration from the south to the north.

The unique circumstance available to many Mennonite (im)migrants is that of dual citizenship in their sending and receiving countries, as most have a claim to Canadian citizenship (although a complicated claim) through the birthright of their parents and grandparents who were born in Canada. In every practical sense, they are immigrants; yet members of this population would not meet Canada's criteria for any immigrant or refugee classification. Their access to Canada and the social welfare system is based solely on the citizenship status, or political capital, they hold prior to migration. As "newcomer citizens," they defy Canada's immigration classifications, eligibility criteria for settlement services, and even informal social categories. They should not exist. The social conditions and migratory practices of Mennonite (im)migrants offer an unusual opportunity to study the intersecting global and local forces of social exclusion, as practices of social exclusion are made necessary in a global neoliberal context.[8]

Why social exclusion?

Questions of social exclusion and inclusion are especially thorny in North American and European societies that are being dramatically transformed by over fifty years of large-scale immigration, primarily and increasingly from countries in the Global South. In Canada, it is projected that by 2031 almost one-third of the nation's total population will be a member of a "visible minority" group and over one-quarter of Canadians will be first-generation immigrants (Caron Malenfant, Lebel, & Martel, 2010). Recent predictions place Canada among the world's top seven countries to receive international migrants (more than 100,000 annually) between 2015 and 2050 (UNDESA, 2015). At the same time, there is widespread recognition of deepening economic and social divides in Canadian society. International comparisons over the past three decades, for example, show that both inequality in household earnings and numbers of people living in poverty[9] have increased rapidly in Canada, reaching a reported thirty-year high, and levels well above the OECD average even in the best of economic conditions (Block & Galabuzi, 2011; Yalnizyan, 2013). Economists report a uniquely dramatic spike in wealth inequality in Canada (Uppal & LaRochelle-Côté, 2015) and a surge (up by 34 per cent) in the share of total gross income captured by Canada's richest 1 per cent

(OECD, 2014), suggesting that the drift towards an increasingly divided society is likely to continue.

There are discernible patterns in who gets ahead and who falls behind in Canada, and the socio-economic organization of individuals and social groups is shown to be stubborn. Both immigrants and racialized communities fare worse than their native-born and white counterparts in a variety of dimensions of social exclusion, and on all indicators the gap is persistent or increasing over time (Banerjee, 2009; N. Lightman & Good Gingrich, 2012; Picot & Hou, 2015). Specifically, for example, research shows that immigrants in comparison with Canadian-born workers earn less, particularly upon entering the labour market (Banerjee & Lee 2015; Mitchell, E. Lightman, & Herd, 2007); are almost twice as likely to experience low income (Shields, Kelly, Park, Prier, & Fang, 2012); suffer negative impacts of a recession first and longer (Picot & Sweetman, 2012); and are not likely to catch up to their Canadian-born comparators in their working life (Banerjee, 2009; Morissette & Sultan, 2013). Other forms of social exclusion show up as uneven access to health services and health outcomes (Raphael, 2010; Sidhu, 2013; Wilson, E. Lightman, & Mitchell, 2009); available social resources and political involvement (Zhao, Xue, & Gilkinson, 2010); and even subjective sense of belonging and trust (Reitz, Banerjee, Phan, & Thompson, 2009). New immigrants and First Nations peoples are over-represented in certain neighbourhoods and regions where there are abnormally high rates of poor health, infant mortality, and overall lack of well-being (Ades, Apparicio, & Séguin, 2012; Gilbert, Auger, Wilkins, & Kramer, 2013).

The social stresses of these coinciding trends – growing inequality alongside new and deepening ethnic, racial, and religious diversity – show up at all levels of societies. Mounting tensions are expressed in heated debates about "reasonable accommodation" (Mahrouse, 2010; Wall, 2005), struggles over – and sometimes backlash against – "multiculturalism" (Foner & Simon, 2015), and aggravated assertions of "ethnic" nationalism (Bloemraad, Korteweg, & Yurdakul, 2008). Moreover, the failure (or even active refusal) to "blend" or assimilate to fit a dominant norm, to the extent possible, has been used to justify otherwise unjustifiable acts of discrimination and marginalization against individuals and groups. As the social and economic diversity of the Canadian social landscape deepens, Canada's shrinking social welfare and public health care systems are commonly portrayed to be overburdened and unsustainable, leading to narrower entitlement requirements for non-citizens, tighter eligibility criteria, and reduced benefits. In this social, political, and economic context defined by scarcity and insecurity, the influx of immigrants, refugees, and migrant workers has led to growing concerns about "integration," "acculturation," and "inclusion" into the economic and social fabric of the nation. Immigration laws and social programs are geared towards ensuring that newcomers are equipped to become contributing members of society rather than a drain on the system. The increasing diversity of clients, students, and patients, as well as social workers, teachers, and health practitioners, is met with new forms of regulation, surveillance, and punishment to manage difference in intensely neoliberal social contexts.

Amid growing international and intra-national economic disparity and social polarization, along with widespread employment insecurity and labour migration, there is an "emerging consensus regarding the limitations of poverty research that focuses solely on income" (Pisati, Whelan, Lucchini, & Maître, 2010, 405). Moreover, social policy scholars note that "a primary focus on poverty no longer fully captures the strains generated by rising inequality" (Banting & Myles, 2015, 11). Familiar frames of reference and defining terms are inadequate to represent these evolving social realities. The dynamic and ever-new complexity of social problems is made manageable through the use of metaphors "because they are devices that allow us to transfer the assumptions of a known situation to an uncharted one" (Blanco, 1994, 184). Indeed, the need for new metaphors of understanding (Blanco, 1994), new cognitive structures (Bourdieu, 1989), is reflected in the (often fleeting) popularity of notions such as a "new poverty," the "underclass," "social closure," and "social exclusion."

These efforts towards fresh models of understanding bring to the fore several "to-the-root-of-the-problem" social quandaries that have bubbled beneath the surface of poverty debates for a very long time and remain largely unexplored. These include questions of choice, or individual and group agency; the paradox of self-imposed hardship or marginalization; the contradictions of difference within a valued common good; and the dilemmas of distinction and belonging. The making of social policy and the delivery of human services within and beyond national borders are directed towards managing and distributing seemingly scarce resources. Determinations of eligibility, entitlement, and inclusion are necessary activities at all levels of service delivery. This is moral work, and much is at stake. It has to do with who ought to get what, and who ought to pay the price (E. Lightman, 2003). Social exclusion as a metaphor for social processes and outcomes offers a framework, or a cognitive structure, for defining what is happening and describing how it happens.

What is social exclusion?

It is generally accepted that René Lenoir, then secretary of state for social action in the Chirac government, was the first to coin the phrase "social exclusion" (see Lenoir, 1974). He identified various social categories, comprising an estimated 10 per cent of the population of France, who were unprotected by or excluded from employment-based social security systems (de Haan, 1998).[10] Social exclusion language spread rapidly through policy and research channels, and subsequently new meanings were imparted to an already vague concept. Social exclusion as an identified social problem has led to new institutes, departments, projects, and conference debates initiated by both government and non-government organizations. The most notable and critiqued is Tony Blair's Social Exclusion Unit (SEU), established in the United Kingdom within the Cabinet Office shortly after the election of the Labour government in 1997. Through the SEU, Blair launched a host of initiatives to combat exclusion from the labour market, education, housing, healthcare, and communities in general. Social exclusion has also been a concern, at least rhetorically, of international organizations with a view towards economic and social development, such as the European Commission's establishment of the European Observatory on Policies to Combat Social Exclusion in 1990 (Room, 1995); the United Nations (United Nations World Summit for Social Development 1995); the World Bank (Gacitua-Mario & Wodon, 2001); the International Labour Organization (Figueiredo & de Haan, 1998); the Organisation for Economic Co-operation and Development (OECD, 1999); and the Asian Development Bank (Sen, 2000b), to name only a few.[11]

Maintaining an unusually long lifespan, social exclusion language continues to frame policy planning for numerous European political institutions.[12] In Canada, the term has found its way into several provincial policy strategies and a research agenda for Human Resources and Skills Development Canada (HRSDC).[13] Highlighting Quebec's unique character in North America, in December 2002 the provincial government adopted Bill 112, a framework law launched by a community group and formulated through an ambitious process of collective action and public deliberation that includes a National

Strategy to Combat Poverty and Social Exclusion in its policy commitment to eliminate poverty.[14] More recently, social policies aimed explicitly at combating social exclusion or promoting social inclusion have been adopted in Nova Scota (2003), Manitoba (2012), and the Yukon (2012).

Definitions of social exclusion are as various as those using the concept. Its theoretical development emerged several years into its extensive use to signify a broad range of social and personal concerns.[15] In its most popular version, the words refer to poverty, homelessness, or unemployment. It is also applied to encounters with prejudice, stigmatization, and discrimination. In the fields of psychology and education social exclusion refers to individual experiences of rejection; feeling marginal, foreign, disaffiliated, deprived; and so on. Today the term is so commonly used in academic literatures, official government discourse, and even everyday parlance that it resounds much like a cliché.

Perhaps the widespread appeal of the term "social exclusion" has to do with its universal invitation; most, if not all of us, can identify with the idea of social exclusion in some way. We know something of what it means to feel left out, to experience the angst of not belonging. In this way social exclusion is normalized as a part of human experience. This universality has tremendous potential for decreasing social distance between those on the inside and those on the outside. Yet I argue that when applied in social policy and human services to address social and economic inequality, it functions to achieve precisely the opposite. This version of the idea, as popularly taken up in social policy and social services discourse, activates a specific "common sense," or widely shared understanding, that is consequential.[16] Most important, common sense social exclusion works to grow gaps – economic, spatial, social, political, and even subjective.

Given the imprecision of the term in practice, social exclusion may seem little more than a passing notion that is quite empty and devoid of substance. Yet I suggest that through analysis of the idea as an idea, and if carefully defined and judiciously applied, it becomes a rich and complex metaphor for seeing, knowing, and understanding the social world.

The concept of social exclusion that provides the theoretical framework for this examination of Canada's human services turns our attention to social relationships and structures and is somewhat paradoxical. Contrary to the common and casual sense of the term, I insist that social exclusion is not about being left out, or even cast out. Rather, social exclusion concerns the relationships between people who are variously engaged with or *inside* society's social institutions and systems. I define social exclusion as "the official procedures and everyday practices that function to draw individuals and groups inside to devalued and dis-possessed places, and thus (re)produce, reinforce, and justify economic, spatial, sociopolitical, and subjective divides."

The problem of self-imposed social exclusion

Whereas the *idea* of self-imposed social exclusion may be almost every-where,[17] and despite a recent "revival of interest in human agency" (Martin, 2004, 79), instances of self-imposed or voluntary social exclu-sion are rarely considered in policy and social research. Most references to voluntary social exclusion pertain to seemingly aberrant individuals (Lund, 1999; Silver, 1994). For example, there are those who are *unable* or *unwilling* to participate in society productively (Pleace, 1998, 50). In some instances, people seem to bring suffering upon themselves, even "collude in their own oppression" and engage in self-destructive behaviour (Gleeson, 1992, 478). Indeed, we know through casual obser-vation and empirical research that people do make choices – in intimate relationships and social networks, for example – that ultimately per-petuate lives of hardship and deprivation.

From a theoretical standpoint the contradictory notion of voluntary social exclusion may be reconciled through definition. For instance, some adopt a relational perspective and attempt to trace the specific processes through which people become caught in a downward spiral of hardship and deprivation, often focusing on its individual subjec-tive experience (Commins, 1993; Room, 1995; Shucksmith & Chapman, 1998). In the application of this dynamic view, social exclusion tends to be reduced to the prevention of participation in the "normal activities of citizens in that society" and the lack of recognition of citizenship rights, which are to be counted as social exclusion only when they hap-pen to people for reasons beyond their control and against their wishes (Burchardt, Le Grand, & Piachaud, 1999; Commins, 1993; European Commission, 2012; Hills, Le Grand, & Piachaud, 2002; Richardson & Le Grand, 2002; Room, 1995; Shucksmith & Chapman, 1998). In other words, voluntary social exclusion is a contradiction in terms. Indeed, some argue that self-exclusion is not social exclusion at all, but some-thing entirely different; that only social exclusion that happens *to* people *against their will* counts as cause for concern; and that voluntary social exclusion represents a concept (and reality) that does not belong in policy and social welfare debates (Barry, 2002; Le Grand, 1998). It follows from this argument, then, that only those who *want* social inclusion can suffer social exclusion. Staying with participation as the basis of social inclusion, others explain voluntary social exclusion through an emphasis on the "distasteful" nature of social spaces of inclusion for certain individuals and groups, and therefore self-exclusion is understood to be merely exercising one's legitimate right to choose non-participation (Hack-Polay, 2008; Hayward, Simpson, & Wood, 2004; Reay & Lucey, 2004). Reducing social inclusion to social engagement offers little insight into expressions of self-imposed social exclusion, the daily life consequences of which are first and foremost material, putting a strain on physical survival.

Moreover, questions of *choice* cannot be sidestepped in contemporary contexts of intensifying transnationalism, as they cut to the core of classificatory schemes defining individuals and groups on the move. Existing categories for migrants are consequential, since they serve to sort the victim from the villain. For example, judgments of choice and free will distinguish the refugee from the "bogus" claimant, the asylum seeker from the "illegal alien," the trafficked from the temporary foreign worker, and the trafficker from the smuggler. Presumed intentions, motivations, and desires are fundamental to how we organize ourselves and behave towards one another. With increasing demands on a pared-down system of social services, determining rules of inclusion and exclusion is a necessary and essential function of all levels of government. National welfare states require tools and criteria – metaphors – to evaluate who is deserving and who is not; whose needs count and who will pay to address those needs through social policy and social services.

Research that considers the everyday realities of those who move across national borders to make a living, thus transgressing boundaries defined by the nation-state, reveals a range of complexities and paradoxes that challenge such simplistic and linear explanations: processes of inclusion and exclusion operate simultaneously, social inclusion is sometimes resisted, efforts towards inclusion may accentuate and reinforce exclusion, and experiences of social exclusion may be evaluated to be both desirable and adverse (e.g., Clements, 2005; Good Gingrich, 2006; E. Lightman, Herd, & Mitchell, 2006; E. Lightman, Mitchell, & Herd, 2005; Wolff, 2005).

Who are Mennonite (im)migrants?

Few historians relate the unique story of Mennonite (or *Dietsche*) (im)migrants in Canada. A complicating factor in precisely tracing their roots is that the Dietsche are not a singular group of Mennonites: rather, they include several discrete groups – emerging in response to the pressures that provoked their migrations – who have desired to remain more traditional in lifestyle and more separate from the world. In his 2013 book entitled *Village among Nations: "Canadian" Mennonites in a Transnational World, 1916–2006*, Royden Loewen carefully and eloquently traces the religious, social, and economic contexts of Dietsche migrations between Latin American colonies and rural Canadian communities. As the only thorough historical account of this Mennonite population to date, it provides important background for this inquiry.

The roots of all Mennonites are religious, originating in the sixteenth century and the Protestant Reformation in Europe. A small group of radical reformers became known as the Anabaptists, departing from the newly formed Protestant church on several points of religious ideology and practice. The central tenets of the Anabaptist movement included believer's (or adult) baptism; the authority of the New Testament scriptures; the "priesthood of all believers," or communal scriptural study and shared church leadership; and definitive separation of church and state. Named after Menno Simons (for primarily pragmatic reasons), who in 1536 renounced the Catholic priesthood and was re-baptized as an Anabaptist elder, the first Mennonites distinguished themselves from other Anabaptists by their rejection of violence, even in self-defence.

Persecuted for their radical beliefs and practices, invisibility and movement were vital to Mennonite life. The first northward migration took one group of Mennonites from the Netherlands to the Danzig-Vistula region, then under the rule of Polish kings (Sawatzky, 1971). Over 200 years later, when the Lutheran church imposed severe restrictions on further land purchases by Mennonites, many moved on to South Russia, where the Russian Colonial Law of 1763 offered these colonists free land, "perpetual exemption from military and civil service, freedom of religion, the right to control their schools and churches, and the right (and obligation) of agricultural colonies to be locally autonomous" (ibid., 5).[18] After almost 100 years of prosperous and self-governed colony life, the privileges of their cultural-religious freedom and isolation began to be withdrawn by the tsar of Russia. Most important, military exemption was no longer permitted, as the Mennonites were required to accept all responsibilities as Russian citizens. The majority of Mennonites agreed to render some form of service to the state, while others understood the compromises demanded by the tsar to be irreconcilable with Mennonite beliefs and practices.

Ideological dissension within the Mennonite brotherhood, coupled with intensifying problems of landlessness and inadequate alternative economic opportunity, enticed many to look to a new land. Between 1874 and 1880, over one-third of the 50,000 Mennonites in Russia emigrated to North America. Most settled in southern Manitoba, where the Canadian government permitted the establishment of closed colonies with little capital expense. Representing four subgroups of the Mennonite communities in South Russia, the Manitoba settlers tended to be the most traditional and impoverished of the immigrants. The *Altkolonier*[19] (Old Colony) constituted the most conservative strand of the Dutch-Russian history, paralleling the Old Order Mennonites (sometimes called "horse-and-buggy" Mennonites) of their Swiss relatives in eastern parts of the United States and Canada. Their quest for isolation – based on the Anabaptist conviction of separation of church and state and the authority of the biblical scriptures – was unrelenting, and they reinstituted their separated colony life in communities known as reserves in Manitoba and Saskatchewan.[20]

But less than a decade after resettlement, the provincial government introduced the Manitoba Schools Act, which required all instruction to be in English and later stipulated that all public schools fly the Union Jack. Internal conflict among Mennonites again flared. Some began moving west, and by 1911 the Canadian census reported 14,400 Mennonites in Saskatchewan and 15,600 in Manitoba (Sawatzky 1971, 18). When both the Manitoba and the Saskatchewan provincial governments implemented the School Attendance Act in 1916 in an attempt to assimilate ethnic groups and eliminate the German language in all schools, Mennonites who did not send their children to a recognized English-speaking school were fined or incarcerated. With the mounting pressures of World War I, military conscription was imposed in 1917. Even under these extreme conditions, the more "liberal" among the Mennonites continued to find ways to adjust to government demands; but the more "conservative" groups – the *Altkolonier* and *Sommerfelder* – became increasingly disturbed by the imposing threats to church authority and community cohesiveness. Beginning in 1922, between 7,000 and 8,000 Mennonites migrated from the Canadian prairies to northern Mexico and Paraguay, where they established traditional colony settlements (F.H. Epp, 1982; Janzen, 2004b; Sawatzky, 1971). In the move to Mexico, Mennonites negotiated certain rights with the Mexican government, known as the *Privilegium*,[21] which included permission to settle in patterns of their choosing, that is, in colonies (Krahn & Sawatzky, 1990; Quiring, 2003; Sawatzky, 1971). With growing concern about the possibility of mandated direct military involvement of Mennonite groups remaining in Canada, a second wave of migrations to Paraguay and Mexico occurred when international travel was made possible following World War II, and more southern colonies were formed in the 1940s and 1950s. Maintaining a structure that had been developed in Russia and reinstated on the Canadian prairies, the Mennonite settlers organized their new colonies in Mexico into villages and numbered *campos* consisting of individual family plots that included shared agricultural land.

Over the course of the past ninety years, the number of colony Mennonites has increased dramatically, in the main owing to their large families. The associated perennial problem of land shortage in colonies has meant that Mennonites have expanded their land base by repeating the paradigmatic migration of the 1920s, establishing daughter colonies in the Mexican states of Chihuahua, Durango, Campeche, and Zacatecas and further south in Belize, Bolivia, Paraguay, and Argentina (Loewen, 2013b).

However, survival within colonies has not been possible for everyone, and an altogether different sort of migratory pattern began within a few years after the mass migrations to the south. Individual families started migrating back to Canada, to the province of Ontario, where seasonal agricultural work was more readily available than on the prairies. In recent years, this northern trickle has swelled to an unrelenting and evolving stream of migrants; over 80,000 members of this "loosely linked pan-American community of some 250,000 Low German-speaking Mennonites" have "returned" from Latin America to various parts of rural Canada and the south-central United States (Loewen, 2013b, 4–5). Today, it is estimated that Mennonites from colonies in Latin America total 50,000 to 60,000 and comprise approximately 20 per cent of all Mennonites in Canada (Janzen, 2004b; Loewen, 2007; Quiring, 2003). The population is concentrated in areas close to the fertile farming fields of southern Ontario, but significant numbers have also been drawn by agricultural work to Alberta, Saskatchewan, and Manitoba (Janzen, 1998; Loewen, 2007).

The Mennonite Central Committee (MCC), a relief and development organization of the broader North American Mennonite church, has had a pivotal role in migrations from Mexico to Canada. MCC, initiated as a mutual aid effort, was founded in 1920 in response to requests for help from Mennonites in Ukraine who were suffering under the weight of war and famine (Juhnke, 1989). Records show that the organization's interest in the Mennonites living in Mexico dates back as far as 1946, when several prominent Mennonite leaders visited Mexico on behalf of MCC and were alarmed by the need for "spiritual awakening" and "cultural grounding" made evident to them in the areas of "religion, education, and sanitation" (Quiring, 2004, 88). A prevalent sentiment among North American Mennonites was that colony Mennonites had regressed economically and religiously, while other groups had made important advancements.[22] Even though MCC's efforts were not overtly aimed at religious conversion but were focused on economic, education, and health initiatives such as provision of seed loans, well digging, food relief programs, medical care, and teachers, colony Mennonites resisted this interference, and MCC personnel left in the early 1950s.

It was not until 1975 that MCC was able to establish more sustained work with Mennonite colonies in Latin America and Dietsche (im)migrants in Canada. Today, provincial MCC offices as well as MCC Canada provide varied supports for Mennonite colonists, ranging from the ongoing publication of a biweekly German-language newspaper called *Die Mennonitishe Post* to the establishment and oversight of addiction centres in northern Mexico. Consistent with its tradition of providing aid and relief in the face of natural disasters, MCC Canada responded to the Durango drought in 2012. Despite facing public criticism over a decade ago for unfairly judging and interfering in the lives of fellow Mennonites (Quiring, 2003, 2004), MCC's involvement with colonies in Latin America continues to extend well beyond material need, seeking to address a perceived "mental, emotional, physical and spiritual vacuum" (Braun 2013, 6).

While it is likely that these efforts to relieve various types of hardships endured by some Mennonites in Latin America derive from sincere concern, their impact on the distinct and separate Old Colony lifestyle has been mixed. Based on a thorough examination of church documents and interviews with Old Colony bishops and ministers in Mexico, Quiring concludes that MCC and other North American Mennonite organizations "have undermined, sometimes inadvertently and at other times intentionally, the integrity of the Old Colony church" (Quiring, 2004, 89).

Migration continues to be a way of life for many Mennonite colonists, moving from colonies in Mexico and Bolivia to rural regions of Ontario, Manitoba, Alberta, or, more recently, Saskatchewan, and back south again. Some migrants are "back-and-forthers," following the Canadian harvest from early spring to late fall and returning south when the agricultural season is over. Others attempt to settle more permanently, making the long drive back to Mexico only for extended vacations in the winter months. And there are some for whom any thought of return, even for a visit with family, is financially and logistically impossible. The nature and meaning of this migration – unprecedented in Mennonite history, yet sharing features with expanding south-north and east-west migrations (Collyer, Düvell, & de Haas, 2012) – and the necessary practices for preserving a cultural and religious heritage in the context of migratory livelihoods are central to the story of self-imposed social exclusion that follows.

Nomenclature that accurately identifies this particular population of (im)migrants in Canada, and thus clearly situates this research in Mennonite scholarly literature, is far from straightforward.[23] At the same time, precise identification is fundamental to sound research and credible knowledge pertaining to the dozens of disparate Mennonite groups residing in North America today. The significance of migrations beyond the boundaries of the colony, or colony *emigrations*, undertaken by those who have more recently returned to Canada from Latin America, tends to be diminished or overlooked altogether in the conflation of groups and histories.

In research interviews, the most common term used for self-reference, especially when distinguishing their own people from others, was Dietsche. For example, when defining ethnic or racial backgrounds of the workers in her workplace, Justina, an (im)migrant woman, noted that she and three others are "Dietsch,"[24] another co-worker is "brown-skinned," and the rest are "English." In Canada, the specificity of the term in everyday discourse is adequate to refer only to Mennonites who have migrated from colonies in Latin America, as no other Mennonite group – even those who speak *Plautdietsch* or Low German – refers to itself as Dietsch. Highlighting their unique migration pattern, I use the term *(im)migrant* throughout the book to signify the Dietsche Mennonite supranational disposition. Their migratory history, which many continue today, and their general resistance to "settlement" sharply distinguish them from more conventional images of immigrants. Accordingly, I reserve the terms Dietsch/Dietsche and (im)migrant to refer to service recipients or "clients" who would identify themselves as such. All Dietsche research participants emigrated from a colony in Latin America to Canada, and continue to claim some affinity with colony life in important ways. Furthermore, a sampling criterion for the Mennonite (im)migrant participants was that they were engaged in return migration or had lived primarily in Canada for fifteen years or less.

The research

Drawing on qualitative research conducted between 2003 and 2013 in rural Ontario and Alberta,[25] I explore the social realities and the idea of self-imposed social exclusion through an analysis of the social field that is Canada's social welfare system. Aiming for a range of perspectives, I made efforts to hear from Dietsche (im)migrants who were engaged with human services in some way, exhibited some measure of economic exclusion, and demonstrated various degrees of settlement and adaptation to "Canadian culture" in the context of transnational livelihoods.[26] Thus, the Dietsche respondents represented a multiplicity of social positions in their own ethno-religious culture and in mainstream Canadian society. Specifically, some research participants had been in Canada for only a few months, others had been there for several years, and some had returned to their colony in Latin America every winter. Still others had settled into year-round employment in Canada. As I wished to explore the ways in which processes and outcomes of social exclusion are gendered, both men and women were interviewed. To provide insight into the trajectory of social exclusion and its meaning over a lifetime for individuals, their families, and their people, I sought out several older persons in the Dietsche population. All but four interviews with the sixty-six (im)migrants were conducted in Plautdietsch, either with the assistance of an interpreter or with a Plautdietsch-speaking interviewer.[27] Interviews with Dietsche (im)migrants were loosely structured and free flowing, intended to invite people to "remembrance" and "testimony" (Simon & Eppert, 1997; Simon, Rosenberg, & Eppert, 2000).

To complement the narratives from Dietsche (im)migrants, fifty-five social service workers and employers were interviewed. The practitioners represented a variety of agencies and services including welfare, health and mental healthcare, child protection, employment services, education, housing, police, and legal services. They worked for publicly funded institutions (such as schools, hospitals, and clinics) as well as non-government, non-profit agencies that were fully or partially funded by federal, provincial, or municipal governments. A number of service providers were employees or volunteers with provincial or Canadian branches of MCC or other Mennonite organizations.[28]

The personal histories and identities of service providers in relation to the Dietsche (im)migrant population are important to the analysis that follows. For example, some practitioners were also Plautdietsch-speaking Mennonite immigrants from colonies in Latin America; some were Mennonites who spoke Plautdietsch, but had never lived in a colony in Mexico or South America; some were Mennonite, but did not speak Plautdietsch; and some were not Mennonite at all. Interviews with fourteen Plautdietsch-speaking immigrant service providers, who were thus both insiders and outsiders, provided unusual insight into the experiences and perceptions of Dietsche (im)migrants, and the meaning of engagement or detachment in various social fields. All Plautdietsch-speaking immigrant service providers had lived in a colony before migrating to Canada. Yet in contrast to Dietsche (im)migrants, all immigrant professionals who were working with the Dietsche population had migrated as children or teenagers, had pursued higher education in Canada, were no longer participants in the Old Colony church or other conservative Mennonite churches, did not retain traditional practices, and had integrated into and were acculturated to Canadian mainstream society. I identify these participants as Mennonite *immigrant* service providers.

The identity of health professionals who spoke Plautdietsch but had not immigrated from Latin America was more difficult to pin down, but most Dietsche (im)migrants spoke about them as more English than Dietsch. These participants, along with ethnic Mennonite practitioners who did not speak Plautdietsch, are identified in the following chapters as *Mennonite* service providers. Finally, service providers who had no historical or ethnic connection with Mennonites are designated as *English* in this book, as they were commonly identified in Dietsche communities.

Such privileged engagement with Dietsche (im)migrants was made possible through my personal and professional identity and experience – as a Mennonite mother, health practitioner, and social researcher. I am a Mennonite by ethnicity, culture, and religious participation.

The Dietsche and I are part of the same "imagined community" (B. Anderson, 2006) linked by a "deeply rooted history," a shared religious and ethnic identity, and a common understanding of "Mennonite ways" including "nonconformity, simplicity, non-violence, and separation from 'the world'" (Loewen, 2013b, 230–1). Yet I am not a part of the Dietsche population. My ancestry resides with the Swiss-German Mennonites rather than the Plautdiestch-speaking Dutch-Russian Mennonites. While we share religious roots and our cultures intermingle, there are definite differences that divide our Mennonite histories and heritages. For example, the language of my parents and grandparents is Pennsylvania *Deutsch*, a dialect of German, as is Plautdietsch. They constitute discrete languages that do not permit communication across this cultural-linguistic divide. Given my Swiss-German Mennonite identity, I am both an "insider," as one who is culturally informed and sympathetic, and an "outsider,"[29] as I am unable to speak Plautdietsch and I occupy a very different social position from Dietsche (im)migrants. Even though I identified myself as Mennonite early on in my research, I discontinued this practice because (im)migrant respondents consistently perceived me to be English and did not acknowledge the ethnic and religious heritage we share.

I first worked with Dietsche (im)migrants in my position as a community nutritionist and program coordinator for a peer-led prenatal nutrition program for Dietsche women, from 1995 to 1997. Although I had participated in Mennonite communities all my life, I had never before encountered the Dietsche population. They had been hardly visible in my Mennonite world. I soon learned that this particular branch of the Mennonite family tree was well known to other Mennonites especially in certain rural regions, and was frequently and openly discussed with derision. "Mexican Mennonites" are known by many as our poor cousins, as "second-class Mennonites" (Braun, 2008), who tarnish our good name. I recognized this common inclination to "box up" (Loewen, 2013a) difference when difference cannot be kept out of sight or erased. Difference is simultaneously brought into existence to be defined beneath and outside, even beneath and outside the human condition. Such dehumanizing self-righteous practices are commonplace and can be observed in a wide variety of social contexts, from interpersonal relationships, to workplaces, to communities and cultures. I became curious about the specific conditions and mechanisms through which such processes of "unmaking" and "remaking" are set in motion and sustained, and I wanted to learn more about the ways in which individuals and groups resist the identities ascribed to them to claim and reclaim self.

A few years later, in preparation for my doctoral research, I renewed and expanded my relationships with service providers and individual members of the Dietsche (im)migrant population through informal conversation and program observation, and I also provided a series of nutrition education classes for Dietsche women. In 2003 and 2004, following approximately eighteen months of frequent visits to various settings in Dietsche communities in order to build rapport and trust, I conducted in-depth research interviews, focus groups, and program observations with service providers and Dietsche (im)migrants.[30] All Dietsche respondents were people I already knew or to whom I had been previously introduced. My aim was to set the conditions for trust and to reduce social distance, for "social proximity and familiarity provide two of the conditions of 'nonviolent' communication" (Bourdieu et al., 1999, 610). Building on established research relationships, I led two subsequent qualitative research projects with Dietsche (im)migrants: one in 2006 with twelve women in southern Ontario; and the second with eighteen women in southern Alberta and Ontario, from 2010 to 2013.

The theoretical lens through which I interpret this case example of social exclusion and its self-imposed expressions is the reflexive sociology of Pierre Bourdieu and his concepts of *social fields*, *systems of capital*, and *habitus*. Bourdieu's sociology offers a methodology as well as the theoretical constructs to study social action, in order to zero in on the *interface* between the subjective and the material, the individual and the social. Bourdieu's concepts and reflexive approach provide the tools and integrative perspective necessary to uncover and examine the relationship between established sociopolitical structures and the mental structures (or ideas) that work to keep both in place. This book is not intended to be a commentary on Bourdieu's work, which has been both widely acclaimed and critiqued. My approach is simply pragmatic: I use his work to the extent that it furthers mine. That being said, I have also attempted to accurately and fairly incorporate his complex ideas and present them in applied ways that are accessible.

The research represents a collaborative effort, as it was conducted in consultation with Dietsche research participants who emerged in the process as key informants, or cultural brokers. In many ways, it is a shared or communal analysis, as the work was done through ongoing dialogue with these individuals. We considered a series of key ideas that recurred in the data, examined how they fit within broader Anabaptist/Mennonite history and tradition according to the litera-ture, and studied them in comparison with our divergent yet similar life experiences. It is an analysis that was conducted in the spaces in between "I and the other," nurturing intersubjective knowing and a mutual coming to understanding.[31]

The book

Janzen (2004b) refers to Dietsche (im)migrants from Latin America as the "rejected conservatives" among Mennonites, as "one could say that many parts of this subject have not even received a first look" (21). While this book is in no way intended to be a cultural study of Dietsche (im)migrants in Canada, I aim to contribute to the noticeable gap in all literatures regarding these migrant communities. This study of social divides and self-imposed social exclusion is deliberately contextualized in the social world through the personal experiences and life narra-tives offered in interviews and focus group discussions with an ethno-religious group of (im)migrants to Canada from religious colonies in Latin America and professionals from a wide range of human service agencies who provide services for this population.

As with any research with people, ethics are a critical and challeng-ing matter. I resisted exposing Dietsche (im)migrants because their dis-position is to stay out of sight. My misgivings about publishing a book about Dietsche (im)migrants – a decidedly noisy mode of "knowledge mobilization" – have hindered the writing of it for several years. Dur-ing this time, it became apparent that, although I was reluctant to draw the "world's" attention to this separate and private people, many oth-ers were not.[32] My silence cannot protect their privacy, and perhaps this is not my responsibility. After years of consulting and working with leaders in Dietsche communities, I committed myself to finish this writ-ing with the resolve to strive for increased mutual understanding, espe-cially in those instances when Dietsche (im)migrants are not able to stay out of sight or invisible – when they are forced to find new ways of being who they are in the world.

I have written this book with a several audiences in mind. First, I anticipate that the subject matter and reflexive sociological approach of this work will be of interest to scholars and teachers who think about the processes and practices that organize those social spaces and define social relations. The applied nature of the theoretical foundations offers practical relevance for practitioners in the formulation and analysis of social policy and in the planning and delivery of human services. Given the tendency for Aboriginal and ethno-specific services to be designed and delivered by "their own," the inside look at the experiences of service providers who are variously positioned in relation to the traditional Dietsche population will be of particular interest to practitioners who identify with ethno-cultural "minority" groups as well as the "mainstream," and feel themselves to be neither in nor out in both social contexts. More generally, those of us who share a history, cultural-religious heritage, or family tree with the Dietsche may find the personal narratives enrich and enliven those common roots. And finally, it is expected that the life experiences recounted here will offer personal resonance for those who know something of the violences of social exclusion.

The simplicity of the stories and the complexity of the conceptual tools are best taken together, as both are necessary to guard against the common dangers of misrepresentation and non-understanding. The situated study of subjective experience and individual agency within material realities and social processes provides analytical precision and depth in understanding the far-reaching and profound implications of social exclusion. This dual focus – the ordinary of everyday/everynight life mingled with theory – offers a necessary point of view in the well-rehearsed debates regarding chronic social ills. And because social exclusion is socially situated in this case, the themes explored go beyond social exclusion. The book is also about habits – the usual, presumed ways through which we consider social problems, policy responses, and "target populations." In this way, the focus of this study is *people* and the relationships among and between us, in particular the social forces that work to marginalize and oppress some and accommodate and elevate others. Whether the issue be named social exclusion, poverty, marginalization, discrimination, or oppression, this is an endeavour to develop and try out a relatively new metaphor that might guide our approach to those social problems, the making of policy, and the delivery of human services. Although not an explicit focus here, the effort to analyse everyday social practices alongside official procedures may inform our understanding of the deeply rooted and specific divides of racism and colonialism that feed so much conflict and suffering in our world. Ultimately, I aim to encourage the imagination of policy and practice responses that promote social justice, shared social responsibility, and social *in*clusion – strategies to reconcile economic, spatial, sociopolitical, and subjective divides.

In the chapters that follow, I offer accounts of people's lives as they were generously shared with me. I incorporate direct quotations in order to illustrate ideas and demonstrate processes of social exclusion. To encourage the reader's more personal engagement with these expressions, I use pseudonyms and identify the participant category. Quotations from the interview translator are simply indicated by the word "translator" before the text. Responses from interviews with married couples are indicated by identifying the respondents as such following the quotation. When the interview was conducted in Plautdiestch and translated into English upon transcription, I indicate this by "[Trans.]" at the beginning of the quoted text.

This inquiry into a case or example of self-imposed social exclusion presents a "particular instance of the possible" (Bourdieu & Wacquant, 1992, 233), as many life circumstances of Dietsche (im)migrants are increasingly commonplace in Canada and other wealthy regions of the world. Boundaries that are made at once casually porous and anxiously fortified invite and manage transnational movements of people. Migrations from situations defined by lack – of work, food, opportunity, safety, hope – to promises of possibility have sculpted new lines and layers in the Canadian social landscape. The movement of Dietsche Mennonite families from the south to the north are positively ordinary in the factors that provoke and sustain them. And the Mennonite commitment to a distinct ethnic, cultural, and religious identity that runs in and through their migrating and settling is shared by individuals and groups from around the world. So in this way, the Dietsche (im)migrant case of social exclusion is both unique and typical, as the dilemmas of inclusion and exclusion, conformity and self-definition, and entitlement and regulation are common to human experience in contemporary globalized contexts.

Chapter Two

Mennonite Migrations and a Common Sense Point of View

Mennonite migrations provoke encounters between peoples and cultures and world views that are mutually unfamiliar and sometimes conflicting. How do communities respond to Dietsche families who come and go, usually staying to themselves but always standing out in their difference? How do Dietsche (im)migrants experience and engage with individuals and institutions in this perplexing environment, outside the protective familiarity of the colony? My research spanning more than ten years focused on the relationships between Dietsche (im)migrants and human services in Ontario and Alberta. Social service workers from a wide range of agencies and organizations discussed their work with the Dietsche.[1] While our conversations varied, I heard definite patterns and commonalities across human service sectors and geographic regions. Thus, there emerged a shared point of view, or a "common sense."

Concepts, such as the idea of social exclusion, are not benign, somehow detached from the social world. To the contrary, the ways in which we think – the "thought objects" constructed to grasp our social reality (Bourdieu, 1989, 15) – directly guide how we organize ourselves and behave towards one another. Even more, it is especially those widely held beliefs and assumptions that are taken for granted, even eluding consciousness, that are most stubborn and defining. We readily refer to such ideas as *common sense*, as if they are indisputable and inconsequential. Yet Sen (2000a) asserts that "unreasoned pessimism, masquerading as composure based on realism and common sense, can serve to 'justify' disastrous inaction and an abdication of public responsibility" (34). Demanding little energy or thought, appeals to common sense too often overrule inquiry and reason.[2] Common sense provides a schema for naming, categorizing, evaluating, thinking, interpreting, and constructing "truth" that is replicated across multiple and various sites through everyday practices.

Through the case example of Dietsche (im)migrants, this chapter considers the common sense point of view in human services that produces representations – "official" representations – of a specific cultural and religious (im)migrant population. In the final sections of the chapter, these official representations of the population are placed alongside self-representations. In this examination of the inconsistencies between how service providers view Dietsche and how Dietsche view themselves, I wish to draw attention to the consequences of common sense ideas or cognitive structures.

Assessing need: Dietsche (im)migrants in Canada

They have their own dreams and hopes for the future. And, I guess more and more, the dream of coming to Canada to earn enough here and go back to Mexico is a broken dream. They have come to the realization that to be a farmer, an independent farmer – which is sort of the ideal to strive for – is not obtainable. [Henry, Mennonite service provider]

Research interviews and focus groups were conducted with social workers, health professionals, employers, teachers and other school personnel, settlement workers, employment counsellors, police, and legal advisors. In Canada, Dietsche (im)migrants are known by human service workers for certain practices and behaviours that set them apart in local communities. Service providers repeatedly and consistently referenced the following concerns: employment, housing, language, education, family systems and social networks, migration and travel, and poverty. I will briefly discuss each issue in turn as social service workers and health professionals described them to me.

Employment

Dietsche (im)migrants most often take up jobs in Canada's agri-food industry. Many men and women work as seasonal labourers in tomato, cucumber, and tobacco fields or in processing plants. Some Dietsche (im)migrants work alongside migrant labourers hired through Canada's Temporary Foreign Worker Program (TFWP), including the Seasonal Agricultural Worker Program (SAWP), and the more recent

Stream for Low-wage Positions.[3] When these temporary-visa workers are required to return to their home countries, as they are permitted to stay a maximum of eight months in any given year for the
SAWP to a cumulative total of four years for those in the Stream for
Low-wage Positions (ESDC, 2015), Dietsche (im)migrants provide
ready labour for large, year-round greenhouse operations in southern
Ontario and Alberta. Some employers expressed an overall preference for Dietsche workers, and others complement their temporary-
visa labour force by hiring more flexible Dietsche workers for a few
months or weeks at a time.

Even though the conditions of employment for (im)migrants in Canada are often temporary and tenuous, service providers seldom cited
unemployment or under-employment as a concern for this population. Social service and health practitioners agreed that Dietsche are
unusually hard-working and generally find paid work quite readily.
However, practitioners expressed disapproval for their apparent satisfaction with – and even preference for – seasonal, low-paying farm
labour. Moreover, the practice of working together as families in these
jobs, sometimes with very young children working alongside their parents or playing in the fields, was frequently viewed with curiosity and
criticism.

Housing

Inadequate housing arrangements raised concern, particularly for
child protection workers and health practitioners. Most Dietsche
prefer to live in secluded rural areas, away from surrounding cities
and towns. Dietsche families have been known to live in old farm-
houses in disrepair, tobacco houses, chicken coops, bunkhouses, and
house trailers. Several families may share a large farmhouse. Word of
a vacancy in such preferred housing in rural regions travels quickly
through the Dietsche grapevine. Since these accommodations are
generally not desirable or acceptable for "Canadians," they are often
passed from one Dietsche family to another. Acquiring a distinctive
appearance over time, they are recognized by local people as "Mennonite" places. In rural areas, it is common for employers to provide
housing, which is sometimes rent free. When housing is partial compensation for labour, it is often seasonal and not fit for occupation
beyond the harvest months, and families are required to move frequently. Dietsche also live in small towns in agricultural regions of

Canada, where they often find apartments above taverns and store-fronts or in congested, low-income housing complexes.

Language

Many (im)migrants speak only Plautdietsch, or Low German. Until recently, this dialect of German has been primarily an oral tradition among this population. Service providers commonly reported that many Dietsche have poor literacy skills, and some appear unable to read or write in any language. Traditionally, the language of the church has been High German, as all religious services are conducted in High German, and German Bibles are used for all instruction – religious and otherwise. However, social service workers observed that most Dietsche cannot read or understand this language, which is distinct from Plautdietsch. English has entered the homes of some who have lived in Canada longer and whose children regularly attend public school; parents sometimes prefer to learn from their children, reinforcing the younger generation's English-language skills. The standard settlement initiative for (im)migrants in Canada has focused on English-language skills, demonstrated by numerous population-specific English as a Second Language (ESL) programs in Ontario and Alberta.

Education

Participation in formal education systems is minimal for many. In colonies in Latin America the general practice is for girls to attend school until they are eleven years of age and boys until they are twelve. In Canada, Dietsche children generally finish elementary school (attending until the age of twelve or thirteen), yet children even younger may not attend school regularly, because nine- and ten-year-olds often work in the fields with the rest of the family during peak harvest seasons. Service providers noted that some parents report to school officials that their children are being "home schooled" to avoid visits from the attendance counsellor; attendance in the public education system cannot be enforced for children who are home schooled. Teachers and school attendance counsellors relayed their suspicion that, in these situations, little or no "proper education" is provided, as they believe that many parents are effectively illiterate and have very limited formal education. Educators noted that some Dietsche parents send their children to "their own" Old Colony schools that have been established in certain areas of rural Canada,[4] but that such schools are reported to be costly, often full, not accredited, and hire unqualified teachers. These Dietsche practices regarding education in Canada, combined with poor literacy skills, were usually perceived to demonstrate a collective and individual devaluing of formal education and knowledge and constituted a focal point for social service intervention.

Adding some nuance to the issue of inadequate education among Dietsche children and their parents, Mennonite immigrant service providers described considerable variability in the quality of education provided in Mennonite colony schools in Latin America. Some colony schools were reported to be quite inadequate according to North American standards, in that it is common for children of all ages to be taught in a single classroom by one untrained teacher, where they receive primarily religious instruction in High German from the Bible as the only text, in a very strict and punitive environment. In contrast, certain colonies are known among Mennonites to provide high-quality schooling that attracts families from other colonies. Mennonite immigrant service providers used this knowledge of colony schools and church influences in education to provide a context for describing schooling practices in Canada and the value (im)migrants place on education.

Family systems and social networks

Dietsche (im)migrants tend to have very large families and generally do not use birth control. It is not unusual for families to include ten to fourteen children. Many service providers identified the patriarchal order of families to be a problem requiring intervention. Some assumed that the Dietsche dedication to a traditional, male-dominated religion and culture is an indication that violence against women and children is quietly condoned. Physical and sexual abuse in family relationships was occasionally mentioned as a controversial characteristic of the population.[5] While some practitioners acknowledged that the incidence of various types of violence in Mennonite families may not be higher than in other population groups, others contended that an alarming rate exists among (im)migrants, and they attributed this to the traditional patriarchal belief system and cultural degradation. Len, a Mennonite service provider, who had worked solely with

Dietsche families for over seven years, characterized the population as follows:

> Now when I say they are lost to humanity, I am not saying that in a negative way. But when we mentioned all the social problems, I didn't mention incest. In my whole life I have never come across where there was so much sexual abuse and incest.[6] And I think that would have to be studied, and it would have to come down to – it's really a matter of them coming so low as a people.

Practitioners generally recognized that extended family relationships are important to most (im)migrants, but they often described these relationships as unhealthy and unreliable, presenting "a lot of complex issues." A strong commitment to family networks and traditional gender roles was considered helpful in providing support and stability, but it was also sharply criticized for contributing to family violence, rigidity and defiance, intolerance and exclusion, and isolation. People who are not connected with family and church are ostracized, and they tend to have more material, social, and emotional needs. While families were generally viewed as supportive of one another, service providers reported that extra-familial relationships are often non-existent or quite strained and difficult.

Migration and travel

Continued migration and intentional separation from mainstream society prevents full participation in the education, health, and employment sectors for many (im)migrants. The transitory lifestyle of some families, in combination with their employment as seasonal farm workers, precludes intervention by formal services and impedes any kind of "tracking mechanism." Even families who have settled more permanently in Canada often travel back to Mexico for four- to eight-week visits in the winter months, sometimes jeopardizing or forfeiting their sources of income.

Despite the difficulties presented by the Dietsche migratory habit, the issue of citizenship, or documentation, was rarely mentioned in discussions of the needs of this population. When prompted, service providers recognized that the first and most urgent need that many have when they migrate is assistance with the complicated and difficult process of obtaining legal status in Canada. Most practitioners recognized that Dietsche depend entirely on MCC to provide this service, and often there is little by way of other kinds of assistance that they can offer until this paperwork is complete.

Most service providers readily acknowledged the desperate conditions that many leave behind in Mexico. Some postulated that Dietsche represent an unusually impoverished group of immigrants:

> They come from very, very poor villages and there is nothing! A doctor called me once because he was sending a woman home having had a baby and he said, "Is the environment suitable?" I said, "Well, no. For you, no. You wouldn't consider it suitable, but for what they're used to, this is heaven. Like, they have floors; they have doors!" [Cathy, English Service Provider]

Poverty

It was inconsistently recognized that, even in Canada, some (im)migrants have difficulty providing the basic necessities for their families:

> When we go into families, we can have a gamut of abuse sometimes – physical abuse, and parent-teen conflict, children's behaviour being out of control, mom not able to cope if dad's not in the home. But we find we can't even address those things until we actually address the level of poverty some of them are living in. It just blows some of my staff away. I mean, you can't work on anything around parenting skills, or setting up structure, or routine in the home without first addressing "When am I going to get food to feed my children tomorrow?" So we find that is a real core issue with quite a few families that we have. [Gayle, English service provider]

On the other hand, some practitioners commented on the extraordinary potential for earnings in a single picking season when several family members contribute. Mike, an English service provider, maintained that a family working together in tomato or cucumber fields could make "over $10,000 in one month." These sorts of claims, in combination with the Child Tax Benefit money collected by many large (im)migrant families, led some human service workers to speculate about "what they do with all their money," that perhaps they are "hiding what they have in bank accounts" [Susan, English service provider], buying properties for their sons, contributing large sums of money to the church or extended family members, or simply squandering their earnings. Susan's false starts and nervous laughter when offering her recommendations for changing Dietsche spending practices suggest discomfort and ambivalence in her authoritative position on the matter.

> They could, in fact, have fairly good incomes with the Child Tax Benefit. So maybe – I guess what I'm trying to get across, maybe they need help with budgeting or maybe – maybe someone needs to work with these people to determine the distribution of their earnings and how they are spending their money. I don't think they would want to do that, but – [laughter]. But that might be an area of assistance for these – [Susan, English service provider]

Compounding need

Social service workers and health practitioners repeatedly described the problems presented by Dietsche families as interrelated and "compounding," in that it was not possible to name issues of concern as discrete and disconnected from each other. For example, large families, transient habits, poor language skills, and low levels of education all contribute to difficulties in obtaining adequate and affordable housing, steady employment and sufficient income, education for their children, good healthcare, and social supports. Dietsche tend to keep to "their own," appearing to want very limited contact with dominant society. Many attend their own churches, prefer their own schools (if they send their children to school at all), and attempt to stay *"totally separate like a colony in Mexico"* [Marge, Mennonite service provider]. Often, Plautdietsch is spoken in the home as well as in the workplace, as certain kinds of jobs are sought, and some employers hire only or mostly Dietsche. Thus, there may not be much incentive to learn to speak or read English, even in the workplace. Often (im)migrants do not access available community resources in spite of profound economic need, and many are reluctant to accept services when offered or mandated. Dietsche clients are frequently described as a "hard-to-serve" population. Nancy, an English service provider articulated the difficulties of finding social housing for this population:

> There's always the problem with language when they come in. It's like, "Do you really understand what it is that we need?" Then, to put them on

the appropriate bedroom-size waiting list – a lot of times in [the nearby small city] the highest bedroom size we have is four, but most of them would want to live in [the small town] because that's where the bigger population of Mennonites is. And there, they go up to five- and six-bedroom-size units. But it's hard sometimes getting them slotted in. They want housing immediately and it's hard to put someone with eleven kids in a four-bedroom house. The other problem we have is getting verification of their current monthly income. Say they've been here four years. With so many kids working, it's hard to get them to understand that yes, we need to know their children's earnings as well if they're not going to be in school. Because part of the process is, like you said, we take part of their earnings. So that can be a real difficulty. And the other problem we have is when they come up from Mexico, some of our applicants and tenants actually own real estate in Mexico and they have to sell their property [to qualify for social housing]. And getting the proper documentation – [laughter]. And, you know, they'll go back and forth how often?

Human service workers seldom agreed on the most pressing social and individual problems exhibited by (im)migrant families. In general (and as would be expected), service providers gave priority to the concerns most relevant to their particular program or service. For example, health professionals were inclined to emphasize dental, reproductive, and infant health issues. Teachers and public education employees discussed efforts to get Dietsche children to attend school and then strategies to keep them attending. Practitioners from Ontario's social assistance or welfare program (Ontario Works) and various employment services expressed the importance of improving job skills and literacy for more secure and higher-paying employment. Mental health professionals emphasized mental and emotional concerns that needed attention, primarily for women. Law enforcement officials and child welfare workers alike identified the need for a more adequate understanding of, and appreciation for, Canadian norms, laws, and the legal system.

Even though service providers did not agree on the identification or prioritization of problems among (im)migrant families, the thrust of needed intervention was articulated with remarkable consistency and resolve: education, information, and knowledge. For example, service providers might acknowledge the "unsuitability" of the living conditions of some Dietsche families, suggesting appreciation for their economic hardship in Canada, but they did not necessarily associate income with such lack. When housing is provided by the employer, as is often the case for field labourers, practitioners speculated that many families unquestioningly accept whatever accommodations are offered in order to get and maintain work. Henry, a Mennonite immigrant service provider, commented that some Dietsche face landlord-tenant difficulties, but they seldom or never raise the issues "because residential tenancies are hard to come by, and you don't want to rock the boat too much." Economic hardship in Canada was also attributed to their inclination towards large families and low-paying, seasonal employment, "because when they have so many children, the income does not cover the needs of the children" [Gayle, English service provider].

Human service practitioners maintained that the inability of Dietsche parents to adequately provide for such large families "according to our standards" demonstrates and reinforces the importance of educating Dietsche towards the goals of limiting their family size, acquiring English-language skills, instilling the value of formal education, securing better employment, accessing and accepting services, and absorbing "Canadian" norms and standards. Thus, the assessed need is made to fit the planned intervention: education. Dave, a Mennonite service provider, explained:

> To me, education is on the very top of the list, because I just think it's an overwhelming issue. We have people coming into this area from Honduras, and I have several clients from that area. And the difference is they may not understand the language, but they're extremely well educated. It's just a matter of getting them into programs where they can secure some English knowledge and be able to speak, and then they're going to be off and assuming professional roles. We have the combination here of Mennonite [i.e., Dietsche] people who are not educated and don't speak the language, which is a real problem, so their mental muscles haven't been challenged for a long, long time, if ever ... Number one, they're uneducated. On top of that, they're proud of being uneducated, and therein rests the key problem. You know, there's this whole issue: "What I don't know, I'm not accountable to God for." You have to get in underneath the surface to make them understand that ignorance isn't blessed, and it isn't necessarily a way to hide from your responsibilities in life. So to me, education is above all else. If they're properly educated, they will find proper housing, and they will look after that housing properly, and they're going to treat their children properly, and you know, there are all those other issues that go with it. So I'm always on my soapbox about education when they come in, which isn't really what they want to hear.

I enquired about the specific sort of education that is needed, and where (im)migrants would turn to for this education.

> Well, the first one starts with life skills, I think. To a large extent, so many of them just have really no understanding in the whole life skills process and what's required on the very basics of life and what's acceptable and what's not acceptable. And understanding workplace conventions. I mean, they just don't have the concept that you go to work at a certain time and you take a break at a certain time and you go home at a certain time. They feel that they should have the choice to do that whenever you want to do that. And they also are quite comfortable in just earning enough money and getting back in their Suburban with the fenders falling off, driving back to Mexico, as opposed to staying here and making a contribution here, back to society. And I'm not saying it in a detrimental way. I'm only saying that it's education they have to have. They don't know any better, and I think that there's work that has to be done in that regard.[7]

While there was disagreement regarding the specific content of the most important information or knowledge required by (im)migrants, service providers repeatedly cited and discussed the following issues:

- appropriate methods of disciplining children;
- birth control, along with the need for encouraging and advocating for the rights and health of women;
- English-language skills;
- Canadian culture and laws;
- community services and resources.

In describing the fundamental need for Dietsche families to be better informed, practitioners emphasized that these specific gaps in knowledge overlap, complicating and intensifying the challenges they confront when trying to help this population. Above all, social service workers stressed that (im)migrant families require education regarding available services and resources. Further, families need to be instructed to access services and resources more readily. "Getting information out" to Dietsche families "is partly educating them to go and get the services that they need, when they need the services" [Janice, English service provider]. Many practitioners related that this population tends not to access services until they are in crisis, or until help is imposed on them. Janice further reported that often it is only "when they hit a roadblock with regard to friction with society" that they accept formal services – for example, when intervention is mandated through the courts or child protection services.

Conversations with service providers revealed that most see the need for education to extend beyond imparting information. Education must incorporate a component of persuasion to alter the way Dietsche think.

> LUANN: Are those issues being addressed? Literacy and high school education?
> KATHLEEN: I think people are trying. I mean, MCC is certainly trying to educate them. They're using the radio station to promote education, the importance of it. When they come into our office, we're promoting it.
> JANICE: They do real literacy courses there.
> KATHLEEN: Yeah. Lots of literacy courses. Lots of opportunities!
> LUANN: So it's a matter of shifting –
> KATHLEEN: Beliefs. [English service providers]

Health and social services practitioners expressed an obligation to address misguided beliefs and values through instruction and, when necessary, coercion.

> And some of the medical concerns also translate into referrals for us [child welfare services], because the parents will use their home remedies to try to correct illnesses or injuries in their children and don't seek the proper medical treatment, for some reason. Somebody else becomes aware of it and then makes a referral to our agency. And I find there are almost two streams. Some are just – it's a lack of education and so you take an entirely different approach around educating them in terms of what they need to do. Which is a lot easier to deal with than a very ingrained belief system that "You can't tell me how I'm going to treat my child. You have no right to do that." And again, that persecution[8] thing comes up. [Gayle, English service provider]

Some service providers commented on observed differences between Dietsche newcomers and other immigrant groups. They suggested that other immigrants tend to come with more knowledge and information about Canadian culture and expectations, and they are provided with this information, including English-language skills, in their home countries before emigrating. Ways of better preparing Dietsche parents for migration were explored.

> VICTORIA: I think it's funny that Ian brought up the idea of education in Mexico. I've been thinking about that for a long time. I really think that that's where it needs to start, before people arrive here. There has to be more information available. "Don't hit your kids!" would be a really great start [laughter].
>
> MICHELLE: Don't give them bottles of fruit juice [laughter]. We have chocolates – three times a day in Canada! I'm sorry, I don't mean to be facetious. But that is such an important element that is missing. And if they knew what to expect when they arrived. I mean, their bad housing. It's – well, pervasive. It's just a huge problem. They come into these horrible places without what they – you know, sometimes without running water and what not. But if they knew what to expect when they get here, what their rights are. But I don't know even culturally whether that's something that even fits for them. I don't know.
>
> VICTORIA: If you could start, at least, the rumour mill –
>
> MICHELLE: The rumour mill, we know, is very effective within this community. So, let's start the rumour mill going in Mexico. So when you come to Canada, you know your kids are going to have to be in school until they're twenty-two or twenty-three, and that you have to pay for it [post-secondary education] after they're seventeen. You know you can't hit your kids. Yeah, just keep it all going. [English service providers]

In contrast, practitioners who had immigrated to Canada from a colony in Latin America stressed the need for education differently. First, they talked about the need for Dietsche to learn their history and heritage. Second, all service providers who themselves are Mennonite immigrants emphasized that lack of knowledge – ignorance – is a shared experience and a mutual problem, because many professionals who work with this population are similarly in need of education. Mennonite immigrant human service workers talked about the need for greater understanding and respect on the part of their English colleagues for Dietsche culture, values, beliefs, and traditions. Reflecting their unique perspective and position in the work they do, these Mennonite immigrant professionals noted that other human service workers often dismiss their work with this client population, along with the needs of Dietsche families.

And it seems like they [Board of Education administrators] are just happy that we [Mennonite immigrant service providers] are dealing with the Mennonite group. "We won't bother them. Let them do what they want. They're dealing with them, so we don't have to." So they feel that way about our work, and it's disheartening. [Peter, Mennonite immigrant service provider]

Designing social services for Dietsche (im)migrants

Community groups and human service agencies, often in consultation with MCC workers, developed a variety of services and programs to address the needs of Dietsche families in Ontario, Manitoba, and southern Alberta. In Ontario, where the flow of Dietsche (im)migrants has been consistent for over five decades, programs specific to Dietsche families have been steadily expanding and evolving since 1977 when MCC Ontario (MCCO) first opened an office in Aylmer to provide the essential and complicated work of assisting with documentation or obtaining secure legal status for Dietsche (im)migrants in Canada (Janzen, 1998). MCC's role in the settlement of Dietsche in Canada is crucial, as the first and most pressing need is obtaining legal status. This documentation process is exceedingly complex, and until 2004 it relied on an obscure loophole in Canada's citizenship law that was identified in 1976 by William Janzen, director of MCC's Ottawa Office, just one year before new legislation was introduced. Following the establishment of the point system in the 1960s, which was used to screen immigrant applications, it was virtually impossible for Dietsche Mennonites to obtain landed immigrant status. Janzen successfully lobbied government officials to change their interpretation of the 1947 Canadian Citizenship Act. This opened the door for Mennonites from Mexico to claim citizenship through what became known as the "delayed registration" provision.[9] While the process of obtaining legal papers was long and arduous, nevertheless thousands from Latin American colonies obtained Canadian citizenship, which permitted them to travel freely through the United States and to take up residence in Canada.[10]

In August 2004 the "delayed registration" provision was discontinued, and the migratory corridor between the south and the north was closed to remaining family members who did not already have Canadian citizenship. MCCO workers report that the impact of this legislative change on the northern migratory patterns of Dietsche Mennonites as a group may not be as significant as was first anticipated. Many in the Mennonite colonies in Latin America who were eligible obtained Canadian citizenship before the law changed. The steady stream of new (im)migrants has continued, but it is composed of younger and often smaller families seeking to retain their citizenship.[11] As new Dietsche Mennonite families from various colonies in Latin America migrate north, the acuteness of their need – their apparent social exclusion in Canadian communities – is refreshed every year.

MCC personnel in Ontario first noticed other needs of the population, beyond documentation, in the late 1970s, particularly when fewer were returning to Mexico for the winters, and serious employment and housing issues became apparent. As the (im)migrant population grew over the years, various service agencies conducted studies with Dietsche residents in southern Ontario to evaluate health and social needs of the population.[12] In the mid-1980s local social service agencies, such as the Simcoe Children's Aid Society, called on MCCO to help address rising numbers of needy newcomers in southern Ontario. In response, MCCO sponsored a number of studies that confirmed serious concerns related to employment, housing, and health (Janzen, 1998). Other social service agencies, such as the Unemployed Help Centre in St Thomas, conducted their own surveys in East Elgin and surrounding regions, which led to several reports documenting unusually high numbers of people (primarily Dietsche [im]migrants) who were working poor, illiterate, and living in inadequate housing (see A. Dyck & Fuller, 1989; Janzen, 1998; McMenamin, 1989). During the following three decades, MCCO, along with other social agencies, expanded their work with Dietsche in southern Ontario to provide housing improvement and development projects, employment training, job creation activities, health education, and personal and family support.[13]

Today, many government and private social agencies have adapted their services for Dietsche (im)migrants, providing a wide range of population-specific programs to address English language and literacy skills, parenting support, cultural and legal expectations, education and school attendance, dental care, and maternal and child nutrition and health. For example, high schools in several rural towns in southern Ontario offer customized programs and schedules to meet the educational needs of Dietsche youth and allow them to obtain their high school diploma while working to help support their families; some mainstream mental health agencies, such as the Canadian Association for Mental Health (CAMH), provide Plautdietsch-speaking counsellors to better serve Dietsche families; and at least two child protection/welfare agencies have created a population-specific pro-tocol in consultation with Dietsche leadership. Maternal and child health programs, often funded in part by federal government grants, target health issues such as iron deficiency anaemia, immunizations, low-birth-weight babies, and mental and emotional health for women (Good Gingrich & Snyder, 1997).

While most of these programs have been directed towards women and children, recent initiatives focus on increasing the employment capacity for Dietsche men. For example, the Linwood English School, opened in 2008, offers family-based literacy programs to both men and women. Cultural and practical barriers are addressed by providing classes in the evening to accommodate men's working schedules, small class sizes geared towards individual learning needs, and childcare. Lit-eracy education is tailored to meet everyday needs of men and women, such as vocabulary related to employment, medical needs, talking with teachers, and food and cooking.

Representing years of cultivating relationships and planning, MCCO turned the leadership and resourcing of their work in Aylmer over to Dietsche leaders in the community in 2008, when the MCCO Resource Centre became Mennonite Community Services.[14] At that time, MCCO shifted its role to emphasize coordination of "Low German" services, and education for service providers and Dietsche newcomers.[15]

In southern Ontario, practitioners and community members have met every year as a well-organized network since 1997, when a small group of social service and health professionals working with Dietsche programs first launched the annual Low German Networking Day (initially funded by Community Action Program for Children [CAPC] under Health Can-ada). The goal of this one-day conference, with keynote addresses in the morning and workshops in the afternoon, is to exchange information between service providers and Dietsche (im)migrants to improve deliv-ery and acceptance of services. Indicating increased interest and perhaps more open communication, over 300 participants, including English-speaking practitioners, Mennonite immigrant service providers, and Dietsche leaders, have attended the Networking Day in recent years. In 2014, having outgrown available venues, it was divided into two days and locations in Southern Ontario. Despite these efforts, the MCC coor-dinator for Low German Programs reported that an ongoing challenge is the lack of uniformity or standardization for services across regions. For this oral culture and highly mobile group, regional differences in both the programs and the names of services present barriers to access.

In southern Alberta, relationships between human services and Dietsche (im)migrants are relatively emergent and sometimes volatile, as significant numbers of Dietsche first settled in this province only about fifteen years ago. Here, the bulk of social supports for (im)migrants are provided by MCC Alberta (MCCA) and are focused primarily on citizenship and immigration documentation, paperwork required for government benefits (such as Employment Insurance and the Canada Child Tax Benefit), and employment services. One MCCA staff person estimated that every month 200 to 300 Dietsche access the job board located at the MCCA office in Taber, Alberta. Since 2012 Citizenship and Immigration Canada has provided funding for MCCA to facilitate "understanding" between the community, local government agencies, and newcomers. MCCA has hosted seminars on the history and culture of Dietsche (im)migrants for federal and provincial government staff (specifically services related to employment, immigration, education, mental health, and police) and local employers (such as Frito Lay). Education sessions for (im)migrants are directed towards helping newcomers understand Canadian laws and mores, "financial literacy," English language and computer skills, and employment matters. Four school divisions in the region have a sizable population of Dietsche children. Each of two of these school divisions, reporting a combined enrolment of 1,600 to 1,700 Dietsche students, employs a half-time "liaison" person to encourage school attendance and has established alternative schools for Dietsche children. A unique, long-standing coordinated effort is the Southern Alberta Kanadier Association, which was initiated in 2001 by Alberta Health Services, MCCA, and the Horizon School Division. Approximately fifteen to twenty-five human service practitioners – including representatives from Taber Police Services and the federal police services (the Royal Canadian Mounted Police, or RCMP) – meet every two months to facilitate networking among service providers working with Dietsche families (G. Epp, 2013).

In Ontario and Alberta, all service providers – whether Mennonite, Mennonite immigrant, or English – agreed that the circumstances and needs faced by Dietsche families are complex, and effective service is costly in dollars and cents, in human resources, and in time. Work with this population was described as "frustrating," "challenging," "demanding, requiring unusual commitment," "convoluted," "unmanageable," "discouraging," "overwhelming," and "disheartening." It is here, at this point, that conflict occurs – when Dietsche families are deemed lacking, and social workers and health providers seek to improve their lives. It is conflict provoked by confrontation between competing ideals and aspirations and, even more, contradictory livelihood practices and sensibilities in the everyday.

Common sense confrontation

Without exception, Dietsche (im)migrants spoke of their gratitude for the support and services they receive in Canada. Life in Canada is good, so much better than life in Mexico or Bolivia.

> HELENA: [Trans.] The whole time we have been here we have eaten like we never did there.

In Canada, there is work. In Mexico, work is difficult to find.

> LUANN: Why did you move? What brought you here?
>
> HELENA: [Trans.] We were so bad off, and we had debt that we couldn't pay. It was so that what we could earn was just enough to eat. To pay some of the debt off, we couldn't do. Now we had to sell everything and pay the debt, and we had long planned to come here. And we didn't know how to do it with our debt. And we couldn't leave our work, so we had to sell everything and pay the debt. And we came here to see how it would be here for us.
>
> LUANN: Debts from buying land?
>
> HELENA: Uh-hmm. [Trans.] And it is too that there is more work here. There, there isn't as much work as here. There they have to drive out [of the colony] to places and that's what we didn't want. We didn't want our people, our children, in amongst the Mexicans. That's why we came here. There's more work here.

(Im)migrants emphasized that they believe it is always better to work for a living, and they would resort to welfare only if they had no other choice. Dietsche men and women generally reported that they came to Canada to find paid employment. The "best" jobs were usually identified to be agricultural, often field work. While many Dietsche are committed to farming work, some said that finding year-round employment was a priority. Thus, working for large farm operations that hire permanent, rather than seasonal, help is desirable employment. Other acceptable jobs include factory work, welding, carpentry or *"framing,"* and cabinetry and woodworking. Many men expressed a preference for "being their own boss," and, because they are accustomed to that position in Latin America, they find it difficult to work for someone else. Most spoke favourably about their employers.

When asked about their income, most reported that here they have "enough." Several (im)migrant narratives described initial difficulties in making ends meet, and debts had to be paid along with the substantial expenses incurred in migrating and obtaining legal status in Canada. Dietsche described these financial responsibilities as burdensome and recalled a sense of great relief when they were debt-free and their wages could be committed to supporting the daily needs of their families and saving for the future.

> LUANN: The amount that you can earn here, is it enough that you can pay
> for everything that is needed?
> KATHERINA: [Trans.] Not much is left over.
> LUANN: Have there ever been times when there wasn't enough money for
> food, or when you needed help with food or clothes or something like that?
> KATHERINA: [Trans.] Yes. Early times were not very easy. We had to borrow
> everything we needed to come here. We had nothing. And then find
> work to pay off the debts. Then we borrow from brothers or uncles. We
> borrow it, and then when we have enough, we pay it back.

In Canada, there is help if times get tough – food banks, welfare, laws, and police. These conditions were presented as a stark contrast to those in Mexico, where respondents described having to go without the necessities of daily living and needing to depend on isolated instances of charity from family and the community.

> LUANN: So [in Mexico] there was no other place to go for help if there
> would not have been enough food? That meant you just had to borrow
> from the store?
> HELENA: [Trans.] There was no other place. We usually just bought with
> the money we had. We didn't want to borrow because of the interest they
> charged us, and we often just bought with the amount of money we had.
> But that was enough for just the necessities. Meat and stuff like that was
> not with it. Very little potatoes. Almost all beans and rice, or beans and
> tortillas, bread and jam ... And vegetables. That was there too, but that
> was so expensive there, the money didn't reach. And gas – if we wanted
> to drive, gas had to be filled up so we could drive again. There it is much
> more expensive than here.

Dietsche (im)migrants were generally positive about the material aspects of life in Canada. Exceptions to their otherwise optimistic accounts were centred on social and cultural discontent rather than physical needs. For example, while living accommodations in towns were usually described as a "good house," families making their homes in these locations talked about feeling uncomfortable and out of place, especially in areas of high-density subsidized housing. Several Dietsche mothers described the close proximity to neighbours as a negative environment for their children and expressed disapproval of things they were learning from their peers.

Dietsche women, in particular, expressed gratitude for a general sense of safety and security in Canada. Many who had migrated from Mexico talked about leaving behind a society of *"lawlessness,"*[16] where even police are corrupt:

> ANNA: [Trans.] I always feel more comfortable here than in Mexico because here there are English people and there, there are Mexicans. I always feel more comfortable here because of stealing and everything. Here I'm never that scared, not when we drive and not … wherever I am.
> TRANSLATOR: And in Mexico you would have had that feeling?
> ANNA: [Trans.] There, I'm always scared.
> HEIN: [Trans.] Yes, always.
> ANNA: [Trans.] On the road one was even scared, because there they would hold people up. It's very bad there. [Dietsche (im)migrant couple]

Another aspect of life in Canada for which Dietsche expressed appreciation was the accessibility to healthcare. Most (im)migrants reported never having seen a doctor during their lives in Mexico, in part because they could not afford healthcare.

Many (im)migrants, especially women, had only positive things to say about their experiences with services and service providers in Canada:

> ANNA: [Trans.] No, I think the police are very good here.
> TRANSLATOR: Anna was just commenting that she thinks it's very, very good. Again, in Mexico, that often would be …
> ANNA: They try to take the money away [chuckles].
> LUANN: Oh, police do?
> TRANSLATOR: They're often corrupt there.
> LUANN: You don't trust police there. If someone was coming new, just coming from Mexico, what advice would you give them about people

like teachers and doctors and Children's Aid? What should they
know?

ANNA: [Trans.] I would say they were good here. Very good. The police are
good. I think it is all good. Right?

HEIN: [Trans.] I would say to adjust. Just adjust to that all is good. [Dietsche
(im)migrant couple]

Most Dietsche parents reported that their school-age children attended school regularly. Many expressed a preference for the Old Colony school in the areas where they were an option, and some made great financial sacrifices so that their children would receive a "Christian" education. Dietsche described feeling more "comfortable" with their own private schools than with public schools, because prayer is a regular part of school, children are not exposed to television, and they *"don't learn things we don't want them to learn."* Some parents related that they would like their children to finish high school. Others, often those with young children, indicated that they have not given thought to how long their children would stay in school. One father recalled that his children were prohibited from attending the local public school for the first several months after migrating to Canada because they lacked the proper "papers," or documentation of their residency status.

Dietsche (im)migrants described significant relationships with extended family members. In general, extended families help each other out and look after each other. For some, the sacrifice of leaving family in Latin America when they moved to Canada was enormous, and the pain was still fresh. Many left relatives in the same desperate conditions that forced their own migration. They expressed their worry for family members left behind.

LUANN: I can tell you're remembering. And it sounds very difficult.

HELENA: [Trans.] It is hard, yes. And then one thinks a lot of the children
[still in Mexico]. They have to struggle. I have said before that one maybe
has it too good here. One doesn't feel worthy of so much help that you
get here. One feels very small. But they are so good here and help one so
much. And one is very thankful for that.

In many cases, family members remaining in Latin America, such as brothers, sisters, parents, and adult children, are unable to migrate to Canada because they have no claim to citizenship, and families become divided.

The moral work of addressing Dietsche need

The allocation of resources in human services – often referred to as "taxpayer dollars," thereby dividing us up into those who pay taxes and those who apparently do not – is a particularly contentious issue to be resolved. Who will pay to address the problem, and who is eligible (or deserves) to receive the service? Attitudes and social values about cause, responsibility, cost-benefit, and prognosis are invoked. The public – or more accurately, those who are *not* clients – may have a limited sense of charity towards those bearing evidence of social ills. There are social and political aims to be gained or lost through the design and delivery details of social policies and human services.

Thus, in focus group conversations, it was not unusual for the concerns of service providers to figure most prominently. Simply put, the delivery of social programs and services is commonly centred on the needs of service providers rather than the needs of service recipients or the identified problem.

> IAN: We need a better orientation to Canadian norms prior to coming. Now I know that's hard, but it certainly would make a big difference when they arrive on MCC's doorstep to say, "We're here!" Maybe that can happen in Mexico or something, but they come here so ill prepared, and it's overwhelming delivery when they arrive, and we just can't catch up …
> LUANN: Right. So, each one of those issues you talk about is interrelated. Where do you start?
> IAN: God, I don't know! [Laughter] [English service provider]

This ironic turn in focus from the needs and living conditions of populations being served to the needs, resources, and effectiveness of social service agencies and practitioners is neither new nor unique. Chambon (2012) identifies this "move away from a broader exploration of social issues for social change" (4) as part and parcel of widespread professionalization in the 1930s, and it is reinforced today in the emphasis on evidence-based practice and inquiry. In the case of human services work with Dietsche (im)migrants, practitioners were concerned with obstacles that interfere with effecting the desired changes among the clients in their caseload. When it comes to Dietsche clients, the hurdles to successful intervention are numerous. In our conversations, service providers focused on the following three issues: language and cultural barriers, transportation challenges, and suspicion of services and professionals.

The need for *translation* or interpretation services contributes significantly to both the complexity and the expense of educating Dietsche (im)migrants. Agency budgets often do not allow for the costs associated with translation services, and most service providers were aware that many Dietsche families cannot afford to hire their own interpreters. Service providers also pointed out that their Dietsche clients generally do not choose to access agency services, especially when translators are not provided; rather, contact is often limited to circumstances in which "the law is involved" and the court has mandated intervention. They also noted, repeatedly, that even more than the translation of language and words, the interpretation of culture and world views is equally important. Language and cultural barriers mean that service workers invest an extraordinary amount of time in issues they deal with but also that the rate with which change can be expected is slow. Interventions that may produce desired outcomes in a few months in most situations could take years with this population, service providers reported.

English service providers identified Dietsche (im)migrants as being in need of a proper understanding of the Canadian way of life. The contrast between "Mexican Mennonite culture" and "Canadian culture" was frequently noted in reference to a host of issues, including providing for and disciplining children; the roles and status of women; seeking medical attention; obtaining acceptable housing; finding desirable work; the value of education; claiming individual rights; planning for the future and establishing employment and financial stability; and engaging with mainstream society. Service providers cited Dietsche cultural norms and religious values as evidence of the need for education, as they were considered to be at odds with, if not offensive to, Canadian society. Translation of language and culture was considered necessary for proper intervention in the reworking of cultural/religious norms.

Mennonite immigrant service providers, in contrast, tended to recognize language and cultural gaps that require bridging *in both directions* in order for services to be more effective and accepted.

> Sometimes there will be cultural misunderstanding. Like, you know, the family will understand it different than the service provider. My role is only to interpret. But sometimes, while I'm interpreting, I can clearly see that there is a misunderstanding because of cultural issues. It's not because

of what's being said. And then I'll say, "It's a cultural issue. The lady or the man answered this way because of their beliefs." And so sometimes, it's also trying to help the service providers understand their culture, and where they come from, as well as the Low German families to understand where the service provider comes from. So it is more than just interpreting. [Tina, Mennonite immigrant service provider]

Human service workers related that *transportation* for workers and clients presents a challenge in delivering services in rural settings. Agency jurisdictions are geographically large and social service offices, which are usually located in the largest urban setting in the county, may be many kilometres from the homes of Dietsche families, many of whom live in secluded areas of agricultural regions. For many services, particularly healthcare and government documentation (e.g., provincial health insurance and driver's licences), people living in rural areas are required to travel considerable distances to larger urban centres.

Practitioners reported that many Dietsche women are particularly isolated, owing to their rural homes, cultural expectations for women to stay at home with young children, and their common reluctance to drive. This isolation is augmented by the complications and expense of transportation in rural regions.

> Last year we had a grant for a preschool program. We only had one kindergarten last year, so we had an open classroom every second day. So once a week, on Thursdays, we ran a group. It was interesting because the Mennonites [Dietsche] were our target group. And we started off. But we quickly went through their transportation and their babysitting money. And as soon as we went through their transportation/babysitting money and couldn't transport these people to the program, we lost the whole Mexican Mennonite group because, in a number of cases, either there isn't another vehicle once Dad goes to work, or Mom doesn't drive, it seems. [Kevin, English service provider]

Emphasizing the compounding challenges presented by Dietsche practices in Canadian society, transportation difficulties are often complicated by the size of (im)migrant families and the language barrier. Some programs for Dietsche women and preschool children budget for school bus transportation. Others depend on volunteer drivers who have access to large vehicles. Agencies such as the Children's Aid

Society (child protection services) occasionally provide transportation to appointments with health professionals, but the standard taxis that they use are not equipped with the required number of seatbelts. Often, workers or volunteers who speak Plautdietsch combine transportation and translation services.

On the other hand, service providers observed that transportation is typically not a problem for their Dietsche clients when services, such as employment programs, are geared towards men. Dietsche men are known for their mechanical know-how, and access to a working vehicle is generally not a problem for them:

> The families usually have two or three vehicles. Like when they do home visits, I know the workers have said there'd be two or three vehicles in the yard, and they'd just get one of them going, you know, by using the parts of all the other vehicles. So they would always have something on the road. [Mike, English service provider]

Providing service to this population is also considered to be costly because of an observed *suspicion*, or lack of trust. Dietsche people were consistently described as "fearful," "suspicious," "defensive" and "distrustful" of professionals, presenting unusual challenges for service providers.

> JANICE: And there seems to be a distrust of all our formal services and probably, historically speaking, because whenever the formal services were brought in, it was brought in from the other end [or mandated], because – because of the cultural and language barriers, and that kind of thing. So Family and Children's Services comes in. There's almost automatically a defensiveness that goes along –
> GAYLE: Yeah, you're not kidding!

Some workers experienced this distrust to be a personal affront.

> JEN: [Sigh] I felt because they didn't know me personally, that they didn't trust me. You know, if I was trying to give them advice, or anything, like they didn't – until you really get to know who they are, and – they don't trust you. I don't – I don't know. [English service provider]

The challenges arising from lack of trust were framed as a lack of cooperation or as resistance to help, which seemed to frustrate service providers.

IAN: And the commitment on behalf of the workers! We don't have a lot of support staff with the Low German language skill base. So you introduce workers into the home situation – there's a whole trust level that has to be addressed before you can even get in the door. And then to have them quit, or leave us halfway through an intervention, it just throws a whole wrench into the mix. So it's a very long-term commitment, with limited resources to make it happen.

LUANN: How do you gain that trust? What works?

CATHY: Just time.

ANDREA: Time. They have to know –

CATHY: You tell the truth. And they know when you say something that is the truth and they can depend on that over time.

MICHELLE: And it's a tenuous trust, too. I think that it doesn't take much to destroy it. Even if you've taken years to build it up, it would take one mistake sometimes, in a cultural way, to undo all of the trust that you've gotten. [English service providers]

Thus, successful intervention in such delicate situations requires time, perseverance, and discretion.

And it takes a long time working together, and also shifting attitudes. If I say, "You know, I think this is why you've run into problems: because you stopped taking medication." Being very, very cautious that they don't hear me disciplining them or telling them that they've done something wrong. Because then it becomes shame and guilt and so on. So it's sort of a fine line there, trying to build that trust, build that collaboration, and yet trying to provide, over time, that education to start thinking about things in a different way. [Sandy, English service provider]

While service providers were generally focused on ways to encourage and support Dietsche participation in social and health services, they noted that when resources are scarce, the complexity of (im)migrant needs can result in services being denied.

MARK: There are just inadequate doctors, healthcare services in these areas.

LUANN: Because you're underserviced, in general.

JANICE: Yes, in general. And then, of course, people with very highly complex needs, they're not the first ones on the list for doctors that are already overburdened to take on. So if they're already way over what they should be for their rostering, you come in with highly complex needs, it's easier to turn you away than somebody who's just going to come in for some regular routine check-up. [English service providers]

Dietsche (im)migrants were described as "a pressure on the system" [English service provider] that is increasingly overwhelmed.

The work of discerning what is best for clients and devising methods to achieve that, involves a series of decisions and judgments, and practitioners must call upon shared understandings, objectives, and values. What ideological perspective guides such moral work, and how is it that social service workers apparently uniformly adopt this perspective, as if it were common sense? When we talk about providing service and planning programs, what pulls our focus towards the needs of the dominant group, the up-group or in-group? How is it that when well-meaning practitioners deliver services, client needs are often obscured to the point of being erased in the process of intervention? Furthermore, how is it that some experienced and committed human service workers seem to sidestep personal and professional ingenuity and habitually arrive at the same worn-out assessment and intervention strategies? I propose that the answer lies in the analysis of common sense, in the ideological underpinnings of the social welfare system and mainstream society – which are not new at all – and how they are put to work.

A common sense point of view

The place to begin a study of social exclusion, it would seem, is to determine the degree to which identified individuals or groups are socially excluded. But what does social exclusion look like? How do we recognize it, and what are its indicators? Various definitions, conceptualizations, and theoretical models (often implicit) offered in social exclusion debates derive from two leading perspectives for the social world: the *categorical* and *relational* points of view. Its most common version – made popular by Tony Blair's Social Exclusion Unit (SEU) – retains a multidimensional focus but functions as a static, categorical point of view that has given rise to a multitude of "people change measures" for identified social kinds (Edwards, 2009; Lund, 1999). This trendy idea looks for quantifiable and static measures, as reflected in the British government's definition of social exclusion: "a short-hand term for what can happen when people or areas suffer from a combination of linked problems such as unemployment, poor skills, low incomes, poor housing, high crime environment, bad health and family breakdown" (Social Exclusion Unit, 2001, 10).

The application in policy of this "weak" version, as it has been identified (Martin, 2004; Veit-Wilson, 1998) is inclined to reduce the social realities of social exclusion to that which is in plain sight – its visible, material outcomes. Such measures are used to define thresholds of lack or categories of need associated with people "on the margins." Social exclusion used in this way is often indistinguishable from more conventional concepts such as poverty or deprivation. This popular and rather simplistic notion of social exclusion calls to mind a *kind* of person, an "objective category that sorts human beings" (Hacking, 1999, 17). The *category* of social exclusion suggests a species, like "the horse," as if various human species or distinct kinds of individuals exist in social reality. Hacking notes that, in the social sciences, the merging of ideas, concepts, beliefs, or theories with epistemologically objective items produces classifications, or kind-terms, of and for people. The significance of this classifying process is that "once we have the phrase, the label, we get the notion that there is a definite kind of person … This kind of person becomes reified" (ibid., 27). This objectivist position treats social facts as things and thus denies the active and interactive nature of people as social agents who "are objects of knowledge, of cognition – or misrecognition – within social existence" (Bourdieu, 1989, 14).

Social exclusion as a kind of person conflates the *idea* of social exclusion with its material outcomes – those things that are "in the world," visible and measurable, such as poverty, homelessness, and unemployment. Because these material manifestations of social exclusion are necessarily attached to human beings, the term is used to classify people – poor people, homeless people, unemployed people. Recognition of "linked problems," as referenced in the SEU definition, does not move this view outside such an individual kind perspective or beyond the poverty paradigm. It simply suggests that multiple indicators may be used to mark the social kind.

The less common relational perspective, rooted in the French notion of *les exclus* (Lenoir, 1974), emphasizes structural or social processes that lead to the rupture of social bonds for certain individuals or groups. It is understood to be "the breakdown or malfunctioning of the major societal systems that should guarantee the social integration of the individual or household" (Shucksmith & Chapman, 1998, 230). This view of social exclusion brings to the fore uneven social engagement, as "some groups experience social boundaries as barriers preventing their full participation in the economic, political and cultural life of the society within which they live (Madanipour, Cars, & Allen, 2000, 17). But the dynamic and relational nature that some attribute to social exclusion is evidenced to be especially elusive in its methodological application (Byrne, 2005; Sen, 2000b). Much of the research that retains a dynamic and relational notion is conceptual or qualitative in nature, ranging from the indiscriminate injection of the term to the more unusual descriptions of the spiralling path of exclusion and testimonies of its experience (e.g., Moriña Diez, 2010). Aiming towards accurate personal accounts, this qualitative, dynamic version runs the risk of discounting social exclusion to the individual subjective experience of *feeling* marginalized and deprived of social recognition (e.g., Stewart, Reutter, Makwarimba, Veenstra, Love, & Raphael, 2008). Furthermore, a relational perspective tends to be unstable, often giving way to simpler notions of social exclusion as a kind of individual. Policy researchers observe: "Both [the] individualist [kind] and social [process] conceptions of welfare have a tendency to rely upon 'outcome measures,' that is, current income or wealth, or position within society" (Pavis, Hubbard, & Platt, 2001, 307). Even from a relational point of view, both the problem of social exclusion and its solution tend to be reduced to an analysis of individual attributes at a fixed point in time.

When a categorical perspective erases the dynamic and relational qualities of the social world, one is left with a simplistic, familiar view of social problems that is replete with assumptions. These assumptions usually remain hidden from conscious awareness, unknowable, such that their meanings and consequences are generally unintentional, but no less forceful. I propose that a series of preconceived and widely held beliefs supporting the categorical point of view and common sense notion of social exclusion follow a sequential line of reasoning, as follows:

- Social exclusion denotes a kind of individual marked primarily by employment and material deprivation.
- Since social inclusion implies an opposite kind, society is presumed to be composed of two oppositional and hierarchically ordered groups: the included and the excluded.
- Given that social exclusion is understood to be inherently bad and undesirable, its inverse is considered an unconditional good, whether desired or not.

- The received version of social inclusion is understood to be universally attainable and is to be achieved primarily through interventions that seek to cajole, coax, encourage, support, entice, empower, educate, or buy excluded individuals into a different economic, social, and moral kind.
- The excluded kind are recognized to be innately different, deficient, or deviant in ways that are reversible, such that transforming the limiting or offending nature of one's self is not only possible but necessary to overcome social exclusion.
- It follows, then, that through the individual kind lens, the primary and consequential source of social exclusion is not externally imposed, but is presumed to emerge from certain adaptable aspects of one's individual character or circumstances – from one's self. In this way, I argue, the common application of the concept is rooted in the veiled assumption that social exclusion is most often self-imposed.

Several clarifying comments are in order here. First, I do not understand self-imposed to be synonymous with voluntary. I argue that the dominant view is implemented in such a way that social exclusion is assumed to be self-imposed rather than externally imposed, but it may not be chosen. Second, the social exclusion debate does address relationships between social exclusion and issues of race, gender, sexual orientation, and able-bodiedness, collective and individual characteristics that are obviously beyond one's control. However, it is commonly accepted that social inclusion is possible for individuals of such social classifications, given appropriate measures of accommodation or self-improvement. From the categorical perspective, the difference that has meaning and consequence is presumed to be something *other than* race, gender, sexual orientation, or disability – a difference that can be overcome with adequate supports, counsel, or programming. The criteria determining inclusion and exclusion go beyond such multiplicities, permitting the illusory and binary organization of the social. Third, this view does not preclude a consideration of social structures and processes, as the path to social inclusion may require the modification or dismantling of barriers that deter individuals from becoming a different kind. For example, Esping-Andersen proposed accessible childcare programs in the European Union to address potential employment barriers for women, to assist in transforming mothers of young children to waged workers (Esping-Andersen, Gallie, Hemerijck, & Myles, 2001).

Ultimately, however, the crucial change happens to and by the excluded individual.

The application of social exclusion as an individual kind through a categorical perspective, fixed on its material outcomes, reinforces and perpetuates the common sense belief that those who suffer the social ills of society – poverty, unemployment, inadequate housing – collude intentionally or unwittingly in their own economic and social hardship. The assumption that social exclusion is self-imposed is apparent in typical policy and program responses aimed at the "promotion of work as the path to personal fulfilment and freedom, and the disparagement of the welfare state as providing an unhealthy dependency" (Benn, 2000, 311).

Whether or not the language of social exclusion is adopted, a categorical point of view is so comfortable and well rehearsed that it is spontaneous – knee-jerk – in various professional and political arenas, popular media, and dominant culture at large. It functions as a spur-of-the-moment vision of the social world, a "folk theory" (Bourdieu, 1989), with its pre-notions that ascribe meaning to people and to social relations. Accordingly, common sense leads to the identification of certain problems, particular understandings of social issues and their solutions, and related intervention strategies. The very foundation of common sense, or the categorical point of view, is the binary ordering of the social world, sorting the good from the bad, the deserving from the undeserving, the victim from the transgressor, the included from the excluded.

Contradiction, conflict, and the contest for common sense

In the case of Dietsche (im)migrants in Canada, a superficial look at social exclusion as need is inconclusive. Practitioners expressed inconsistent and often conflicting views regarding the extent to which members of Dietsche in Canada exhibit need. While the problems among (im)migrants were identified as substantial and complex, some service providers commented that most do quite well, taking full advantage of selected benefits Canadian society has to offer, even as they maintain a life that is closely tied to their colony in the south. To some professionals, they are a people who live in misery, enduring severe deprivation. Other workers expressed confusion and suspicion regarding their observations of the economic choices made by some (im)migrants. Dietsche people were described as hard-working and willing to take the jobs that most Canadians refuse. Yet they were represented as a hard-to-serve population in Canada's provincial workfare programs.[17] For example, their "strong work ethic" was admired, yet disapproval was expressed for their apparent lack of ambition, as Dietsche men especially are sometimes too eager to accept "dead-end" jobs and too content to stay in those jobs.

Most service providers agreed that Dietsche (im)migrants believe it is important to work for a living, but some observed that Mennonites know how to "milk the system," to get more while rejecting appropriate employment practices and goals. Social service workers acknowledged that the housing conditions of some Dietsche families are well below Canadian standards, but they insisted that Dietsche are happy with their homes and, furthermore, that their labour is important to the local economy; so it is in the best interests of everyone just to "look the other way."

The Mennonite commitment to community and family was portrayed for the most part as admirable. Service providers noted that Dietsche women exhibit extraordinary resourcefulness and intuition in raising children. Yet they identified Dietsche as a high-risk population for child protection services. Even as some service providers identified their lack of relationships and support for one another as a necessary point of intervention, others expressed suspicion that too many Dietsche are directing large amounts of money to their church and community. The unusually efficient "Mennonite grapevine" was recognized to be both an asset and a nuisance in providing service for this population.

There was general agreement among practitioners that Dietsche (im)migrants place little or no value on education. They were represented as a people unusually lacking in knowledge, even ignorant and backward. Service providers described the inordinate creativity and energy required to ensure that Mennonite children attend school. At the same time, Dietsche children have been refused access to public school systems until the costly and lengthy process of obtaining citizenship or landed immigrant status was complete. Ironically, human service professionals also reported that many Dietsche people are very eager to learn. Service providers remarked that when (im)migrant children do attend school regularly, they frequently prove themselves to be quite capable, and they do very well, even to the point of excelling. Instances of extraordinary resourcefulness, inventiveness, and entrepreneurial know-how were described. Some non-Mennonite professionals commented on the remarkable ability of Dietsche (im)migrants to survive great hardship and on an unusual capacity for "making do" with very little.

Dietsche narratives offered little clarity regarding the question of their social exclusion or its experience. (Im)migrant men and women expressed appreciation for ample employment, adequate income, acceptable housing, supportive social networks, and generous assistance from local agencies and programs. In contrast, most service providers agreed that interventions for Dietsche Mennonites need to be geared towards changing their behaviours and attitudes related to employment, housing, healthcare, and education. It is clear that Dietsche (im)migrants understand and define *need* in terms that are quite different from most human service practitioners.

In addition to inconsistent reports regarding the extent of social exclusion among (im)migrants, the legitimacy of social exclusion claims and any associated need for this population was called into question by a wide range of service providers. They frequently asserted that the conditions within which many Dietsche families live result from individual and group *choice*. Furthermore, their observed refusal to access and accept services was seen as reinforcing the voluntary nature of their possible social exclusion. Human service workers attributed this reluctance to accept help from professionals to cultural and language barriers, the Mennonite history of persecution, "extreme views" regarding certain medical and mental health conditions, ignorance and misinformation about proper treatment and healthcare, and a general fear and distrust of outsiders. The Dietsche "religion" or belief system was frequently offered as an explanation for bewildering behaviour and imprudent choices and was identified as a barrier to providing effective service.

Despite the decisive role attributed to culture and beliefs on the part of service providers, they expressed conflicting opinions regarding the nature and quality of Dietsche "religion." On the one hand, the population was depicted as a people defined by their religion, their church. On the other hand, it was reported that some have discarded the religious identity of Mennonite, and refer to themselves as simply Dietsch. Their belief system was described as "fundamentalist," "male dominated," and "conservative." Some represented Dietsche religion as having eroded to an arbitrary and oppressive system of rules, which was not considered to constitute a faith at all. On the contrary, many Dietsche (im)migrants described religious practices, such as prayer and church affiliation, as extremely important, guiding decisions regarding where they raise their family, employment, education for their children, and daily life practices.

In general, professionals repeatedly cited the Dietsche way of life – their culture, language, and beliefs – as the singular reason for (im)migrants' lot in life. Interventions, therefore, are targeted towards supporting changes in culture, language, and beliefs through information, education, and various forms of persuasion. Ironically, refusal to access certain services often resulted in mandated interventions, and families were forced to "participate" in society and the amenities it has to offer. Hence, the needs that might define this group as socially excluded were often considered to be unconvincing, illegitimate, or self-inflicted. Dietsche need falls out of view and difference becomes the focus of attention. If we apply the common sense idea of social exclusion to this particular population, it appears to fit best as a voluntary, self-imposed expression.

When the markers of social exclusion function to differentiate and categorize individuals, their potential for consistently identifying legitimate need is undone. Even for those deemed deserving, it appears that common sense social exclusion cannot be definitively recognized and assessed, as its material outcomes are imprecisely interpreted and inconsistently judged. In other words, to discern and examine social exclusion by looking only for its material outcomes is to invoke the underlying belief that such want and deprivation result from one's self. And self-imposed suffering is suspect, minimized, and disqualified, and it does not count as social exclusion at all. At a basic level, social exclusion as a category – as common sense – is a conceptual paradox.

This is not to say that the observation and judgment of self-imposed expressions of social exclusion as described by service providers are entirely unfounded. Such indications of collusion in one's own social exclusion, one's own suffering, provide the primary focus and motivation for this work. I maintain that both manifest expressions and latent assumptions of self-imposed social exclusion are pervasive. Among Dietsche, in particular, evidence of self-imposed social exclusion is uncommonly apparent and extraordinarily visible, as it is exhibited through overt and intentional choices having to do with dress, lifestyle, employment, education, health practices, and so on. However, the accounts of human service professionals reveal that common sense assessments of social problems, of social exclusion, do not contribute to meaningful understanding of exclusion-by-choice. Common sense suggests that people instinctively act in their own best interests. Capitalism, as both an ideology and an economic system, rests upon this belief in human nature. Apparently self-defeating yet intentional "choices" contradict this common sense.

In the uneven social relations of human services, contradictory points of view are not merely differences of opinion. This is conflict – a struggle for self-identification up against official representation, a contest for common sense, "for the monopoly over legitimate naming"(Bourdieu, 1989, 21). From a categorical point of view, the only explanation for self-imposed social exclusion, for counter-intuitive behaviour, is individual or collective deficiency or deviance. Such a simplistic indictment of a whole group of people is to waste an opportunity to deepen our understanding of culture, values, difference – ourselves – as fundamentally social beings. This requires, I argue, reversing our gaze.

Critical self-consciousness: Reversing the gaze

The common sense point of view reads difference on the surface. Without access to and understanding of counter-cultural practices and meanings, one "stops short at ... the 'sensible properties'" (Bourdieu, 1984, 2), and the work of discerning social exclusion is contradictory and inconclusive.[18] To simply equate social exclusion with its observable symptoms permits only a cursory consideration of the ailments of our society and obscures – even justifies – the processes and social relations that result in such brokenness. Moreover, since social exclusion is assumed to be inherently bad and undesirable and its inverse unconditionally good, exclusion-by-choice defies familiar liberal notions of rational self-interest. A categorical concept of social inclusion and exclusion as individuals or conditions of binary opposites – regardless of the cause or source of exclusion – leaves little room for understanding apparent choices for bad rather than good. Even the relational perspective contributes little to our understanding of those who refuse to take advantage of public or private goods and services, thus reinforcing their own difference and disadvantage. Aiming to protect its dynamic character, yet borrowing the binary underpinnings of the categorical perspective, some insist: "'Exclusion' is something that is done by some people to other people" (Byrne, 2005, 2). From this point of view, to *choose* social exclusion is not only nonsensical, but impossible.

Whether the self-imposed nature of social exclusion is assumed as a given (from the individual kind model), or dismissed out of hand, a deeper understanding of such manifestations is not available through the categorical point of view. Furthermore, to promote such common notions is "to impose at the same time principles of visions of the world that legitimize inequality by making the divisions of social space appear rooted in the inclinations of individuals rather than the underlying distribution of capital" (Wacquant, 1998b, 225). This is to say that conventional ways of thinking about poverty and social suffering – whether viewing the poor person as a deficient and deviant individual or as a powerless victim of social structures and processes – serve to advance the often veiled assumption that people behave in ways or have tendencies that ultimately lead to their own fate in life as well as to their inability to change it. From this rudimentary belief, whether deriving from the established right or the left, social positions and their associated material realities are made to be self-evident, even self-inflicted, and social divisions are fortified. This is of great consequence. In this way the idea of self-imposed social exclusion – often remaining concealed, spontaneous – has implications that far exceed the quandary presented by a few deviant individuals who choose to be "social drop-outs" (Silver, 1994, 545) or by peculiar ethnic groups that desire to be defined by difference. These "collective representations thus fulfil political as well as social functions: in addition to permitting the 'logical integration' of society ... classification systems serve to secure and naturalize domination" (Wacquant, 1998b, 225).

Finding social exclusion is not only about identifying need and points of interventions. We cannot move from the "primary stratum of the meaning we can grasp on the basis of our ordinary experience to the stratum of secondary meanings ... unless we possess the concepts which go beyond the sensible properties and which identify the specifically stylistic properties of the work" (Bourdieu, 1984, 2). In this case, understanding is to be found beyond – and through – the apparent markers of Dietsche (im)migrant difference, and the necessary concepts are made available through conscious and self-conscious literacy of our own common sense. This requires us to reverse the gaze, to recognize the necessary and everyday *practices* of cultural competence on which the dynamics of social exclusion and inclusion rely – competence in knowing and reproducing the symbolic economy of the market-state social field in order to maintain and improve one's position in that field. For instance, the superficial reading of difference is consequential, owing to the intuitive cultural competence of the market-state system of capital followed by human service practitioners. Like a work of art, difference "has meaning and interest only for someone who possesses the cultural competence, that is, the code, into which it is encoded" (Bourdieu, 1984, 2). To borrow the words of Paulo Freire (1998), the cultural competence that is crucial for accurate social analysis, effective policy formulation, and viable human services delivery is the "critical examination of [one's own] received wisdom, not as a storehouse of eternal truths but as itself situated in its own historicity" (14). To distinguish this concept from the more common push for the researcher or practitioner to acquire cultural competence of the Other, I refer to the reflexive practice of "critical self-consciousness."[19]

The analysis of social exclusion as both processes and outcomes – interdependent social structures and relations – requires a shift in focus, in at least two ways, from the more habitual categorical point of view. First of all, we must recognize that exclusion happens by people and to people, as "there are processes which include and exclude, but there are also social actors who both include and exclude" (Rodgers, 1995, 51). Thus, if we intend to strive towards more dynamic thought, the practices and processes that function to make the opposite of the excluded kind – the included kind – must come into view. Second, it is far too simplistic – and ultimately unproductive – to merely turn our gaze in the opposite direction, with feet firmly planted on a categorical standpoint. For example, many scholars and social activists denounce the injustices of social exclusion and oppression of all sorts, invoking values and goals that vigorously challenge prevailing thought and practice. Yet ironically, anti-oppressive projects that linger within a categorical mindset are likely to accomplish little more than pointing fingers and laying blame. Efforts to expose, even correct, historical and contemporary atrocities – variously named Colonialism, Western Imperialism, White Supremacy, Orientalism, and so on – tend to get bogged down with assigning guilt and virtue, and thus sorting oppressing elite from oppressed victim. Even though various "anti-" approaches redefine places of honour and disgrace and reconfigure "us" and "them", social divides are sustained, if not reinforced. Consideration of the social world from a categorical vantage point is not – cannot be – transformative in the end, because the taken-for-granted "vision of divisions" remains protected, concealed, and uncontested.

So I insist on shifting our attention, not to condemn, but because the excluded cannot exist without their counterpart. de Haan (1999) makes the point that the notion of social exclusion is a way of conceptualizing the *whole* of society, "including (and with a focus on) the processes of deprivation that are part and parcel of that society" (8). The heart of the matter, I assert, is not the excluded and the nature of their deviance or deficiency or difference, or even the transgressions of the included, but the essence and meaning and consequences of presumed social practices – "habits-of-mine" (Chambon, 2005) – we all subscribe to and abide by.

The foundation of critical self-consciousness is reflexivity: to accept the absurdity of claiming a "bird's-eye-view" (D.E. Smith, 1999). A reflexive view compels us – as researchers, professional helpers, or concerned citizens – to consider the ways in which we think and talk about people and social problems as if we occupy a place *outside*, as if we have no place in this social world that we are trying to articulate. The practice of reflexivity acknowledges the "I" – or the I/Eye of the beholder (Corrigan, 1991) – that takes in and comprehends the realities of a physical and social space to be inescapably "encompassed, inscribed, implicated in that space" (Bourdieu, 2000b, 130). Seeing and theorizing and evaluating the social world – which we do in daily life without thinking, and social practitioners are required to do as professionals – must involve recognition that we are seeing and theorizing ourselves. The place from which my I/Eye casts its gaze, *and* the point on which it lands must move from a divided social, from "us" and "them," from the "excluded" and "included" to a collective "we" and the social systems and processes in which we all participate and the social order in which we are all interdependently positioned. These are the strategies for critical self-consciousness that are put to work in the chapters that follow, as we turn our attention from client groups – the Other – to the social relations and practices that make up human services.

Chapter Three

Market Logic and the Order of Social Space

It is within a precisely ordered social context that social exclusion *happens*. Further, the processes and outcomes of social exclusion are inevitable, even necessary, in the structure and function of certain social spaces. Although it may seem ironic on the surface, through the case example of Dietsche (im)migrant engagement with Canada's human services system I argue that the organizing principles of the social spaces that make up the state – in particular, the welfare state and all its related services and institutions – operate to propel processes of social exclusion and reinforce its outcomes. The organization of our schools, universities, hospitals, social services, courts and prisons, and even neighbourhoods is based on a shared set of values and assumptions that direct daily decisions of eligibility and entitlement. In these public spaces, the market and the state merge to form a closed loop: a singular social field and system of capital. This is social exclusion by design.

Point of view matters

Peter emigrated from a colony in Mexico to Canada when he was a teenager. He has devoted the past several decades of his life to walking alongside Dietsche newcomers. He described how a passing glance of need becomes the basis for excluding difference in Canada's human services.

> LUANN: You mentioned some of the dichotomies in the community. What do you mean by that? What are you referring to?
> PETER: Well, I think dichotomies, or lack of consistency between some of the social agencies. There have been cases in the past where a family ... Let

me see if I can remember the case correctly. A family came, and their sons and daughters were supposed to be registered in the public school system so that they could get family benefits. Family Allowance. But they couldn't issue immigration status until they were registered, and they couldn't register until they showed that they were immigrants. And who was going to make the first move? And the same with the judicial system. There are people who work diligently in trying to get these kids that are compulsory school age in the school, and attending and receiving adequate instruction at whatever level. And then you get someone like the provincial attendance counsellor who says, "Just tell them that they're collectively home schooling." Or, you'll take an attendance case before the court, which has happened in the past, and the judge says, and rightfully so, "These are some of the hardest-working people in our community, and to bring an attendance issue before this court is a waste of time ... They do fine. And so thereby, I'm not charging this person with truancy." The whole judicial system is based on the will of the judge presiding over the case. Are they going to fine him?

LUANN: Individual discretion.

PETER: Exactly. And so, those types of inconsistencies really thwart any effort to see some real substantive things happen.

In this chapter, we shift our focus from the evaluation of individual and group need to relationships – to the dynamics and structure of social exclusion. We move beyond the idea of social exclusion as an individual kind, while taking this common sense point of view seriously. I propose an *integrative* perspective of the social world for investigating the contradiction and conflict arising when a common sense categorical point of view is set in motion in human services. An integrative point of view draws our attention to the individual intersection with the social, the interface between personal agency and structures, the subjectivity of objective conditions, and the contradictions of self-imposed social exclusion. Aiming to preserve a dynamic concept of social exclusion, an integrative perspective brings into view spaces of exclusion and inclusion and the ways in which their inhabitants are both producers and products of those spaces.

The default nature of the categorical perspective is consequential, as it conjures up a particular social order, a "vision of divisions" (Bourdieu, 1989), that is presented as indisputable and absolute and therefore is commonly accepted as truth. Thus, an integrative point of view pushes us to reconfigure common social categories of and for people as dynamic social *processes* that function to make groups and order social space. And perhaps most important, an integrative point of view encourages us to probe familiar binaries in our professional and personal lives and wonder how these binaries of thought and language serve to position us in certain ways in relation to certain others – notions of good/bad, deserving/undeserving, oppressed/oppressor, victim/perpetrator, voluntary/forced, knower/known, helper/helped, and one who gives/one who receives. The general binary of better than/less than operates in almost all social settings and groups, including classrooms, workplaces, families, and playgrounds.

Social exclusion, then, shows up as a kind of individual and a kind of structure that is composed of dynamic systems of social relations that work to define and set apart individuals and groups. Cycling processes and outcomes function to keep people in place. Social exclusion as both kind-and-process sheds light on the profoundly social and relational nature of social exclusion, revealing that groups – social kinds – are not inevitable and natural; rather, they are *made* through official procedures and everyday practices that direct the accumulation and exchange of various types of assets in social space (Good Gingrich, 2010b).

We turn now to consider the human services system as a *social field* that functions according to a market *system of capital* that is organized and maintained by four forms of social exclusion – economic, spatial, sociopolitical, and subjective.

Conceptual tools for seeing, knowing, and understanding

Bourdieu's approach to social inquiry is well suited to a dynamic concept of social exclusion. He advocates "structuralist constructivism" *and* "constructivist structuralism" (1990a, 122), with the use of "relational reason" so that we see the "'thing-ness' of social facts" only insofar as they are products of "*processes* that permit the mutual penetration of the subject-ive and the object-ive realities of society" (Wacquant, 1987, 75; emphasis in original), or "the internalisation of externality and the externalisation of internality" (Bourdieu, 1977, 72). Bourdieu's linked concepts of *fields*, *capital*, and *habitus* are useful in seeing and understanding how processes of social exclusion are put to work. Designed to "grasp the *mode of production of social practices*" (Wacquant, 1987, 75; emphasis in original), this set of ideas draws our attention to the processes by which groups and social systems make themselves and are made, whether they be social classes, ethnic and religious communities, human services and related professions, or even the whole of the public sector and the welfare state. Further, Bourdieu's notions of social fields and systems of capital permit the *tracing* of symbolic power.

The social world is neither static nor arbitrary, as suggested by a categorical perspective. Various spheres of life such as science, religion, the market, politics, and human services form distinct (yet overlapping) social systems or microcosms that are highly structured, and are produced and organized according to specific principles, norms, and forms of authority. Each structured social space, or *social field*, expresses a history of growth and change over time, imposing its "specific determinations upon all those who enter it" (Wacquant, 2007, 8). A field (or *champ* in the original French), very similar to a field of play in a highly competitive game or sport, is defined by its own *system of capital*, both material and symbolic, as individuals and groups compete for available resources that are effective and valued in that social field. The system of capital functions like the rules of the game, the values and agreed-upon practices that guide the ways in which individuals get ahead or fall behind; the rules that determine the allocation of all available resources in this social field, including those that are material or economic and those that need to be converted to have material value. It follows, then, that a social field is an arena of struggle, a battlefield, between those who defend the field's principles of judgment that reinforce the existing distribution of capital, and those who seek to improve a dominated position or reverse a downward trajectory through introducing foreign standards or criteria of evaluation (Wacquant, 2007).

Capital is the various types of assets, or valuables, that are at play in any social field: "A capital does not exist and function except in relation to a field" (Bourdieu & Wacquant, 1992, 101). The value of capital, and the profits and relative social positions that are made possible through its possession, is determined by the rules of capital production and exchange. Space and place thus are organized according to the legitimate means of appropriating and moving capital in a social field and the resulting types and volume of assets possessed by individuals and groups. Occupants of all ranges of positions in social fields seek, individually or collectively, to safeguard or improve their place and to impose principles of profit and exchange most favourable to their own (individual or collective) material and symbolic property.

Bourdieu defines three primary and broad species of capital, or "the energy of social physics" (Bourdieu, 1990b, 122)[1] that provide the basic working elements of social exclusion. These types of capital, which are circulated and reproduced in everyday social relations and practice, are as follows:

a) *Economic capital* refers to the legitimate access to and accumulation of all kinds of material possessions – money and property. This form of capital echoes Marxist ideas of social organization, which are effective in understanding economic exclusion. Economic capital (in its different forms) usually provides access to other species of capital, and other types of resources are useful to the extent that they can be converted into material assets.
b) *Social capital*, referring to valued and useful social connections, is made up of all the resources that can be called upon simply by virtue of being part of a network of durable social relations. Social capital concerns "who you know" when "who you know" counts.
c) *Cultural capital* draws attention to the means or instruments through which scarce symbolic goods, skills, and titles are generated or appropriated. Cultural capital may exist as personal characteristics (such as language skills or familiarity with art); as objects of possession (in books, paintings, machines, etc.); or as certification or recognition provided through diplomas or credentials.

The structure and volume of an individual's holdings are not static. Rather, assets are accrued and divested, valorized and devalued through dynamic social processes that are organized by a system of material capital that works in favour of those who hold large volumes of capital in a social field. In this way, the game is always rigged. This is the power of a fourth and more general type: *symbolic capital*. The notion of symbolic capital appreciates that any form of capital – economic, social, or cultural – can be put to use in ways that conceal its value and power, thus making all sorts of social unevenness appear natural and inevitable. Symbolic capital concerns the prestige, honour, or social credit achieved through the use of other types of capital, but the profits (or losses) of such transactions are denied and unrecognized. Its meaning and effectiveness are in its subversive quality.[2] At the same time, symbolic capital is readily converted into material capital and back again. Further, the display of material and symbolic strength (e.g., through prestigious associations and family relations) is likely, all on its own, to bring in material assets (Bourdieu, 1990b, 119). Operating as a form of credit or a kind of "advance," symbolic capital is recognized as valuable only through the specific social economy – or the rules of the game – that grants its value in the first place. The system of symbolic goods production, or "the system producing the producers," designs the procedures and practices that reinforce the existing social order (Bourdieu, 1990b, 133). Symbolic power is decisive in determining social trajectories and thus is vital to the processes and outcomes of social exclusion.

The market-state social field and system of capital

The state, including all that comprises the government or the public realm, can be thought of as an ensemble of social fields and subfields, each with its own peculiar, yet related, system of capital (Bourdieu & Wacquant, 1992, 112). The state as a social field, indeed as a field of power, is central to understanding common sense views of the social world, as it is the agency that "'possesses the power of legitimate naming, i.e., the power enabling official imposition of the legitimate view of the social world'" (Bourdieu, 1984, as cited by Wacquant, 1987, 79). This is to emphasize that the social space constituted by the social welfare arm of the state is a structured and self-perpetuating system of social relations. The welfare state's "official" representations of individuals, groups and social problems of all sorts (expressed in social policies and networks of services) can be demonstrated to reproduce its own respective social order according to a specific system of capital.

Many theorists agree on some notion of the global market, globalization, or advanced capitalism as the primary ideological thrust in developed liberal welfare regimes the world over, including Canada.[3] *Neoliberalism*, as the prevailing ideological context is often named, is a "rascal concept," as it is "promiscuously pervasive" (Brenner, Peck, & Theodore, 2010, 184) yet "elusive and contested," and "often invoked without clear referent" (Wacquant, 2009, 306). I use the term with intention to refer to an evolving ideological, political, and economic paradigm that consolidates and normalizes free-market imperatives in everyday social interactions and institutions (Hay, 2004). Borrowing terminology coined by Macpherson (1962), Byrne (2005) describes the neoliberal perspective to be founded on the doctrines of possessive individualism, which emphasize the "negative liberties of the self, the optimizing function of the market," and the "residual role of the collective sphere" (19). The essence of neoliberal logic is summed up in four foundational and crucial assumptions:

- that markets are the best and most efficient allocators of resources in production and distribution;
- that policies and practices must remain wary of the "moral hazards" of welfare states;
- that societies are composed of autonomous individuals (producers and consumers) motivated chiefly or entirely by material or economic considerations;
- that competition is the major market vehicle for innovation.[4]

The overriding ethic of possessive individualism shows itself to be a powerful defining and atomizing force that structures not only economic institutions, but political and social relations as well. Discourses of "fiscalization" and "marketization" have served to justify a wide range of "reforms" to social programs that are aimed towards economic goals of international competitiveness, and expenditure restraint through economic restructuring (Prince, 2001, 6). Such reforms have resulted in varied applications of *welfare residualism*. The residual model of welfare "construes our collective social obligation very narrowly, and places great reliance on the private economic market as the optimal means to meet needs and allocate resources" (E. Lightman, 2003, 63). For some countries, this trend has meant primarily staying – or extending – the course. For others, such as Canada, welfare reform has ushered in and justified the contraction of social assistance, the introduction of welfare-to-work, or workfare, and the outsourcing of services and programs to for-profit business. It is a widely held belief, and goes without saying, that all aspects of state function, including what is left of the welfare state, should be managed like a business. Most high-ranking politicians emerge from the world of international business and finance, and it is assumed that the knowledge, skills, and values that made them successful in that world will make them competent managers of the state (McKenzie & Wharf, 2010).

This is not to say that a well-managed state, guided by economic principles, is undesirable or even new. The foundation of Canadian society is market capitalism, based on fundamental notions of individualism and private responsibility, and the Canadian social welfare state was intended to be a complement rather than a substitute, mediating market forces through extra-market allocations (Doern, Maslove, & Prince, 2013;

E. Lightman, 2003). Price (2007) argues that the threat of privatization (as in turning over services to the private sector, or outsourcing) promotes government performance and productivity. E. Lightman (2003, 5; emphasis in original) writes:

> It is assumed that the vast majority of the population will address their income needs through paid work, in a context of full employment and good wages. This *primary distribution* of resources occurs without direct governmental involvement. For those unable to cope in the private market, particularly those excluded through no fault of their own, *secondary* or *redistributive* government social programs come into play – but only *after* the primary distribution of the market has been found deficient.

What is new, however, "is the intensification of designing social programs on the ethic of the economic market" (Doern et al., 2013, 123) by channelling all goals and means of benefits and services through paid market employment, "ensuring the centrality of market consciousness in everyday life" (E. Lightman, 2003, 64). This "commodification of the welfare state" (E. Lightman & Riches, 2000) produces a transformed market-state social field in which resources are scarce and money is of crucial importance.[5]

Welfare residualism and market-based social services are commonplace in developed capitalist societies worldwide (OECD, 2005). Perfectly in tune with austerity measures that are widely criticized yet the preferred solution to failing economies (Stiglitz, 2013), market-based social welfare aims to increase economic self-reliance by redirecting people towards paid work and market consumption and away from state-funded social services and assistance. Policy and program measures include curtailing benefits, tightening eligibility, mandating employment related activities, and punishing recipients for noncompliance (E. Lightman, Mitchell, & Herd, 2010; Martin, 2010). The alleviation of poverty and social exclusion through employment activation programs is a fundamental principle of social welfare in the United Kingdom, the United States, and Canada (Evans, 2007; OECD, 2005; Peck, 2001).[6]

This unqualified and exclusive alignment with the logic and (im)morality of the market, or the economic social field, has given expression to an important international ideological and political shift of welfare states over the past three to four decades. This represents more than a collaboration or partnership between the state and the market – it constitutes a corporate takeover of sorts, whereby the state and all its constituent parts – including, most consequentially, the welfare arm of the state – has been bought out by global market interests, thus fusing social fields and integrating systems of capital and imposing the market as the only game in town. This market conquest is the very essence of neoliberalism. Clearly extending beyond ideas to structures and practices, neoliberalism is demonstrated to be a "*transnational political project* aiming to remake the nexus of market, state, and citizenship from above" (Wacquant, 2009, 306; emphasis in original). The principles of neoliberalism direct the fused market-state social field, functioning as a unified system of capital. In this field, self-sufficiency through economic productivity – narrowly defined in labour and consumer market terms – is a moral imperative.[7] When the market and the state function according to the tangled ideals of consumerism, competition, and individual self-interest, the whole of social life is reduced to market participation, and social problems – managed through policy responses composed exclusively of market mechanisms – necessarily dissolve into private troubles.

Presented as inevitable, as are all ruling ideologies, market-state fusion is "pregnant with the possibility of immense social regression" (Wacquant, 1998b, 228). Ideologies such as neoliberalism owe their organization and potency to social fields, as they are produced and circulated through the specific functions they fulfil in the struggle to acquire symbolic capital and define the rules and regulations of capital distribution. In the course of competition for the various species of capital – especially the pursuit of symbolic domination – "ideological legitimation (or naturalization)" of social divisions and class inequalities is accomplished (Bourdieu & Wacquant, 1992, 106). Thus, it is through the operation of a singular market-oriented system of capital that the market and the state come together to form a closed social order, and it is the corresponding practices of production and reproduction that set into motion and constitute the self-perpetuating processes and outcomes of social exclusion.

Circulating capital and forms of social exclusion

The particular ideological foundations that define the social order of a social field are not merely personal ideas or values. Ideology *occurs* as functioning systems of capital. A system of capital organizes all sorts of physical places and social spaces, and in this way ideology can be perceived, traced. Neoliberal market ideology, as the prevailing system of capital, orders the market-state social field and related subfields (such as the labour market, schools, healthcare, and social services) through economic processes involving all species of capital. These economic exchanges position people and groups in relation to one another. People are characterized by the place they occupy, the relative position of these locations, and the extent of physical space (as in properties owned) and symbolic space (e.g., in law) they take up. In other words, individuals and groups are distributed in social space according to the overall volume and structure of capital they possess over time.

The crucial mechanism through which the four forms of social exclusion are realized – economic, spatial, sociopolitical, and subjective – is the dispossession and devaluation[8] of all types of capital in dominant social fields. The composition and capacity (or symbolic power) of economic, social, and cultural capital held by and accessible to individuals and groups serves to order social space and physical place, demarcating intersecting and interdependent forms of social exclusion that exist "on the ground." These forms of social exclusion are manifested in tangible and material occasions that can be meaningfully observed and measured at one point in time and over time.

The remainder of this chapter is an empirical inquiry of the social space in which the state and the market merge – by design – and resulting outcomes of social exclusion that operate for "eligible" individuals and groups. The everyday and ever present realities described by Dietsche (im)migrants and service providers who work with them provide evidence of the economies of the spaces Dietsche occupy as social service "clients" and social policy "targets" in the social field of the welfare state. Thus, I aim to provide a *mapping* of the ideological distribution of capital and the objective structure of relations between positions in the fused market-state social field. I investigate the regulations of circulation and allocation of various species of capital that produce forms of social exclusion. Through the case example of Dietsche (im)migrants in Canada, my focus is turned to the empirical consequences of its system of capital.

Social exclusion shows itself to result in economic, spatial, sociopolitical, and subjective divides, permitting its recognition and assessment through relevant indicators or species of capital. In the ordered space of Canada's market-state social field, the objective, material outcomes of social exclusion correspond with certain species of capital. Whereas they are not clear, linear relationships, I understand the dynamics of the four forms of social exclusion as follows:

- limited access to the economy of material goods manifests itself primarily in economic and spatial exclusion;
- the divestment of social capital results in spatial and sociopolitical exclusion;
- barriers to cultural capital operate in the production of sociopolitical and, ultimately, subjective exclusion;
- symbolic capital, as unrecognized capital, secures the economic, spatial, sociopolitical, and subjective order of the social field, thus defining trajectories and the possibility for movement, especially to higher ground.[9]

The following discussion of the manifestations of the four forms of social exclusion is based primarily on data from my first research with Dietsche conducted in Ontario from 2003 to 2005. The explicit focus of the work was the outcomes and processes of social exclusion experienced by this population, thus providing more complete and detailed pertinent data. The largest of my three qualitative projects with Dietsche (im)migrants in Canada, these data include in-depth interviews with twenty-four Dietsche (im)migrants; follow-up life history interviews with four (im)migrant women; and individual interviews or focus group discussions with fifty-four service providers (fourteen of whom are Mennonite immigrants) who work with Dietsche in Ontario.

Economic exclusion

Economic exclusion primarily involves income and wealth. This is the most familiar and widely recognized form of social exclusion. Measures of poverty are usually determined according to annual income rather than overall wealth. In Bourdieu's terms, economic capital is closely related to various forms of symbolic capital and goes well beyond the notion of income. He defines economic capital as the form that is "immediately and directly convertible into money and may be institutionalized in the form of property rights" (1986, 243). The idea of wealth recognizes assets as "resources from which we can generate a flow of income" (E. Lightman, 2003, 15). Similarly, Bourdieu's concept of economic capital makes plain the means by which various versions of material and symbolic assets are accumulated and subsequently converted into "flow," or further access to money, thereby boosting the potential for gain in an endless, positive feedback loop.

In a study of social exclusion, the distinction between wealth and income is important, as in the Canadian sociopolitical context the distribution of power corresponds directly with the distribution of wealth. Further, wealth is the primary vehicle through which inequalities are sustained from one generation to the next (Stiglitz, Sen, & Fitoussi, 2009). While we study incomes regularly, surveys of wealth in Canada are uncommon (E. Lightman, 2003; Yalnizyan, 2000). Yet the procedure of means-testing in a marketized welfare system attempts to determine eligibility based on assessments of income plus material assets, or personal wealth.[10] As a result, service recipients are routinely asked to report details regarding not only the flow of money into the household from all sources, but also any *potential* for income. Judgments of eligibility for benefits are based on adequately low levels of income as well as material assets, or economic capital, which can be liquidated or converted into flow.

I approached conversation about financial matters with Dietsche (im)migrants with some caution, as their custom is to keep such personal details private. Furthermore, I was aware that as social service clients, many of the Dietsche people I interviewed are routinely required to disclose all particulars related to money, and I wanted my inquiry to be distinctive from a client intake form or risk assessment. I intentionally posed questions of income in relation to day-to-day experiences, such as current employment, wages, hours worked per week, and the usual number of months in the year of waged work. The precarious nature of the work in which many engage was made evident in the complex and variable methods employers use to compensate them for their labour. For example, wages could not be simply recalled and reported, as farm workers are often paid in cash combined with housing accommodations and by the piece rather than an hourly wage. I accepted, without probing, the responses offered and avoided direct requests for information regarding annual income, assets, investments, debt, and so forth. As a result, there are significant gaps in the data, and only estimations of monthly or annual income are possible. The following is a summary of reported details regarding the wages and income of these families as estimated at a particular point in time:

- A family working in the fields, with at least two family members picking, typically earned from $12,000 to $20,000 in a picking season. There are many variables, such as the number of pickers, crop yields, and the payment of wages by the hour or volume. Wages earned by each family member were generally pooled, contributing to the household income.

- Others who had more permanent employment, such as welding, carpentry, factory work, or working as a hired farmhand, reported making between $10 and $14 an hour, which was estimated to total an annual income of $19,000 to $28,000.
- Some families also collected the Canada Child Tax Benefit (CCTB), which was reported to range between $700 and $1,100 per month.
- The estimated annual income of working families interviewed, including the CCTB when applicable, was between $20,000 and $36,500 per year.

Dietsche (im)migrants rely on unreported income from a variety of sources, especially money (or material goods) from family members and wages paid in cash. Discussions of earned income suggest that many Dietsche do not distinguish between the formal and informal economies. It is all paid work.[11]

These income estimates are meaningful to the study of social exclusion in relational terms – for example, in comparison with monetary resources deemed necessary to live in a certain geographical region or in relation to the income of others in a society. Such determinations are subjective in nature, requiring judgments to be made. Thus, the work of measuring poverty is value laden, setting into motion assumptions and beliefs that can be traced to specific ideologies and views of the social world. "Choosing a poverty line depends on how high or how low we set our sights for the well-being of the materially disadvantaged in our society" (deGroot-Maggetti, 2002, 16). The diagnosis of poverty as a social ill is also contentious, as the standard or "normal" targets by which symptoms are to be compared and assessed are hotly debated. As a result, there are countless ways of measuring income adequacy, and a thorough consideration of the various approaches would constitute an imposing project in and of itself.[12] In this case, I have used Statistics Canada's Low Income Cut-Offs (LICOs) for 2003 (corresponding to the year of most of the data collection) to make some comparisons.

Taking into account the place of residence and size of family units, it is estimated that most Dietsche (im)migrants had incomes ranging from 57 per cent to 100 per cent of these poverty lines. Nine out of the thirteen working families interviewed earned less than 89 per cent of the low income cut-off. Only two families had an estimated combined income (wages earned from non-seasonal work and the CCTB) matching the LICO. Of the twenty-four (im)migrants interviewed, only four representing three families depended solely on government assistance for their income. Two of these families were headed by single mothers, the only Dietsche single-parent families in the study. One man and his family were living on welfare, owing to his profoundly debilitating condition, and to that point he had been refused assistance from the Ontario Disability Support Program (ODSP). He spoke with considerable emotion about being unable to work. While providing an adequate income for his family was important to him, it was even more important that he work to provide that income, whether adequate or not. He was continuing to try to find ways of making work for himself.

In striking contrast to working families, all social assistance recipients in this study reported that their income was not adequate to meet the needs of their family. One widowed woman, who had given birth to sixteen children and still cared for five at home, had lived on welfare since the death of her second husband in 1995. Her application for ODSP was approved about one year prior to the interview. She reported that this support resulted in an increase of $200 to $300 every month, which often was still not enough for her family. Reported income for these families living on social assistance ranged from $950 to $1,500 per month, or $11,400 to $18,000 annually.

Four of the thirteen working families interviewed depended on income from seasonal field work. The older children in these families (ten to fifteen years of age) were reported to work alongside their fathers, and sometimes their mothers, during peak harvest months. Income calculations for these families were especially difficult, as the earnings fluctuated from day to day, owing to unpredictability in the type of work, amount of work, and number of family members contributing. Of these working families, only three of the women were engaged in paid work. One woman, whose husband was recently injured in a work-related accident, was just beginning to sew piecework in her home. Another woman had recently acquired a part-time job in a plastics factory, and the third was helping with field work. Of the nine men supporting their families with steady, year-round employment, only two had worked in that job for more than one year. Families relying on seasonal farm labour, even when several family members contributed, reported significantly lower incomes than the LICO poverty line.

Of the sixteen Dietsche (im)migrant families represented in this study, six did not collect the CCTB for various reasons. Several reported that they were waiting for paperwork to be finalized, as service providers explained that mothers in families are required to have documented citizenship or landed immigrant status for one full year before they are eligible to collect the benefit. One father reported that they had not received cheques for two or three months. He suspected that the lapse was due to their change in address (two years previously), and his efforts to rectify the situation had been unsuccessful.

During my ten years of research with Dietsche (im)migrants, only a few working families admitted that they had relied on welfare for a brief period of time upon arrival in Canada before employment was secured. Accounts from service recipients and providers revealed that the Dietsche who do access workfare are likely to be unusually short-term clients. When there is not enough money for the necessities of life, Dietsche first seek financial support from extended family members. Family income is often cobbled together, in that sources of income are usually numerous and varied, including an assortment of paid work situations, government assistance, and extended family support.

In summary, economic exclusion was evidenced not only in the meagre income of most Dietsche families, but also in the precarious and inconsistent nature of their financial situations. While it is important to remember that these findings cannot be used to make claims about Dietsche in general, they are consistent with income and employment data from other studies of Dietsche (im)migrants in Ontario (e.g., Brooks, 2002; Touzin & Thompson, 1993). More important, the character of economic exclusion is illustrated with some precision. Perhaps contributing to the pervasive and perpetual debates surrounding poverty rates in Canada, the day-to-day realities of (im)migrants demonstrate that precise annual income calculations for individuals and families experiencing economic exclusion are impossible. The decisive factor in economic exclusion appears to be an insecure attachment to marginal sectors of the polarized labour market. Here, in the secondary labour market, the growing demand for cheap labour means that jobs are often short term, working conditions are commonly unsafe and unregulated, and wages may be paid in cash, or sometimes not paid at all. People frequently move from one job to the next when the work runs out, illness or injury precludes physical labour, or news of higher wages or job permanence promises greater economic stability elsewhere. Thus, access to material capital is unpredictable for Dietsche families in Canada, demonstrating processes and outcomes of economic exclusion.

Spatial exclusion

Spatial exclusion has to do with social and physical distance and divides, achieved through the amount and type of physical and geographic space occupied by individuals or groups. Large holders of economic and social capital not only tend to take up large amounts of space in their dwellings, businesses, and so on, but often have rights to multiple homes and work spaces (e.g., cottages, summer and winter homes, commuter condos), thus permitting easy geographic mobility and simultaneous alternate residency. At the opposite end of the asset spectrum, a primary indicator of the dispossession of economic and social capital is substandard housing circumstances, congestion, and geographic segregation. Factors related to housing conditions considered in my research are consistent with those used by the Canada Mortgage and Housing Corporation (CMHC) and include housing availability, adequacy (reasonable maintenance, basic fixtures and appliances), suitability (acceptable number of bedrooms), and affordability (shelter costs consume less than 30 per cent of before-tax household income).[13] A household is deemed to be in core housing need if its current housing falls below at least one of these standards and the family would not be able to afford local market housing that meets all three standards (R. Lewis & Jakubec, 2004).

The same gaps in the data that preclude precise analysis of economic exclusion prevent a detailed assessment of housing affordability, suitability, and adequacy. The primary obstacle to such an analysis is the notable transience of Dietsche families. People move frequently, most often motivated by the pursuit of employment or a home in the "country" (i.e., rural area). Specifically, thirteen of the sixteen Dietsche families interviewed reported having moved within the past year. Second, calculations of affordability require housing costs to be compared with household income within a concurrent stretch of time. Many, especially those working in seasonal jobs, relied on a variety of sources of income, both documented and undocumented, such that even estimates of income over a few months would have required in-depth questioning and investigation. In several instances, the information provided regarding housing and income details, such as alternative sources of income, rent, and cost of utilities, seemed incomplete or unlikely. Giving priority to the quality of the research relationships rather than the data, I did not pursue that line of questioning if an opportunity did not present itself.

Although detailed and accurate numerical information may not have been readily available in these research interviews, Dietsche (im)migrants shared their experiences of spatial exclusion in their stories of everyday life. Indeed, in this study of a particular case of social exclusion, spatial exclusion is perhaps the most conspicuous form. Dietsche homes in rural southwestern and central Ontario, particularly in the fertile agricultural regions close to the northern shores of Lake Erie, can often be identified by their distinctive features. Many Dietsche families live in employer-owned farmhouses that are old, visibly dilapidated, and structurally unstable. For example, it is not unusual for these houses to have broken windows that have been boarded up, unsteady and uneven concrete or wooden steps leading to the front door, a sagging roof, and rotting window and door frames. Some buildings used to shelter large families are very small and box-like, appearing more like sheds than houses. Poorly insulated and very small house trailers frequently serve as homes for (im)migrant families, and many can be seen on farm properties in certain regions of rural Ontario. While efforts have been made to monitor housing provided by employers in the past two decades, some Dietsche families still live in chicken coops and bunkhouses.[14]

Service providers reported that more Dietsche families were beginning to buy houses in Ontario. Yet all (im)migrant families in this study rented their homes. Thirteen out of the sixteen Dietsche families lived in market rental accommodations. Of these, nine lived in rural areas, miles away from even small villages and towns. Rent for these rural accommodations ranged from $500 to $750 per month. Two men employed as hired hands for large farming operations received housing as partial compensation for their labour. In one instance, the family did not pay rent, but paid $200 per month for utilities. Rental accommodations for families living in villages and towns tended to be marginally cheaper, ranging from $485 to $685 per month. Recognizing the limitations of the data, I estimate that most working families living in private rental accommodations paid 24–40 per cent of their before-tax income in shelter costs. Not surprisingly, two of the families on social assistance and living in market rental units spent an inordinate percentage of their reported income on housing. One of these families, which was waiting to be approved for ODSP and living on welfare, recounted paying rent of $625 out of a monthly income of $950, or 66 per cent. Three (im)migrant fathers, all living in housing that was not affordable according to the CMHC definition, stated that their rent was "too high."

Only three families resided in social or rent-geared-to-income housing. Two families lived on wage income, while one relied on welfare. Owing to availability, all subsidized housing for these families was in small urban centres. The few social housing situations represented in the study met all standards, as they were affordable (by definition), adequate, and suitable. Without exception, all families living "in town" spontaneously expressed their desire to have "more space," or to live in "the country." Most respondents who had experience living in rent-geared-to-income housing acknowledged that it was a "good house," but there were "too many people" in the housing complex, and "not enough space" outside for the children to play.

Tenants living in social housing paid a sliding scale of 30 per cent of their income in rent. Therefore, in order to calculate the rental rate, Dietsche families living in social housing were required to report all household income, including the earnings of any children not registered in school and over sixteen years of age, every month. Dietsche respondents noted that when they had no income to report, they paid $85 per month for rent. Some families, however, could not afford to live in rent-geared-to-income housing. Elisabeth, a Dietsche single mother living on disability benefits, described her predicament when her son quit school.

> It's okay at this place. At first, at [a subsidized housing complex], it was good, too. And the rent was low. But my son quit school when he was sixteen and he started working, and then we had to pay $725 a month there. Me and my son together. Utilities were separate. We lived there over a year.

When the cost of rent in social housing was no longer affordable for Elisabeth and her son, their extended family network helped them find a place to live that was within their means. Ironically, even though the explicit goal of government-subsidized housing services in Ontario is to provide affordable living accommodations, their rental costs were significantly less when they moved from social not-for-profit housing to market for-profit housing.

The adequacy and suitability of Dietsche (im)migrant housing varies, but certain trends among families were apparent. For example, observation and participant responses suggest that at least five of the thirteen market housing accommodations were not in good repair. Families lived with rotting front steps, broken windows, doors with broken hinges and without doorknobs, unreliable running water, and poor and unsafe heat sources. During an interview in a small village apartment above a store, for example, the propane heater in the corner of the living room periodically let out a loud and startling "bang" that was apparently its habit, as such outbursts went unnoticed by the mother and the young children who live there. In a rather dilapidated building, this apartment, which provided shelter for a family with four children under the age of six, had no central heat source. It was equipped with two electric baseboard heaters and this seemingly short-tempered propane heater. Two of the families – one with four children and the other with five – lived in rural, two-bedroom homes. Each family divided their children between two beds in one bedroom. The thirteen children of another family, ranging in age from three weeks to eighteen years, shared four bedrooms. Similarly, a family that routinely travelled to Mexico for the winter months rented a rural home year-round. Seven of their eight children, from nine to seventeen years, shared two bedrooms.

The factors considered in assessing housing tend to overlap, such that availability, adequacy, suitability, and affordability are often linked, and deficits occur concurrently. Therefore, parents find themselves in situations in which multiple impediments to providing shelter for their family are confronted at once. Even though housing for (im)migrant families was reported to be scarce, the Dietsche network is so effective that most families found their own housing through tips from extended family members.

> My sister-in-law moved out, and she told me about this place. It was good. But it's hard to find good places to live. At first, when we came here in 1990, we moved to my brother. They had six children. We had eleven. We lived together for a little while. They helped us find a house and find work. [Annie, Dietsche mother]

Because rural housing accommodations are often provided by employers as partial compensation for farm labour, news of employment opportunities travels through the same grapevine. In such cases, housing is provided for the duration of employment, which is limited to the harvest season. Many of these homes lack insulation and heating.

Families usually migrate north in the spring or summer and need to find accommodations immediately. Most often, the options available to them will be "bunkhouses or barns or little shacks behind the farm-houses." Marge, a Mennonite service provider, went on to explain:

> And at this time of year, we've just had all kinds of movement because people can't stay in these homes past about October, maybe November if they're really pushing it. And they have to find something else.

I asked, "So, where do they go?" She replied:

> Some will just go back to Mexico, when they can't stay here any longer, especially if the work is pretty much done. And they'll take whatever money they earned here in the summertime, and that actually gets them through, not too badly, the winter months in Mexico. Especially if they've got a little house there still, so they've someplace that they can stay. And then they'll come as soon as the work begins in the spring, and they can live back in the same decrepit housing again. So that's one option. Another option is that there are a number of families now that go to Leamington for three months or so over the winter months, because the offshore workers [temporary visa workers] are only allowed to stay in Canada for nine months of the year,[15] and their greenhouses need workers twelve months of the year. So there's always that three- to four-month period when employers don't have their offshore workers, and they will hire the Mennonites from Mexico to cover for those three months. And then they fire them immediately when the offshore workers come again ... The other option is that they'll look for housing in town, so we've seen many coming in looking for whatever they can find.

While any sort of rural housing is scarce, affordable housing in rural areas is especially hard to come by. Social housing is available only in relatively congested parts of town. When a choice must be made between location and adequacy or suitability, living in the country was clearly identified to be the primary consideration for Dietsche families. Social service practitioners confirmed this preference for rural living.

> CAROL: They will accept a substandard house because it's cheap, or cheaper, and because it's out in a rural area. They don't really want to live in town, where their children are exposed to other influences. They really want to be isolated ... They have however many children,

sometimes, in one bedroom. Sometimes there might be three children sleeping in one bed.

RUTH: My friend at the trailer – there are four children sleeping in one bed. And one of those children is nine years old. I wouldn't want to live where this woman is living. I don't think you would, or Carol would. There are six children and two adults living in that tiny, two-bedroom trailer. [Mennonite service providers]

Many Dietsche families are on the move, continuously, so that available homes are passed from one (im)migrant family to another.

MARGE: There's always some housing available in the fall because there are always people who leave for Mexico or Leamington then, and they lived in town. So then that opens up some housing in the fall. But there's not much, you know. And what there is available in town is also not good at times, in terms of overcrowding, and people have to pay way too much for housing that is also decrepit and substandard.

LUANN: So this is beyond subsidized housing?

MARGE: Yes, because subsidized housing units are always full. We were talking about that the other day. We've had houses – I think they were developed about eleven years ago – two sets of subsidized housing, one with fifty units. They've been full, steady, throughout that time.

LUANN: When they go to Leamington, where do they stay? Because the housing that's provided by employers is usually for single men, right?

MARGE: That's right. They have to find housing there and it's a problem. A co-worker was telling me this week that one family is driving one hour, one way, because they couldn't find housing any closer. But there are a number of families living around there, so the men are pooling together to drive to the greenhouses. Some of the motels will take them in the wintertime. [Mennonite service provider]

The factors contributing to spatial exclusion are numerous and intersecting. In many cases, housing that meets established standards is considered undesirable and unacceptable according to service recipients and providers alike. In a number of rural towns, rent-geared-to-income housing developments were built to address housing shortages, but new problems emerged as these units have come to be occupied predominantly by Dietsche (im)migrant families. Debbie, an English service provider described the tensions that have arisen in social housing complexes.

It's created a lot of difficulties right there in those little communities. And people want to get out. They might be thankful that they have a place to live that is decent, and it's geared to income. So it's something they can probably afford. But I know women that don't let their children play outside because of all the other children. It's typical when you take a whole bunch of families and stick them in one block. And there's no privacy whatsoever. Some have no income, so they already have difficult problems. Only to complicate this, there are eight to ten kids per family. It's created a host of new problems.

The implications of geographic segregation are severe. Will, a Mennonite immigrant service provider articulated that spatial exclusion is about much more than the dispossession of economic capital.

When we wanted to build family housing, we had government funds to build fifty units. And we didn't want to clump them all together in one place because these people have such large families and they don't come from that background. It would create problems. So we wanted to have some units in one little hamlet, and the other one at a different location. We had the land, we had the resources, but people put up a petition in both places, saying "We don't want those people here." And then we asked, "Who are 'those people'?" And they wouldn't say. We conditionally bought a place outside of town here. And then those neighbours, they were up in arms. "We don't want those people here." And we ended up buying four acres in town here that was already zoned for high density. And people couldn't object. But now we have fifty units, up to six-bedroom apartments on a four-acre complex, and that's just way too many people in one place. And to hear the attitude expressed ... It was being built around the time of the Iran-Iraq conflict, and it was nicknamed immediately "Little Iraq." Outside people still refer to it as Iraq.

Spatial exclusion was manifested in inadequate, unsuitable, and unaffordable housing on the one hand, and conflict-ridden and insecure neighbourhoods on the other. Many Dietsche families are forced to choose between these two schemes of spatial exclusion. In addition, and perhaps more important, spatial exclusion is evidenced in the volatility and vulnerability of their lives, specifically, the frequency with which families move, within Ontario and beyond, to find employment and satisfactory housing. While some families reported a preference for regular migration between Mexico and Canada, such movement is available primarily to those who own property in Mexico. Sustained mobility within and between rural regions of Ontario was portrayed as involuntary hardship, often accompanied by a longing for more stability. Thus, spatial exclusion is associated with the denied recognition of and access to economic and social capital.

The challenges confronted in analysing the data for the most objective indicators of social exclusion – various types of economic capital – provide meaningful evidence of the extent and intensity of spatial and economic exclusion. When employment is precarious, income is meagre, and housing is unsatisfactory, people are forced to live unsettled lives, making it difficult – if not impossible – to precisely compare data with the customary measures of employment, poverty, and core housing need. The concealing and suppressing of characteristics of social exclusion work to make individuals and whole groups of people *invisible*. This is sociopolitical exclusion. Consequently, the recognition and analysis of social exclusion that stops short at its material outcomes – outcomes having to do with income and wealth, employment, and housing – is necessarily fraught with inaccuracies and imprecision, resulting in conflicting observations and erroneous conclusions.

Sociopolitical exclusion

Sociopolitical exclusion is evidenced through the strength and effectiveness of social and cultural currency in private and public realms and in various social fields. Social capital is composed of social obligations, or social connection. Its value is found largely in its conversion to economic capital in certain conditions. Specific kinds of stable relationships or affiliations of shared recognition are linked to actual or potential resources. These relationships are often institutionalized, such that each "credentialled" individual member of a group or network enjoys all the symbolic and material benefits of the collectively owned capital. The bulk of social capital held by an individual depends on the size of the network of connections that one can effectively round up and on the volume of the capital (economic, cultural, or symbolic) carried by each of those to whom he or she is connected (Bourdieu, 1986). In this way, social capital works together with cultural capital to define sociopolitical exclusion.

Bourdieu identifies three dimensions of cultural capital: "an embodied state, that is in the form of long-lasting dispositions of the mind and body; in the objectified state, in the form of cultural goods; and in the institutionalized state, resulting in such things as educational qualifica-tions" (Lovell, 2000, 38). To hold cultural capital is to embody the "sche-mata of perception and action, principles of vision and division, and mental structures" – that is, to demonstrate cultural competence – in the particular field that defines its conditions of acquisition (Bourdieu, 1996, 5).[16] Integral to the market-state field are all sorts of education and training systems that award qualifications, thus "durably consecrating the position occupied" in the structure of differentially distributed cul-tural capital (Bourdieu, 1990b, 125). Schools, universities, professional associations, credentialling bodies, practitioner colleges, and trade unions make up the specific social subfield that produces and organizes the exchange of cultural capital. These institutions and systems of rela-tions define the rules of the game in the market-state social field and, ultimately, inscribe subjectivity for its actors.

Sociopolitical inclusion is made manifest in a high degree of visibil-ity, legitimacy, and protection under the law and ample symbolic space and mobility in a range of official capacities in social and political are-nas. Sociopolitical exclusion is the dispossession of social and cultural capital, most often achieved through discrediting the functional value of these assets in material and symbolic exchanges. The processes and practices of sociopolitical exclusion operate to make particular groups and individuals illegitimate or invisible. People are thus *un-made*.

In the case example of Dietsche (im)migrants, the precarious employ-ment circumstances upon which many families rely for their liveli-hoods is evidence of sociopolitical exclusion. Specifically, some families support themselves with wages earned by family members (sometimes teenagers or younger children) who work in low-paying, often sea-sonal, agricultural jobs. It is not unusual for employers to compensate pickers by the piece and in cash. Some Dietsche workers recounted the experience of never receiving pay for a full day or week of work. It is clear that the so-called Standard Employment Relationship "never took hold" for many people, especially for the "predominantly women and immigrant workers in small and decentralized workplaces in the service and competitive manufacturing sectors" and in Canada's agri-business (Cranford, Vosko, & Zukewich, 2003, 7). The growing number of marginalized workers who are disproportionately women, immigrants and migrants, people of colour, and youth are thus less likely to benefit from labour laws, as they are made insignificant and invisible in relevant policies and legislation (Fudge & Vosko, 2001). This is sociopolitical exclusion that operates in tandem with all other forms.

The most basic credential in any society is that of "citizen." This is one of the few forms of sociopolitical inclusion that most Dietsche accept without hesitation. Canadian citizenship is highly valued. For Dietsche (im)migrants, as for all other immigrant or migrant groups who do not (or cannot) remain perpetually out of sight, the most crucial social category to be achieved is that of a legal resident – to obtain *status* as a citizen or landed immigrant. (Im)migrants and service providers alike recognized the need for proper documentation. For many Dietsche families, hope for survival is found in getting their "papers," which are necessary to prove their existence, place and date of birth, gender, ethnic category, and marital status. The official documents required by Canada often had not been produced in Mexico, and the process of obtaining even this little bit of sociopolitical power can be long and costly.

Sociopolitical exclusion was evidenced in instances of rationalizing or showing indifference to substandard housing, truancy, child labour, denial of benefits, and unfair and unsafe employment situations.[17] With the aim of exploring the invisibility of sociopolitical exclusion, I asked this question:

LUANN: This is something that has come up before, on a number of issues, like housing and education. There's a kind of silent agreement that everybody looks the other way. And, what is that about? I mean, we have standards in Canada, and what we think is okay for children and adults, as far as housing is concerned, and education. And laws. And we sort of look the other way when it comes to this particular population. Why?

MARGARET: Well, especially employers. There are child labour laws, and they choose to ignore them, even when you point them out to them.

PETER: And their defence back, though, is "We hired the parents, and they brought their kids."

MARGARET: And "We're not paying the children." They pay the parents, but they don't pay the children.

PETER: That turning away – I think a lot of that is based on racial prejudice. You know, the thinking is "That's just how they operate. That's how they want it. They want their kids out working." And if you ignore the problem, maybe it'll go away. That type of mentality. And second to that – This happened probably about ten years ago. There was a lot of light shed on housing issues. And it really caused a lot of divisiveness, both among the employing community and the Mennonite family. People were cast in a very negative light, and they didn't appreciate that – farmers and the school system, and others. And that's what compelled some action to be taken. And the flip side of that is the whole issue of advocacy. You know, who or for what reason are these things being brought to the fore? "Who sent you?" kind of mentality. Some of the Mennonite families that do come here are perfectly content and want to capitalize or take full advantage of the opportunity to live in a house and have the whole family work, and to make some money in any of the given harvests. And then for someone to come in and rock the boat, someone who may not have had any permission, as it were, or licence to advocate for these people, really is a delicate subject. And I've faced that myself. When I've gone to the Board of Education on certain issues, it's "Who sent you?" "Who told you that these parents are going through this, or that they want this or don't want that?" And the Low German families will say, "Who sent you?" And so there's that whole ownership of advocacy, and who starts the ball rolling, and for whose interests is that person doing what they're doing? Is it for the Mennonite family? Is it for the Board of Education? Or is it for the local farmer? And there doesn't seem to be a cohesive mindset as to what is the best interest of everyone involved. Because everyone has a vested interest in seeing that their goals are being met from the Mennonite community. You know, the Board wants the numbers and wants the enrolment, but they don't necessarily want all the baggage that comes with it. And the employers have their vested interest of getting cheap labour. And the families, especially recent immigrants, have their goals and ambitions in mind – their family goals, the reason they have come to Ontario to begin with. To have the freedom to work, as a family unit, maintaining a lot of the family habits that they would have had in Mexico. They are now being transposed into a system where kids are a little bit more monitored in health, or child labour is more monitored. There's a conflict there. And how to serve whose best interests? And to try and get all of those three constituents on the same page is difficult at best. And then, as I said earlier, "On whose behalf are you speaking? And what gives you the right to be an ambassador for any one of those parties involved?"

LUANN: Who invited you?

PETER: Right. [Mennonite immigrant service providers]

Although invisibility and illegitimacy are sometimes thrust upon Dietsche (im)migrants, it is here, in the sociopolitical processes of society, that expressions of self-imposed social exclusion are most apparent. Numerous and varied instances of voluntary sociopolitical exclusion from the benefits and resources available in Canadian society were reported in interview conversations. Most Dietsche have never voted. Several service providers observed that many in this population seem to be ignorant and weak-willed in claiming their rights as citizens. Dietsche people were criticized for not participating in and contributing to their local communities. The Dietsche disposition for a distinctive collective identity, separation from the broader society, and self-sustaining colony life was identified as a problem to be overcome rather than "catered to" if they wanted to stay in Canada. Service providers saw the Dietsche insistence on maintaining even remnants of the traditional way of life to be stubborn defiance that prevented proper integration into Canadian society. Moreover, some interpret their migration to be wilful desertion of the colony in Latin America and rejection of the traditional way of life. Thus, it appeared to some human service workers that many Dietsche refuse meaningful engagement in both the traditional colony life and Canadian society. Service providers generally perceived the self-imposed nature of Dietsche (im)migrant sociopolitical exclusion – which is necessarily economic in its consequences – to be strangely absolute and patently foolish.

Perhaps the most obvious example of self-exclusion was the rejection, by some Dietsche (im)migrants, of the public education system, thus apparently refusing the primary legitimate means for accruing cultural capital in Canadian society. Recognized credentials and titles function as cultural capital, which is readily transferred into social and economic capital. This type of cultural capital, however, is available only through the "official" education system that is sanctioned by both the market and the state. Of the sixteen Dietsche families represented in this study (2003–5), none had children with a high school diploma. Twelve families sent their children to the local public school, but all families with teenage children reported that their older children did not attend regularly, or not at all.

When asked about high school education for their children, parents of young children remarked that they had not thought about it, or they insisted that their children will do "as we did in Mexico" – attend school until the age of twelve or thirteen. While school was most often reported to be "good" or "okay" for their children, some Dietsche parents related experiences of cruel bigotry.

> HELENA: [Trans.] That trouble we did have for a while. We had to work with it. In the beginning, for three weeks, we had to put him [her son] in a new backpack each week, because they would rip it, and they would

kick him and everything. So I went to the school with a lady that helped me, and I talked to the principal. He was supposed to find out what they did, if my boy made trouble, or if they just did it. Because they always named him "Mexican." They would yell, "Mexican!" And once we had to pick him up, and we stopped by the curb close to the school. And he came walking and two boys came behind him and kicked him and pulled on his clothes. When he came close to us I called him and the boys saw that, and left.

TRANSLATOR: How long did that last?

HELENA: [Trans.] In the beginning, quite a while.

TRANSLATOR: A couple of months?

HELENA: [Trans.] That could be. Then once, one boy had kicked him in the ribs. Then I had to go to the chiropractor with him. He had pain, and then they found out. We had to tell them what was wrong, and then they did something about it. And from then on it was different. At one time, he could barely walk home freely because they would do it to him on the way. He would find another route so he wouldn't have to walk with them – a long way around so he could walk home. And at last it was different.

Dietsche (im)migrants explained that not only English children participated in such verbal and physical abuse. Sometimes Dietsche children, those who have been in Canada a little longer and perhaps felt a little more English, taunted other Dietsche children with jeers of "stupid Mexicans" or "dirty Mexicans." Because of a shared understanding of the social organization of the Dietsche social field, both tormentor and tormented recognized such insults to be hostile and wounding. Dietsche mothers expressed fear and grief for their children who suffered such cruelty when they sent them out into "the world."

Albeit many Dietsche voluntarily exclude themselves and their children from the public school system, rejecting a core societal value of free and equitable education, external barriers to the legitimate accumulation of cultural capital were evidenced to be significant. For example, a Mennonite immigrant service provider explained that access to public education is made costly and formidable for many.

LUANN: So they have to have some kind of documentation before they come to school?

WILL: Well, one of the parents has to have status. And all of the children have to have status. It can take a long time.

MARY: We had one mother, she got her Canadian citizenship last month. So now I registered her child in school. But now they said, "Oh, we first have to have proof of the father's status."

WILL: They don't need that, but many of ... It's so hard to convince the schools. So what we've done is we've got the member of Parliament involved, and it helps.

LUANN: They don't want the student, or what?

MARY: Well, it's past their funding. The logistics make a difference in their funding.

LUANN: It's too late in the school year to get funding for them to go to school. So they don't want them.

MARY: Well they don't say that, our government.

LUANN: So what are they supposed to do while they wait?

WILL: Well, many of them are in limbo, at home, bored. And you ask how long it would take? A lot of it also depends on money. Because the parents have to have a medical, the children each have to have a medical. And the family has to pay for it. They have to pay so much for visitors' permits, so much per application. What is it, a couple thousand dollars that it can cost an individual to get all that documentation done? And then you have a fairly large family. And sometimes that takes a lot of money. And even though otherwise, they might be okay. But then they work for a while because they just don't have funds to pay for it. And so often by the time children start school, their two years of qualification for ESL [English as a Second Language] has expired.

LUANN: So they have to have been here for two years or less to get ESL?

WILL: For ESL, yes. And so if they start school after their two years here, even though they haven't been able to learn any English at home, they don't qualify.[18]

MARY: I have a big beef about that, because little children can't get ESL. And if mother doesn't know any English, then it doesn't matter how many years they've been here. The children start school not knowing any English, but they can't qualify for ESL. And from the start, there's a big language barrier.

Ironically, Dietsche (im)migrants are harshly criticized for denying their children a proper education, yet it is not unusual for their entitlement to be questioned and access denied, resulting in sociopolitical exclusion. Education for all children and youth under eighteen is both a right and a requirement according to international, national, and provincial law. Specifically, for example, denying access to elementary or secondary schools violates the Universal Declaration of Human Rights, Canada's Immigration and Refugee Protection Act, and the Ontario Education Act. Protection under the law does not guard against this form of social exclusion.

Five of the twelve families who sent their children to public schools stated a strong preference for their own Old Colony church schools. Dietsche religious schools have been established in regions of Canada where the population of Dietsche (im)migrants is most concentrated.[19] These private, unaccredited schools offer grades one through twelve. Since their teachers are not certified and the curriculum is not provincially approved, students graduating from Old Colony schools do not receive a high school diploma. While most instruction is in English, teachers were educated primarily in colony schools in Mexico for the customary five or six years. Dietsche (im)migrants expressed confidence in these schools, owing to what is and is not imparted to their children. They want their children to receive a "Christian education," and a key component is prayer in school. Specific disapproval was expressed for television or videos, and sex education in schools. It was evident that the four families sending their children to Old Colony schools did so at considerable financial sacrifice. For example, one family relying on income from seasonal field work and sewing piecework reported paying almost $3,600 a year for their four youngest children to attend an Old Colony school. One Dietsche father, who was physically disabled and had no other option but to depend on welfare to provide for his family, was struggling to pay $215 per month for his two daughters to go to the local Old Colony school.[20]

Families living outside geographical proximity to Old Colony schools in the concentrated Dietsche regions of Ontario expressed markedly more confidence and satisfaction with local public schools. While all (im)migrant parents expressed a disinclination for their children to go to school beyond the required age of sixteen,[21] families in Waterloo, Wellington, Dufferin, and Grey Counties described positive and comfortable school experiences for their children. Discussions with adults and children alike in these regions suggest that Dietsche children do not endure the prejudicial attitudes and malicious attacks that were described to be common in public schools in towns such as Aylmer and Port Burwell.[22] Four families in the study sent their children to a public school in a rural region of south-central Ontario. The mothers of these children expressed approval and trust in the school staff, curriculum, and social environment. This unusual rural school, established in the 1980s, offers

kindergarten through grade ten to children from several different traditional Mennonite groups in the area. Both service providers and Dietsche
parents who are familiar with this particular public school remarked that
it seemed to be regarded by Dietsche with respect and comfort similar to
those accorded Old Colony schools. Since the entire student population
consists of Amish, David Martin Mennonite, or Dietsche (im)migrant
children who customarily do not attend public schools, certain adjust-
ments have been made. A school employee explained:

> KEVIN: Probably over 60 per cent of our school at the present time is from
> this [Dietsche] population, and it's actually growing …. Because the
> school has grown as much as it has, we've got six portables there now.
> Actually, as a percentage of the school population, the other groups are
> declining. Other groups are just staying the same, while this group is the
> growing one. We've noticed the transient nature of the group. They move
> into the area and then possibly move back out. A lot of them seem to, by
> word of mouth, have heard about the school, and they'll attempt to get
> rental accommodation in the area where they can come to the school.
> And our program is run – I always compare it to a French Immersion
> school. For French Immersion schools, you bus your kids over a long,
> long area, past other public schools to get them to a French Immersion
> program. We do the same thing. We have kids changing buses to make
> connections to come to this school … We might have one field trip per
> class. Whereas if I were in another setting, let's say mid-Toronto, and I
> had kids from all different cultures coming in who didn't speak English,
> I'd have them experiencing things that they haven't experienced before.
> And that's not what we're about. We're about numeracy and literacy.
> They value those two things. And I do think they do value it, to a certain
> point, so that their kids are able to read and do math.
>
> LUANN: But as far as experiencing the outside world, that's not a part of
> what they want?
>
> KEVIN: Well, I think it partly seems a threat, because the more you go into
> that type of thing and the more you watch movies and things on TV …
> We don't use movies as an entertainment thing. We have computers, and
> there's no problem with using computers. I've never had an objection,
> but it's with an educational purpose. It's not for entertainment in any
> way, shape, or form.

While many Dietsche parents described utmost ease and trust in
their own Old Colony schools, some reported that they could not

afford private education for their large families. Others have been refused enrolment in Old Colony schools, as the demand exceeds the supply and families are often told that schools are full. On occasion, children from certain families are turned away from an Old Colony school because they are not "suitable." Maria, a Dietsche single mother, understood her experience of rejection by Old Colony school officials in this way:

> LUANN: I have heard about an Old Colony school in the area. Did you ever think about sending your children to the Old Colony school?
> MARIA: Yeah. I wanted to do that last year, in September, when the school started. And then, first they say yeah, they think that should work. Then later one day they called me and say no, they can't. I was very upset about that. Then they say, "No. Then the Children's Aid will come here to our school." And I told [my CAS worker] that they don't like the Children's Aid coming to the school. And she said she wouldn't go there. She would just come to our home after school, when the kids are home, to see them. And I told them that. But they are afraid of the Children's Aid.

Education for Dietsche children as well as adults was given high priority by service providers. In the social field structured to maximize market production and consumption, cultural capital and the associated means of accumulation have to do with distance – geographically, economically, and socially – from the necessities of life. Such distance is expressed in leisure time and activities, professional (non-manual) forms of work, attention to aesthetics, concern for the abstract, and discussion of ideas and opinions. Practitioners routinely suggested that the shortcomings of Dietsche (im)migrants could be addressed through education and professional credentials; encouraging the taste for music, art, and popular culture; engagement in the world; a goal-oriented and planned view of the future; adequate leisure time and its appropriate use; and distance from necessity in the form of monetary savings, private property, household budgets, and retirement planning.

The appropriation of cultural capital is necessary for Dietsche parents to prove their competency according to child welfare risk assessment standards. Parents must demonstrate that they are properly credentialled parents by supporting and encouraging their children's prolonged participation in the formal education system, providing opportunities to play sports, purchasing music lessons, and supplying stimulating leisure activities in the form of popular toys, games, and equipment. When cultural assets are lacking, or when parents refuse suitable cultural engagement, their social networks and family systems become suspect and vigilant monitoring of all members of the group is warranted.

The fear of losing children was palpable in some Dietsche homes. I reluctantly approached the subject of "Children's Aid," as some parents became visibly agitated when asked about their experience with this agency. Conversation with (im)migrant parents about interventions by child protection workers was usually veiled and stilted for all involved, providing much more meaningful data in the "feel" and absence of words than in substantive content. Perhaps finding some sense of safety in distance and deference, many mothers initially denied even knowing of Children's Aid or their involvement with Dietsche families, and some anxiously defended the practice of apprehending other people's children, while emphasizing the proficiency and devotion with which they cared for their own. Sociopolitical exclusion is efficiently accomplished through procedures of surveillance and policing, as these are the instruments that work to devalue and undermine all forms of Dietsche capital.

As demonstrated by the physical and social actualities of many (im)migrants, some prefer disengagement and distance. It is apparent that many Dietsche families recognize a certain safety in invisibility, and they are content to be "die Stillen im Lande" (the quiet in the land). For example, two Mennonite immigrant service providers recounted their experience while conducting a survey of all Dietsche families in their county several years earlier. "From my cultural background, I know where they live. I know to go to bunkhouses and barns. We know where they hide." To remain unnoticed, "the unobtrusive ones," is to elude the watchful "I/Eye" (Corrigan, 1991) of the human service worker. A security of sorts is offered in the invisibility of social exclusion, as people escape the judgments of eligibility and entitlement that are imposed on the excluded kind who make themselves known in the market-state field.

The dynamics of sociopolitical exclusion produce paradoxical outcomes that show up in the complexities and ambiguities of tallying the poor, unemployed, homeless, and other minority groups. As an example, Statistics Canada circumvents incomplete and atypical data by omitting them from its reports on Canadian housing conditions.[23] Furthermore, national and international studies that seek to assess the prevalence and depth of poverty and social exclusion are commonly based on Census data or national surveys in which those groups made the most marginal – such as some Aboriginal peoples and temporary residents – are not represented at all (Cormack, Cosgrove, & Stalker, 2012). Bowker & Star (2001) claim that a "central fact about the modern state" is that "a good citizen is a citizen who can be well counted – along numerous dimensions, on demand" (423). National survey data are limited to information about people who can be located for counting, are able (and willing) to complete the questionnaire, and self-identify according to prescribed and arbitrary categories.

The appropriation of cultural capital – even the very basic and minimal cultural capital associated with being counted as a member of a nation or society – is practised primarily through the display of sufficient economic capital and market participation. Measures of production and consumption are based on assumptions of reliable and enduring paid work and income, place of residence, and profitable social networks. A significant degree of stability and consistency in the daily practices of life is taken for granted. The tools used for counting in the market-state field are firmly anchored in marketized notions of inclusion.

In contrast, economic and spatial exclusion are shown to force transient, precarious lives, yielding the invisibility of sociopolitical exclusion. Paradoxically, those who have been made the socially excluded kind are most likely to be completely absent – cut out, excluded – from the very practices and procedures that claim to verify their existence and address their social exclusion. This descent into silence and invisibility through the succession of economic, spatial, and sociopolitical exclusion is at the very crux of the common sense classifying of the social. This erasure – annihilation – is the culmination of sociopolitical exclusion and begins the process of subjective exclusion.

Subjective exclusion

The subjective experience of social exclusion has received significant attention in research. For example, social exclusion is commonly measured as the individual, subjective experience of economic hardship.[24] Low self-ratings of overall health and well-being and reports of economic stress or material deprivation are also regularly used as indicators of social exclusion.[25] Others propose a "consensual" definition of social exclusion based on statistical agreement between objective conditions and subjective assessments (e.g., Till, 2005). Subjective attitudes and feelings about the local society and one's place in it – such as perceptions of "poverty stigma" and marginalization – are key for some, and social exclusion is thus reduced to a personal sense of belonging.[26]

But consideration of the subjective experience of social exclusion raises some sticky questions for us. When the objective conditions and subjective perceptions fail to line up, how do we make sense of and respond to such incongruity? What is the relationship between feelings of belonging, self-perceptions of material deprivation, and social exclusion? Specifically, if individuals who lack economic, social, and cultural capital in objective terms still feel as though they *belong* to society, are they excluded? Moreover, if economically disadvantaged people don't *feel* deprived (or poor, or homeless, or underemployed), do they still suffer from social exclusion? Is social exclusion contingent only on the subjective, personal experience of marginalization, discrimination, and social rejection regardless of one's economic standing? Or is social exclusion primarily about the subjective experience of objective, material conditions? If people are content in their misery or, more to the point of this project, if people seemingly *choose* their misery, is that something altogether different than social exclusion?

When perceived through an integrative perspective that brings into focus the intersection between the subjective and material realities of space and place, the questions that are perplexing on the surface become meaningless. Contrary to a more intuitive understanding, subjective exclusion is the most profound and consequential of all forms of social exclusion, as it represents the completion of exclusionary progressions, and its force is exerted in everyday material realities against whole groups of people. The power of dividing practices is secured through the function of unrecognized capital, or symbolic power. It is the self-perpetuation of social, economic, and subjective divides, such that space and place become self-organizing. Conversely, the subjective dimension of social exclusion is necessary to all other forms, as it defines social trajectories that are marked by the dispossession of all species of capital and are justified through the denial of symbolic capital. When individuals and groups are stripped of economic, social, and cultural capital in the market-state social field and are denied means of accumulation, their prospects for upward social mobility are indeed dismal. The subjective outcome of market-state fusion is that people are made *stuck* in space and place.

More important, there is a powerful subjective element of social exclusion, but it has more to do with subjective constructions of reality that direct everyday behaviour (Dangschat, 2009; Wacquant, 2009) than with the subjective experience of social exclusion. The dispossession of symbolic power denies the ability to know and name social reality – most decisively, to know and name self and others – and works to deepen divides in social space. Subjective exclusion reinforces and expands distance: economic, physical, social, political, cultural, and subjective. Such social processes are at once simple and excruciatingly complex, and they form the bulk of the remainder of this book.

If sociopolitical exclusion can be understood to be the *un-making* of individuals and groups, subjective exclusion is the set of processes and practices through which people are *re-made*. The primary means through which this is accomplished in any social field organized by market logic is the transformation of all livelihood strategies, all of life, even one's self, into market commodities. For example, (im)migrant men, women, and children are reduced to migrant workers or imported discounted labour in the uneven trade of resources and capital between the south and the north (Good Gingrich, 2010b). Subjective exclusion expands (and profits from) all sorts of global divides by making and keeping people tied to and dependent on market production and consumption.[27] Such processes work most forcefully for the most dispossessed, because they lack the symbolic power to define their own lives. The processes of subjective exclusion operate all over the world to sustain distance between individuals, groups, regions, and nations.[28]

Self-sustaining spaces and places of social exclusion

The precisely ordered social spaces defined by market logic are self-sustaining once the forms of social exclusion are realized. These forms generally are not found as discrete manifestations, as one form is bound to all others and each one spontaneously initiates and propels processes that produce the others. The manifestation of social exclusion demonstrates a compounding effect, such that the polarizing, self-perpetuating character is generated in the synergy between its forms. For example, service providers and recipients alike noted that, contrary to popular belief, paid employment is not a reliable pathway to spaces of entitlement in the market-state field. The economic profits of wage labour are inadequate to reverse the dispossession of all other forms of capital.

Moreover, the rules for legitimate appropriation of various species of capital in the market-state field change frequently through various "reforms" and are thus withheld from those confined to dominated locations. From the client position, there is little possibility of gaining access to transactions that allow the conversion of economic capital into social, cultural, and symbolic capital, and these transactions are crucial in the continued accumulation of economic capital.

> There are barriers everywhere. You see, illiteracy is such a real problem, everywhere. I mean, it has economic ramifications in places you wouldn't even think of. And that is, for example, if you don't read the contents of what's in a can, you buy the name brand that has the picture on it instead of the no-name brands that are cheaper. And therefore, their living expenses are more, and their income is less. They get inferior housing because they have large families and people don't want their houses ruined by children. And the other aspect is that legally you're not supposed to rent your place to a family that has more children than bedrooms. And there are no homes that big, and if there were, they're totally unaffordable. [Jake, Mennonite immigrant service provider]

Once the axes of differentiation have claimed some within and named many without, navigation across the divide is made difficult, if not impossible.

> MARIE: That's where, when you look at all sides of it, it just feels to be overwhelming oppression.
> SUZANNE: It seems that those with poor social connections, that they are much more in that category, I would think. Some come here, they have no family. They don't have a strong church connection. They're poor. They seem to have a lot more things against them. Those are the families who I am usually called to, who are in trouble with the law at some point, or they've been charged with abuse or incest, or drunk driving, or whatever. It happens more often in those families with poor social connections. [Mennonite immigrant service providers]

The course that is charted for clients is through social services and programs. While such government benefits – cash, goods, services, and even credits – are dressed up as citizens' rights and public goods, free to all, in welfare residualism they exact a toll. There are costs associated with accessing services, with making one's self visible. Even the illusion of inclusion must be purchased. Compliance – something much different from inclusion – has a price.

> They want some control. To a large extent, it's a very proud community, that doesn't want handouts. There are the exceptions that come here to simply live on welfare. But, to a large extent, that's not what they come for. So, they will only come for help after they've exhausted their own options. And so that's why they come here with their hydro bills after they have notice that it will be cut off. That's why they come here when they have a court date set for driving without a licence or insurance. Most will try to solve it themselves first. [Will, Mennonite immigrant service provider]

When compliance is enforced through a specific mandatory manner of participation in society, meaningful resistance from spaces of exclusion requires unusual vigilance and fortitude.

> NETTIE: The fear that they bring with them is, "Am I gonna be able to keep my children here?" Their first thought is, "If I let anybody into my house, my children will be taken from me."
> LUANN: And how do they get that idea? This must be a story that makes its way even back to Mexico –
> NETTIE: Yes.
> LUANN: – in these isolated colonies.
> NETTIE: I believe that is what must happen. But I have tried to find out, and I can't really find the root. Why they would bring something … a thought like that with them. But that is their first fear. Second is, "Well, if they're gonna take my children, how can I send them to school?" How can they now open the door and send them to school? Everybody has the ability to go and get them there. It's just a tremendous fear that they bring with them. From my thinking, even bigger than what we brought with us [as immigrants from Mexico years ago]. I mean, for us, everything was new and scary. But for these people who are so isolated, they are seriously afraid of [not] being able to keep their families together.
> LUANN: Why would they come, then, if they think they may lose their children here?
> NETTIE: It's a risk that they take, because they have no money where they come from.
> LUANN: Things are so desperate.
> NETTIE: They are **so** desperate.
> LUANN: Economically.

NETTIE: Right. My husband's brother was one of those. He was in the group. He married into a family that was in that part of Mexico. And they still don't send their children to school. They have lived here now for over a year.

LUANN: They don't go to school at all?

NETTIE: No.

LUANN: What a choice to make, eh?

NETTIE: It is.

LUANN: To come risking, believing, that you may lose your children –

NETTIE: Yes. But, another thing that they believe, "If we keep our doors shut, then we'll be okay." And that means to everybody. They don't know the difference from someone wanting to help and someone wanting not to help. [Dietsche (im)migrant service provider][29]

For some, the cost of engagement is too high, and promises of inclusion never materialize. And they return to the south.

LUANN: It's a story of diaspora in many ways.

WILL: It is. Very much so. And as a co-worker likes to call it, an uncontrolled migration. And some of the migrations south are church organized, but some of them aren't. And it's not just that they go from Mexico for the south, there's a whole group from here that started a colony in Campeche, Mexico. They had been here for quite some time. Their kids had gone to school here, learned English. Some of the kids were born here and educated here. They suddenly up and started a new colony.

LUANN: What takes them back? What would you say?

WILL: Well this particular group, of which my nephew is a part, it seems to be a desire to be independent. They would like to take a lot from here along, including [a more "progressive" or acculturated] church. They know the comforts of here, but they want their independence, I guess.

LUANN: I realize this is asking for a generalization again, but when they come to Canada, would you say that most seek to be separate from the rest of the world?

WILL: That's hard to say. Ideally, yes. Many would. But their economic situation has become so desperate that many of them can't. I worked with a family last week, nine in the family, all in one motel room here. They had enough money for one night. And they didn't have money for food, lodging, any of that. They came for help, into the office here, wondering if we can help. We were able to put them in contact with their church, one of the very conservative churches here. They took care of them. [Mennonite immigrant service provider]

As exhibited by the force with which space and place are ordered towards the four forms of social exclusion, groups are not passively made. Social exclusion *happens* through the uneven distribution of available resources and the differentially recognized reproduction strategies for accruing capital in the market-state social field. Furthermore, the economic, spatial, and sociopolitical outcomes of social exclusion are secured through the denial of legitimate means of accumulating capital from dominated social positions within the social field. In this way, the distribution of capital functions as the precondition for further appropriation of all types of capital, feeding and justifying the specific social conditions of reproduction and circulation orchestrated by market logic. The uneven access to and distribution of all dimensions of capital puts people in place, "durably consecrating the position occupied" (Bourdieu, 1990b, 125) in the market-state field. Thus, it is through the operation of a singular market-oriented system of capital that the market and the state come together to form a closed social order. And the forms of social exclusion are not only outcomes: they are processes that serve to perpetuate the specific organization of social and physical space. The precise procedures and practices made necessary in the left hand of the market-state social field will be explored in more depth in the following chapters.

Chapter Four

Everyday Practices of Social Exclusion

The market-state, as a social system, shows itself to be self-preserving, as access to all forms of capital from places and spaces of economic, spatial, and sociopolitical exclusion is denied. But much more decisive than the uneven access to resources is the lopsided recognition or evaluation of assets already held. Meaningful engagement in the various economies of a social field hinges on both the quantity and quality (or social value) of personal holdings, as one's assets *and* ability to reproduce wealth must be sufficient in order to be a player. And all types of profits and their functional capacity in social interactions are divvied up according to the prevailing logic, rules, and regularities of perception and practice. In this way, the market-state social field, as for all social fields, is organized three-dimensionally, according to the "volume of capital, composition of capital, and change in these two properties over time (manifested by past and potential trajectory in social space)" (Bourdieu, 1984, 114). Thus, social exclusion cannot be accurately measured through only the appraisal of material, social, and cultural resources, or its outcomes, in one moment of time. Social spaces, and therefore the manifested forms of social exclusion, always reflect specific social histories and possibilities, as social space is defined by social hierarchies *and* trajectories.

Our attention is now turned from the outcomes of social exclusion to its *processes* consisting of "normal" everyday practices and ways of being in the world – practices and procedures that are used to address social problems, to *help* those who are socially excluded; practices that derive from neither benevolence nor malevolence. They are simply practical, made necessary in the market-state social field to reinforce its system of capital and social order. Through an examination of the intensely familiar, I aim to show that processes of social exclusion, in particular its subjective form, are automatic or habitual, thus often escaping our notice.

In conversation about their work with Dietsche (im)migrant families, English social service workers described standard procedures through which they assess, manage, and monitor legitimacy, risk, and need, and thereby classify individuals as client, patient, student – or otherwise:

> LOUISE: That particular family, actually, the daughter works and gives all her money to her parents. That poses a problem for us sometimes. Because if we find out about it and it's going in to a parent's account, we're going to look at it as income. And if it's an adult child – we call them dependent adults or independent adults if they're making more than a certain amount of money – we're going to charge that as income as well.
>
> LUANN: What is that certain amount of money? Is there a definite line for determining who is eligible for social housing?
>
> LOUISE: There's an asset level and an income level. Yes. And it's based on family size.
>
> MIKE: And for the unit of an adult, it's the equivalency of …
>
> LOUISE: Of $520 a month.
>
> MIKE: … $520. They have to be making over that for it to be considered net family income. I don't know why it works that way [laughter], but that's what the Ministry has told us to look at.

Coordinating benefits requires stringent reporting and careful calculations of a family's resources, which can become quite complicated when all members of the family work and live as an economic unit. In this exchange, Nancy, who is a caseworker for social housing, and her Ontario Works colleagues try to sort out the rules for keeping track of who is entitled to what:

> LUANN: So if they have an income of more than $520 per month, they're not eligible for social housing?
>
> MIKE: They'd be taken off the family budget, and we would impose a minimum border allowance against the family unit, where the person would be expected to pay a minimum of $100 a month to the parents.
>
> NANCY: Or fair market value of at least 100 a week, which is like 400 a month, could come off their [welfare] cheque. If that independent adult

is making $1,000 a month, we wouldn't just accept the minimum. I mean, we're going to look at what the average room and board would run.

LUANN: And then that much would be deducted from the cheque – whatever the family would get? Dollar for dollar?

NANCY: Yes. Well no, I shouldn't say that.

MIKE: I think it's 40 and 60.

NANCY: It's not dollar for dollar; it's 40 and 60; 60 per cent of it's simply room. And 40 if it's room and board. So, if they're providing food and lodging, it's 40 per cent off. No, it's not dollar for dollar … The other problem we have is getting verification of their current monthly income. Say they've been here, you know, four years. So, with so many kids working, it's hard trying to get them to understand: yes, we need their children's earnings as well, if they're not going to be in school. Because part of the process is, like you said, we take part of their earnings. So that can be a real difficulty. And the other problem we had was when they come up from Mexico, some of our applicants and tenants actually own real estate in Mexico and they have to sell their property. And getting the proper documentation! [Laughter] And, you know, they'll go back and forth how often –

LUANN: You mentioned that income of children is considered in the application for how much rent they pay? Is that right?

NANCY: Yeah.

LUANN: All children?

NANCY: Well, only if those children aren't in school. If you're in school and have earnings, it's exempt.

MIKE: Same as us [social assistance].

SUSAN: Same as us [social assistance].

LUANN: And what kind of verification of income do you need? Pay stubs?

SUSAN: You don't usually get that. They usually get paid cash.

NANCY: So there's no documentation to prove what they're getting or what they're not getting.

LUANN: And so you take their word, I guess, then?

MIKE: Well, we can look at bank deposits. You can get the farmer that they worked for just to write down on a note how much they paid.

NANCY: That's what we usually do.

SUSAN: Yeah. And that's difficult as well. Because the farmer –

MIKE: The farmer doesn't want to get –

NANCY: He doesn't want to get in trouble.

LUANN: Because he's hiring children, right?

NANCY: Yeah, exactly.

LUANN: Challenging, eh? It gets to be complicated.

NANCY: But we have to go through the same process again, trying to get information – because we have to ask for all these verifications – income tax, etcetera, again, once a year –

Beyond work preferences and living arrangements, Dietsche culture in general complicates determinations of eligibility and entitlement, as a whole host of everyday practices fall outside expected norms.

LOUISE: My feeling is too that, I mean, when they settle, they settle into their community with other Mexican Mennonite families … So maybe they're limited in not wanting to assimilate into our own culture. They're holding onto their culture because that's the culture they were brought up with and they believe in it.

MIKE: Certainly in other immigrant groups, you'd see that with the older immigrants who come and stick to their own cultural group. But they would encourage the children.

NANCY: But with these families, kind of not wanting the children to break out of that mould.

LUANN: So their wanting to hold onto their culture and way of life is a problem for them.

NANCY: Well, maybe not for them, but for organizations trying to help them.

MIKE: Yeah, it's hard to watch them say, "My daughter's no longer going to school. She's turned twelve. She's got her grade six. So take her off the bus." What's her future?

LUANN: And you'd think about that, whereas the parents may not be thinking about that.

MIKE: Yeah. For them it's quite normal, right? You know, she's almost, you know, getting ready – getting all her kitchen skills and stuff, or whatever, so she can get a husband. And then she'll continue the tradition.

NANCY: How to break that cycle. Because to a twelve-year-old, they're very influenced and controlled by their parents, that this is your way of life, right? But to an eighteen-year-old that's been through – you don't have a whole lot of say. Do you know what I mean? How could you break that cycle? That would be the challenge, right?

SUSAN: I have clients that, when I did home visits and so forth, and I've talked about the schooling. And the child might have been six or seven, and I'll say, "The child has to be in school. You have to register the child in school." And they'll say, "No, no. I'm home schooling." In the meantime, the parents have a grade six education, and I'll say to them, "You may think that home schooling is the best thing for your child. But really, how can you home school them to our standards of education so they can move on, and go beyond that?" They want to home school. A lot want to home school. That is the barrier.

MIKE: That reminds me of another barrier. They have their own schools too, but they're not recognized by the Ministry of Education. And so they want to send them there. When they come to us [social assistance], they want to send their kids to these schools and we say, "No. That's not acceptable. It's not recognized by the Ministry. You have to send them to another school."

LUANN: So, in order for them to be on Ontario Works, their children have to go – they can't go to an Old Colony school, is that right?

MIKE: Right. There's a couple of them around here. Or, as I said, when they want to home school, they have to have their school authorized – their curriculum. They have to go there and visit and talk to the children and evaluate their school program. And a lot don't ask –

NANCY: And they move around, following the harvest. So it's really hard to keep them on our waiting list when they keep moving and we can't reach them.

LUANN: Right, right. How long is your wait list?

MIKE: Long! [Laughter]

NANCY: Oh you're asking the wrong person, but we're looking at usually a year plus to get anywhere from a one bedroom up to a four bedroom. It's always over a year –

MIKE: Probably depends on the size of the family, too. The singles are more available than the larger homes. They seem to be more available.

LUANN: And your housing is all in town? Any rural?

NANCY: No. Well, in [one township] rural housing would be on the coordinated access waiting list.

LUANN: So if you were to prioritize the needs of this group, what stands out as the most urgent or most important need or problem for this group?

MIKE: Everybody pretty much says language barrier.

NANCY: And education.

SUSAN: Education.

This exchange reveals the breadth and complexity of challenges that confront service providers in their work with the Mennonite (im)migrant population. Efforts to help must go beyond tackling one or two specific issues, because it is who they are and how they live – the Dietsche disposition – that does not make sense in market-state terms and thus requires change.

Habitus and symbolic power

Bourdieu provides conceptual tools to examine practices and their practicalities: *habitus* and *symbolic capital*. To see and understand our own social norms and patterns – that which seems mundane and inevitable – requires us to think in ways that push us outside of the everyday and ordinary. This takes some effort, because the necessary concepts are unfamiliar. We are not accustomed to examining the assumed practicalities of daily life. Yet thinking beneath the taken-for-granted surface enters us into a deeper level of self-awareness and opens up space for difference.

Habitus, the Latin word for "habit," refers to "a tendency to perform a certain action or behave in a certain way; a usual way of doing" (*Collins American English Dictionary*, http://www.collinsdictionary.com/dictionary/american). Bourdieu's concept of habitus does not depart from the dictionary meaning. He situates this notion in social contexts in order to trace patterns of practice that correspond with and produce the order of social fields and systems of capital. Habitus challenges the common sense binary of self and other, of the individual versus the social. Habitus is my social preconscious disposition, or "habits-of-mine" (Chambon, 2005).[1]

Bourdieu's habitus presupposes that much of human action, or what is commonly referred to as individual "agency," is spontaneous or improvisational, yet regulated or structured by patterned social forces. Choices are continually made – choices that direct actions or practice, such as the kind of food we eat, the clothes we wear, where and how we walk, the words we use and our way of speaking, the people we befriend. Such choices are not arbitrarily made, but neither is each one deliberated over and decided with intention. These practices are motivated by likes, dislikes, leanings, or enthusiasms, and they are simply practical, as they preserve or increase the volume and structure of capital we possess.

Individual agency or subjectivity, therefore, cannot be accurately conceived of outside time and place. Contrary to the ideal of neoliberal individualism, the individual, the subjective, is revealed to be social and collective and historical: "The habitus is socialized subjectivity, a historic transcendental, whose schemes of perception and appreciation (systems of preferences, tastes, etc.) are the product of collective and individual history" (Bourdieu, 2005, 84). We carry within us the knowledge that *works* for us according to the structure and function of the various social fields in which we participate. Thus, many of life's day-to-day and moment-to-moment choices are not really choices at all, but rather inclinations, or embodied *habits* that are adjusted to established social systems or economies.

An understanding of the social economy of human service delivery – and there *is* an economy of human services – and the necessary practices (or habitus) of various players, is made available through tracing the *flow* of capital in the market-state social field. This economy is hidden, as it functions primarily in symbolic assets. Habitus and symbolic power function hand-in-hand, as the work of representatives of the welfare state – social workers, healthcare providers, educators, employment counsellors, and so on – corresponds with the symbolic profits available in marketized human service systems. The positions occupied by human service professionals are dependent on the performance of explicit ideas and implicit ideals in routine practices. Even more, the caseworker is the "repository of common sense," fulfilling official classifications and holding sufficient symbolic power to impose recognition, to "make things with words" (Bourdieu, 1989, 22). Thus, the service provider habitus provides a window into the social field, its system of capital, and how it functions in ordinary day-to-day relations.

The helper habitus and the classifying habit

The neoliberal project of government withdrawal is consequential, as it has provoked a crisis of power (Offe, 1985). We might understand this as the depreciation of government symbolic capital. Residualism views the economic concerns of the state and social needs of its citizens to be at odds, in competition for the public's loyalty and investment. Relying on the wholesale appeal and inherent virtue of eliminating risk, danger, and disorder, the current neoliberal trend – noted especially in the United States, Britain, and more recently in Canada (Currie, 2004; DeKeseredy, 2011; Wacquant, 2009) – is to reduce and refashion social policies into laws that are geared towards the "punitive containment of the poor" (Wacquant, 2000, 117). The norms of residualism are enforced through increased authority and faith invested in the *right hand* of the state, which is made up of all legislation, agencies, and social actors linked to financial markets – both international and national. This investment is accompanied by diminishing commitments – of power, status, and money – towards all organizations and efforts associated with domestic social equity concerns. This is the *left hand* of the state, constituted by all sorts of people who deliver social services and programs, especially those who are called "social workers." The left hand of the state is "the set of agents of the so-called spending ministries which are the trace, within the state, of the social struggles of the past" (Bourdieu, 1998, 2). Invoking feminine, maternal characteristics, its primary responsibility is *caring* for its citizens.

These unevenly privileged departments and positions – and therefore, people – are often in open conflict with one another. "I think the left hand of the state has the sense that the right hand no longer knows, or, worse, no longer really wants to know what the left hand does. In any case, it does not want to pay for it. One of the main reasons for all these people's despair is that the state has withdrawn, or is withdrawing, from a number of sectors of social life for which it was previously responsible" (Bourdieu, 1998, 2).

In the context of residualism, the business of the right hand's agencies and agents – "the technocrats of the Ministry of Finance, the public and private banks and the ministerial cabinets" (Bourdieu, 1998, 2) – is, paradoxically, to ensure the market is free to function unfettered by government intervention. The widespread trend is for the redefined and divided state to abdicate its roles in the production and distribution of social resources for its citizens.[2] Such responsibilities are consigned to the labour market, consumer markets, informal networks, the family, and, above all, each individual. The feminine left hand of the state is split off and handed over to various private sectors, thereby boosting the potential for market growth. The left hand of the state and all its representatives are thus transformed into the handmaidens of the dominant right hand. Faced with devaluation, even contempt, the left hand willingly turns – or returns – to the right hand for some efficacy and approval. There it finds various tools and procedures that, when put to use, earn a portion of symbolic power.

The scientific activity of classification by kind-terms and the related medical technique of diagnosis hold unmatched social authority in the properly modern, civilized, secular, and even moral state (see, e.g., Bourdieu, 1991; Hacking, 1999; Rorty, 1988). Similarly, the social order defined by global capitalism necessitates classification schemes of various sorts (Lugones, 2007). Social classifications form the basis of population studies (censuses, needs assessments, opinion polls), application forms (for a job, a driver's licence, a credit card), and intake and assessment questionnaires (for welfare, family services, healthcare). A multitude of everyday accepted social categories and designations confer or withhold all sorts of legitimacy, or symbolic capital: man/woman, citizen, spouse, father/mother, graduate, employee, homeowner, taxpayer, investor, and so on. These "frameworks of interpretations" (Bourdieu, 1996, xviii) are, quite literally, everywhere. This is how we determine what's what and who's who. In the social welfare system, for example, it is necessary to know who is entitled to claim the rights and privileges of citizenship, who is eligible for what services and benefits, and who will foot the bill. The habitus of the professional helper, therefore, is inclined towards classificatory work and a categorical point of view, as such practices are associated with the corresponding economic, social, cultural, and symbolic assets of their position in the market-state social field.[3]

In the case of Dietsche (im)migrants, classificatory work shows itself through the following routine procedures:

- *Risk assessment*, or diagnosis, through practices such as repeated means-testing or screening, followed by classifying or naming, so that everything and everyone is universally recognized for what they are;
- *Case management*, or regulating behaviour, through directives, orders, prescriptions, and various people-change strategies that tell people what to do according to what they are;
- *Outcomes evaluation*, or valuation and containment through continual monitoring and authorized accounts of what people have actually done and therefore, what they are and where they belong.[4]

Risk assessment

As the welfare state gives way to the penal state, scholars note that *risk* is "displacing class as an organizing concept for state welfare policy, a shift that would mean social goals of minimizing danger rather than of redistributing wealth on the basis of need" (Swift & Callahan, 2009, 12; Beck, 1992). In order to support and protect economic growth, interventions are targeted towards "people marked as deviant, bad, risky, or different in some socially selected way" (Swift & Callahan, 2009, 40). With the masculinization of the left hand of the market-state through punitive polices and activities, only those needs that pose a threat to the economic interests of the state, through triggering immediate expenses and/or long-term dependency, will receive service (Lewis et al., 1995, as cited in ibid., 229). In other words, social services are reserved for "risky-need."

Practitioners from a variety of social service settings, including healthcare, education, and child protection, described the technical work of risk assessment to be essential to the delivery of their programs. Risk assessment tools, carefully administered by professionals, are designed to gather specific information regarding individual and family circumstances and precisely evaluate selected variables according to established criteria. The consequential feature of assessing risk is the "conscious or unconscious implementation of explicit or implicit schemes of perception" (Bourdieu, 1984, 2). A group of service providers described how applying certain professional schemes of perception function to make specific meaning from difference.

> SANDY: The idea that – The questions that I have to – I'm supposed to – I don't. The questions that I'm supposed to ask families. It's like, because you're low income, because you're high risk, you don't have the right to keep this kind of thing to yourself. You're not as – You just don't have that right to –
>
> STEPHANIE: That right to privacy?
>
> SANDY: To your own – Yeah. Because if you're poor, and you want to use our services, then you have to give us the information we want. And so then these poor families are paraded around to all these different agencies who are asking all these different, horribly personal questions. And where is the dignity in that?
>
> RACHEL: And the other thing is, even just saying, "You're at risk. You're poor, so you're at risk." [Sandy, English service provider; Stephanie and Rachel, Mennonite service providers]

The everyday work of assessing risk has serious implications in the lives of families, and Sandy's false starts and questioning reveal her ambivalence in fulfilling this expectation of her job.

Identifying and assessing risk or need, or risky-need, is the process of deciding on what is *wrong* or *dangerous* and, in this way, we tacitly agree on what is *right* or *safe*. The basis of assessing risk, individual or social, is an established comparator, a "normal" or "standard" set of measures, characteristics, or behaviours by which to evaluate all visible indicators.

The practice of risk assessment is analogous to diagnosing an illness, and its relationship to this more familiar medical procedure helps us recognize the comparative and value-laden nature of the work. The diagnosis of individual physical ailments, for example, is based on convention that includes normal ranges for blood values, standard measures of organ function, and criteria for typical and atypical clinical appearance. Similarly, mental illness is detected according to diagnostic categories of abnormal behaviours and thought processes (though the effectiveness of this diagnosis is disputed). Reference manuals, such as the *Merck Manual of Diagnosis and Therapy* and the *Diagnostic and Statistical Manual of Mental Disorders*, provide comprehensive and detailed descriptions of "abnormal" in relation to a presumed "normal."

The assessment of *social* ills or risk is a different matter altogether. Recall that the typical indicators of social exclusion are measures of income, employment, and housing. Undoubtedly, Dietsche (im)migrants are recognized to be needy, requiring multiple forms of material assistance from a wide variety of government and voluntary human services. It could be argued that social exclusion as a multidimensional measure of deprivation and limited social engagement is obvious and can be assumed in this case example. But for such social issues, the standards for comparison – the "normal" ranges to serve as guides by which "abnormal" or "at risk" can be measured – are a subject of intense and enduring debate.[5]

In the absence of accepted diagnostic tools for social ills or criteria for identifying risk in marketized human services, difference is judged against a presumed norm that comes in the form of an ideal human image derived from the market. The *economic habitus*, or "ensemble of dispositions of the economic agent" (Bourdieu, 2000a, 25) is the personification of neoliberalized social inclusion.[6] The formation, evaluation, and accumulation of all forms of capital in the market-state field are associated with individual bodily expressions of "self-interested calculation" (Bourdieu, 2000a, 26), competition, and self-sufficiency. This so-called rational economic agent is perfectly in tune with the market-state social field and supplies the invisible yet idealized comparator for all other deficient and deviant identities produced in social policy and related services. He serves as a social archetype, and the everyday practice of classification is, ultimately and most importantly, social prototyping, or subject formation.

The assembled social archetype is maintained by indications of "norm-infractions, what is wrong (in behaviour or thought)" (Corrigan, 1991, 319). The particular attributes of the idealized included subject are reinforced through expressions of *difference as risk* – individual and collective shortcomings – and the subsequent (and inevitable) dispossession of capital. For example, the classifying habitus knows that the entitlements ordinarily associated with citizenship are superseded by market rules and values:

> MICHELLE: Going back to something you said before. Certainly, what we recognized is that this is a very unique population in that we keep having waves of people who are coming. And certainly, when you've been around as long as some of us have, we remember when, you know, you needed to be able to speak Portuguese to offer services in this region. We had a high Portuguese population. That's not an issue any more, now that population has come, and there are enough people who speak English, so it's not an issue. And certainly, back in the eighties, maybe, when the Cambodian refugees came, we had a huge initiative at this Health Unit of one person, whose job was to work with Cambodian refugees and to find out about the culture and all that. That's no longer an issue. But the Low German issue has been, and continues to be, a concern within our community. And I think the difference is that they haven't come in a group, and stopped coming. They continue to come, in waves. They go back to Mexico; they come back. It's just – it doesn't stop. It just keeps happening.
>
> LUANN: So the need – the severity of the need – doesn't decrease over time?
>
> MICHELLE: No.
>
> IAN: But the other thing too is that the countries that those other populations are coming from, they've been proactively promoting ESL in their countries, prior to those with interest coming over. So they have the basic language before they even arrive. Where I'm sure that's not happening in Mexico.
>
> CHRIS: Well, like you were saying, the immigrants that come from other countries, they have criteria they have to meet before they can get into Canada. Where these people are Canadians; they just come. So –
>
> CATHY: Well, and any immigrant that's settling in this region now, they've got money. Like, they're coming from Germany and Holland and they're buying up big farms and they've got money. The new immigrants, they have money.
>
> CHRIS: Yeah, they do. They've already got the education and they know what they're coming for.
>
> CATHY: But not this group.
>
> LUANN: It's a different kind of clientele.
>
> CHRIS: Yeah. [English service providers]

In their work with Dietsche families, all service providers agreed on one thing: Dietsche (im)migrants are different. They were described as different from other client groups, from other Mennonites, from other immigrants or newcomers, from "English-speaking people," from Mexicans, from other Canadians. But not all difference counts. *Treatable* risky-need must be extracted from demonstrations of difference. To qualify as a social concern, the problem must be perceived to be changeable. In the left hand of the market-state social field, the goal of providing publicly funded services with a "businesslike" efficiency engenders strategies such as "rationing," "targeting," and "externalizing" costs, so that the health and welfare needs of certain sections of the population fall outside the business of the state (J. Clarke, 1999). Available interventions or treatments are limited in their number and scope. Risk is determined through judging the suitability of residual benefits[7] and targeted services. These are the treatment options, thus limiting the diagnostic options. For example, poverty as inadequate access to material resources, when recognized as a problem, is not routinely addressed by human services. In this case, few service providers identified insufficient income in Canada as a point of intervention in their work with Dietsche families. When necessary, referrals are made to MCC, food banks, "or whatever community resources you can find" for immediate material assistance. Practitioners reported that services may be delayed until the urgency of such need has been alleviated. Individuals and families who are assessed as having financial need are referred to social assistance for "job readiness, training and skill redevelopment" (Prince, 2001, 6), funnelling all social services through waged labour in order to encourage full and rapid conversion to the economic habitus.

The difference of the client category is also *deserving* difference. Extensive government withdrawal of financial and symbolic support for social equity concerns necessarily coincides with more and more policies and procedures that disentitle and delegitimize certain social groups and ideas, thus limiting eligibility. Those deemed to be "at risk" from a known deviant individual (rather than social circumstances) are most deserving of protection and services. Therefore, women and children are most often framed as "victims" in need of intervention, but their status may shift to "villain" as new risks or needs emerge (Swift & Callahan, 2009, 103). The allocation of diminishing services and benefits necessitates sifting the worthy from the unworthy through the continuous and meticulous scrutiny of individual personal details.

Abe and Eva, Dietsche parents of four children, described their assessment experience soon after they arrived in Canada, before they had found paid work:

LUANN: So what do you remember about applying for welfare? What was it like?

ABE: That was very weird, because we had to answer all kinds of questions, what we are not used to. They had all kind of questions – stuff that was none of their business. [Laughs] But we answered them anyway. They want to know if you had a house. And how long and what kind of job you did. And how much money you made. And we thought that they shouldn't ask us that. But – I know it's important. They think it's important. Because sometimes I find there are people – I'm not very lazy, but some people, they could have a job, but they feel like they want to have the money. Some people refuse work and think it's easy to go on welfare.

LUANN: So at that time, did you have to do anything to collect the welfare cheque?

ABE: Oh, yeah. We had to go to the farm, asking for a job and, you know.

LUANN: So you had to show that you were looking for work?

ABE: [Laughs] Not only me. I was working. But Eva had to do that! [To his wife] You remember that, Eva?

LUANN: And you had young children at home, too?

EVA: Yeah.

ABE: But you even had to do that. At that time we thought … it was not fair. And the welfare – the person who came to our house – she had a lot of papers to fill out. A lot of papers! I don't know why she would do that.

Classifying clients through risk assessment based on difference is finicky and imprecise work, as one difference blends into the next, and the specific diagnosis or risk, the justification for intervention, and the ultimate goal of services cannot clearly or singularly be derived from the presenting symptoms or indicators. For example, some service providers observed that underemployment is a problem because the work taken on by many Dietsche tends to be seasonal. At the same time, it was speculated that the percentage of (im)migrants receiving social assistance is unusually low.[8] Furthermore, it was noted with disapproval that many Dietsche who work in the fields *choose* to return to Mexico for the winter months, seeking employment income in Ontario only during the harvest seasons. Concerns expressed for the prevalence of employment in low-wage and seasonal jobs, suggesting inadequate income for their large families, were countered by stories of their extraordinary earning capacity in a short period of time. Some practitioners expressed appreciation for the apparent Mennonite preference for menial work, as it simplifies and expedites the job placement process. Yet Dietsche people were criticized for their complacency regarding their station in life, as most do not aspire to "better themselves."

Eligibility for targeted, means-tested, and often punitive social services offered by the state functions to cancel rights. For Dietsche (im)migrants, classification as a citizen or landed immigrant is a prerequisite for eligibility, which inevitably – and paradoxically – marks them as adequately dispossessed and therefore disentitled. More important, eligibility reinforces the opposite as uniformly "normal" and moral. Teachers and social workers distinguished Dietsche Mennonites from typical hard-working and committed immigrants and expressed their disapproval of the perceived absence of Dietsche commitment to the nation and local community:

> We need to get them more integrated in our community. I sort of feel sorry for our merchants here. This is a beautiful little community. The people are driving to Mexico every month to get all the material they need because they sew all their own garments. I am sure none of their money ever goes to the store across the street here, which is a really, really nice clothing store. And that is only one example. [Len, Mennonite service provider]

Dual citizenship status and a migratory inclination give Dietsche (im)migrants access to their "home" country, allowing them to take advantage of the resources and opportunities available to them in both places. Such flexibility might be regarded as unusual and courageous instances of adaptation to a globalized market economy. Rather, service providers generally viewed Dietsche migratory patterns to be "milking the system," implying judgments of unethical or immoral behaviour. "A lot of the Mennonites, they are looking for a better life, but if it doesn't work out here," [then] they can pack everybody up into a vehicle and they can drive there and be there in a few days" [Janice, English service provider]. She went on to muse, "My understanding is that they can come up here, they can make a lot of money and go back to Mexico and live like kings." To be deemed to have material need – to be at risk of "becoming a drag on the marketplace" (Swift & Callahan, 2009, 53) – is cause for suspicion, indicating illicit activity.

Assessment takes on profound complexity and consequence when it moves beyond the external and is applied to internal difference – the self – of each individual member of a whole population in one fell swoop. This is how risk assessment of a whole group or category of people sounds:

> LEN: Well, it is kind of sad, the conclusion I have come to. See, I think that due to the loss of part of their culture and being caught up in that legalism of their religion, you know, and the poverty and all the hardships, I think they have lost a lot of their humanity. And all their social problems and the way they view themselves all come from that. Now mind you, in one regard, there is a contradiction. They still feel superior with an essence in their total being. They do feel superior to anyone around them, but that again is something that comes by indoctrination from the legalistic view of religion. They really feel superior as a human to anyone on the street.
>
> LUANN: Because of their religion?
>
> LEN: Yes.
>
> LUANN: Okay. So spiritually superior.
>
> LEN: Right. What I would say, secondly, is social and psychological. Now, by social I mean there is really no social life. Now, I worked with well over a hundred families and usually it is a large family, and that includes the extended family. To give you an example: in my first year here, there was a lady here from another county. And finally I asked her one day – she was a victim of abuse – and I asked her, [Trans.] "Do you ever have visitors? Do you ever socialize?" She said never. No getting together for anything social. Just totally starved, totally deprived. Now when I say they are lost to humanity, I am not saying that in a negative way. It's really a matter of them coming so low.
>
> LUANN: As a people.
>
> LEN: As a people.

Risk assessment processes are critical throughout all stages of service delivery. Progress towards the desired outcome is measured through repeated assessments, and intervention is concluded when risk – or the appearance of risk – has been eliminated or adequately minimized (ibid., 193).

Case management

The tools used for people-change measures in the market-state are variously named. Following the initial assessment, practitioners identified their work as treatment, intervention, education, training, mentoring, and counselling. However, the nature of their programs and services was consistently described to be work of regulating behaviour. In the following exchange, for example, three service providers described coming to an awareness that the management of risk (which, in this case, means being poor) is achieved through telling people what they can do – or not do – according to what they are.

> STEPHANIE: I remember the issues with the new baby program, with public health, [Dietsche] women saying, "They must think I don't know how to look after my baby! Well, I know quite well!"
> SANDY: Aren't they [public health nurses] kind of saying that?
> STEPHANIE: Exactly, they are.
> SANDY: "You screened not so well on our screen, so we're pretty sure you can't take care of that baby!"
> RACHEL: [Laughs]
> STEPHANIE: Exactly. I was in those interviews, and I set the nurse straight. But …
> RACHEL: Well, when you think of what they've survived! I mean, coming from a country with no language, nothing else. They've got these amazing survival skills. And we're telling them, "Sorry, you guys, you don't know how to do it!" [Sandy, English service provider; Stephanie and Rachel, Mennonite service providers]

Case management involves directing or controlling individuals and families rather than the conditions or circumstances faced by them. Once the individual is assessed and deemed to be an eligible client – adequately particularized and positioned to take on "rational" economic behaviours – social services are delivered according to the complicated management tools that evaluate activities and direct behaviours. Clients are to be made into producers and consumers, professional practitioners operate as technicians and clerks, and managers ensure cost-effective, efficient minimization or elimination of risk (Tsui & Cheung, 2004). The risk management tools available to practitioners are varied, and may involve manipulation or force. Cathy, an English social service worker, admitted to her ability to use coercion if the situation called for it.

> I know the Low German-speaking attendance counsellor with the school board here, and for years we worked together. He's trying to get the kids in schools. He'd call me and say, "What can I do? What can you say?"

Well, I can hold a [welfare] cheque if the kids don't go to school, or I can cut them off. I told him, "Let them know I can do this." Because the more education they get, the better the chance that they will break the cycle, you know.

During the past two decades in most Canadian provinces, reforms of many sectors in human services such as child protection, welfare, education, and healthcare have imposed market language, goals, yardsticks, and procedures. For social workers, teachers, and healthcare providers, the quality of their work is based on counting "outcomes," measured by "the ratio of output to input" (Tsui & Cheung, 2004, 439), time-study logs, standardized tests, and cost-benefit analyses. The successful management of cases is highly technical work that demands constant revision and updating, and thus requires professionals to undergo repeated in-service training sessions. Val, an English social worker, described the technical procedures through which social assistance is delivered – or managed – in Ontario:

VAL: Luann, first of all a client has to phone the ISU. They are screened by the ISU. If the ISU determines that there's some eligibility, then they schedule an appointment in this office. Our appointments with our clients now are just, ahh, verification.

LUANN: ISU is intake?

VAL: Intake Screening Unit. This was part of the reform. And the SDMT[9] came in, in 2000, and this was another part of it. They do the initial screening. They determine whether or not people are eligible, based on an assessment – a financial assessment. They schedule them into our office. A client comes in, they do the verification. And then we determine them eligible or not eligible. If they're eligible and it's determined that they are a participating member, they are sent up here. They do a questionnaire. There is an employment resource worker they see, fill out the back part of the questionnaire, and then they're scheduled for another appointment to see one of our employment staff. We have our employment staff specializing. We have taken all the different components of employment, and put staff with certain components that they deal with. We believe that if they are specialists in the field, they would be able to offer the client more information than doing it as a generalist. And we used to do it that way, and we turned it around this way, and we think that it's working better. If clients are going to school, or they are volunteering and they have a child under school age, that's when they would see the childcare worker. What we try, because we've got these three programs, we try to make them interrelate, so that the client can come into the office, they can get financial assistance, they can get employment assistance, and if required, they will get childcare assistance. So now, by devolving all these programs down to us, we have more programs to offer our clients. So, in fact, after the initial work is done, and all the bumbling is aside, things are working much better for us. We have now control over those programs, and we can make them work much better for our clients. So, we're quite happy now, in hindsight, looking back, that we were given the opportunity to have that control. Because, in fact, what we are is consolidated service managers. We manage them – the programs.

The efficient production of "widgets" – closed case files, A-students, discharged patients – cannot be monitored without a complex system of documentation. The voluminous quantity of paperwork required to demonstrate good business practices has introduced the management technology of assessment and monitoring tools, and judgments of student learning, parenting competence, patient health, and employability can be made by simply checking boxes and filling in blanks.[10] Forms figure prominently in classifying work, as described by a group of English service providers.

NANCY: There's all sorts of forms!

LOUISE: I think it's the medical forms that we [at the hospital] get involved in. It's the self-report that they have to do that's a bit challenging.

NANCY: Oh, you're talking about ODSP [Ontario Disability Support Program]?

LOUISE: Yes. Yeah, yeah.

MIKE: And there's the medical form that we [Ontario Works] have that they get their doctor to complete – the special diet forms.

SUSAN: We [Ontario Works] have an application form. We also have the planning forms that we need initially at the Intake.

NANCY: Now there are more forms! [Laughter] We're supposed to become a paperless society.

MIKE: In fact, we're full of forms!

SUSAN: It's terrible. I mean, that is a barrier to those clients we service. There is so much information!

LOUISE: I've seen your forms. It's overwhelming.

SUSAN: Just that consent form alone. The wording on it. Oh, my goodness!

In the field of human services, the benefits of "managerialism" (often equated with good management) in the design and delivery of social programs are rarely disputed (Tsui & Cheung, 2004). Some, however, critique the emerging "managerial state" and the remaking of social welfare in business terms (J. Clarke, 1999, 2003). Ursula Franklin (1992) identifies the "prescriptive technologies" of production – extended into areas that are not production at all – that have created a culture of compliance and conformity, along with a necessity for management and control. The increasingly technocratic management of people and their lives is not accidental. In all areas of human services, "outcomes-based" research, practice, evaluation, and even budgeting earn significant symbolic and economic profits.[11]

The delivery of service according to the prescriptive technologies of production reduces both the objectives and quality of professional intervention to outward impressions. *Appearances* are seen and known, and subsequently managed. In this line of work, there is no need to scratch beneath the surface. The categorical point of view assumes that we can know a great deal from outward deviations, as they indicate internal, deeply personal difference – thus potential risk – in those being assessed. The classifying habitus reads practices and behaviours as conscious and intentional *choice*. From this vantage point, we presume that people are free to choose and are therefore in control of most or all conditions of their lives. Personal liability for risk is thus assumed. Further, subjective characteristics such as motivations, intentions, aspirations, and even needs must be supplied by service providers through detailed assessments of conduct and precise documentation of any omissions or infractions of mandatory performances. Hence, on-the-surface group tendencies indicate the need for individual intra-psychic modification. For example, practitioners described their interventions with Dietsche to be directed towards "shifting value systems," modifying beliefs, and influencing culture in order to instil more appropriate values and attitudes.

MIKE: I think you need to overcome the language barrier, so you can make more inroads into education, you know.

SUSAN: But that's not their priority either, so you have to change their priorities. The fathers right now may not see education as a priority for their children. Maybe the children will start seeing it. But if the children are taught to go out and work and education is not made important at that level, what are the chances that the child, at thirteen or fifteen, is going to think education is really important? I mean, particularly if they are just doing general labour or farm work, they can get those jobs without having the education. [English service providers]

Education is essential to case management. Through processes of education – the most urgent need and preferred intervention strategy identified by service providers – workers seek to "shape minds and mould desires from within" (Wacquant, 1996, 161). In the case of Dietsche (im)migrants, service providers repeatedly referenced the vital role of teaching parents and children a precise set of behaviours consistent with "Canadian" expectations, or the system of capital in the market-state field. English social service workers explained:

> SUSAN: The big issue that I find is education. The majority of the Mexican Mennonites have very, very limited education. I usually find it's maybe grade six. And of course we will not add a child under the benefit unit if the child isn't in school. So, they could lose out on money there.
> MIKE: And they do that. They choose not to send them to school.
> SUSAN: And it's hard for them to understand under our laws that they, in fact, have to have their children registered in school. So I see that as being a problem – the educational part, their priorities being different. It's just about having the hands to do the work that's needed at home. I mean, it generates money, but it's the labour that they want, even if it's not paid. That's their culture, and I wouldn't impose our beliefs on them, but when they're here, their children aren't having the opportunity of being children, you know? We can't impose that but they do have to follow certain rules, you know.
> LUANN: So education, you think, is important. Is that enough?
> LOUISE: I don't know. It would be helpful.
> SUSAN: It's a cultural shift. It is a cultural shift.
> LOUISE: But it's a beginning.
> SUSAN: No, you have to start that way.

Sometimes, deals must be struck with Dietsche parents to ensure their children are properly educated.

> MIKE: That reminds me of another barrier. They have their own schools too, but they're not recognized by the Ministry of Education. And so when they come on to OW [Ontario Works], they want to send their kids to these schools. And we say, "No. That's not acceptable. That school

is not recognized by the Ministry. You have to send them to another school."

LUANN: So, in order for them to be on social assistance, their children have to go to a public school. Is that right?

MIKE: Right. [English service providers]

Education through the public school system, employment services, custom-designed language and health programs, individual instruction by a range of professionals and paraprofessionals, and even informational spots delivered over the waves of the Plautdietsch radio station are directed towards encouraging or forcing changes in the way Dietsche parents raise their children and live their lives.

In addition to education, a range of managerial technologies such as compulsory "volunteering," computer tracking, and standardized testing afford the providers of service certain and consequential *credentialling* powers, which operate de facto to *de-credential*, discredit, and dispossess clients. Deficiency and inferiority, confirmed through adequately passive and submissive behaviour, may meet the qualifications necessary for client legitimacy and entrance to predefined spaces of the market-state social field. Dietsche parents who presume to know what is best for their children – who decide it is more important to teach them to work than to send them to public school, or insist that it is best to work to put food on the table than to lose a day of pay to take children to the dentist – are deemed delinquent and defiant. In such circumstances, agents of the left hand of the state are required to remove children from the home, trading in paternalistic strategies for more blatant punitive measures. In some cases, families are reunited only when all parental authority and judgment is relinquished and parents submit to close supervision and surveillance by case workers.

WILL: There was a case this last week again where – children were taken again away from a mother, and they're just hounding her. And I think the reason they took them away is because she has a medical problem. And rather than allowing churches to take them, they just bring them to their foster homes, and most of our people don't qualify to be their foster parents because they're unwilling to sign the papers saying they will not ever use corporal punishment on their own children, and so –

LUANN: So often children are removed from the home and taken completely outside –

WILL: And sometimes they want to take them out of the community, and I'm not sure why. Like this family I'm talking about right now. Very conservative background. They're away for three months. The little girls came back with earrings. If that's being culturally sensitive, I don't know. Even though I have no problem with earrings, I have some problem with cultural insensitivity. [Mennonite immigrant service provider]

In these more extreme situations, the only variety of symbolic capital available to the dispossessed client is tied to the profits accrued by their social workers and teachers, and the only means of appropriation is through repeated demonstrations of conformity and submission to the rules of the game in the market-state social field. Maria, a young Dietsche mother who is a client of child welfare services and social assistance, explains:

MARIA: The way it is now, if I don't sign everything in every month, like how my worker wishes, then she sends everything back. She mailed everything back. And when I gave her a call and asked her about the matter – One of the things – I had signed in the lower part of the hydro bill, and she wanted it signed in the middle part. One time I sent the middle part in, and then she mailed it all back. So I wanted to know what was going on. Then she wanted the part where my name and address is.

LUANN: So it is hard to get it just right.

MARIA: Yeah. For a while I liked her, but sometimes it's hard to find.

LUANN: Why do you think she is that way with you?

MARIA: I don't know. I was so surprised the one time I got everything back. And then I called the office and I asked why it's like this. And then she said she needed a rent receipt with my name and address, and where it says $700. Not just the seven and the two zeros. Like you are writing seven hundred. And then I say, "Well this is the same receipt that I have sent in every month for a long time already and Mrs B. never sent it back to me." Then she said I need to do it.

LUANN: So you do it the way she wants it.

MARIA: Yeah. Mrs. B., my other worker, she never did that to me. She was so nice. She isn't my worker anymore. She is a supervisor now.

LUANN: How do you think your worker sees you?

MARIA: Well, I didn't do anything bad to her. [Trans.] I don't even know if I've ever seen her.

TRANSLATOR: She doesn't come here?

MARIA: [Trans.] No. They don't anymore. They have changed it now. They used to come once a year, or every two years, to check up on the house and everything – papers and like that. But they have changed everything now. Now I have to go to the office and there is someone else, other than my worker, that I have to see.

Outcomes evaluation

As "quality assurance" programs and notions of "evidence-based practice" are commonplace in an ever-expanding range of social life, evaluating the outcomes or products of the work that has been done is a central focus of all human services, from universities to elementary schools to police services to prisons to hospitals to welfare agencies. Practices of evaluation, or valuation, are necessary to justify preferred interventions and account for the spending of resources. Evaluation can be applied to client or patient outcomes, student outcomes, satisfaction outcomes, practice outcomes, service or program outcomes (Gambrill, 2013). It is at this point that the highly contentious nature of human services work is brought to the fore, as various groups within and outside service organizations "battle for their views of what are permitted programs and desired outcomes" (Swift & Callahan, 2009, 94). The goals of service – both manifest and latent – expose the system of capital that is at work in the market-state social field.

A group of English practitioners discussed the dilemmas and contradictions encountered in precisely determining the objectives of their work with Dietsche clients.

MIKE: And the success story for us is getting them off assistance. That's not necessarily success for the family. I mean, I was just thinking of a family. Came up from Mexico with three kids. They stayed in a trailer on a farm with another Mennonite family. We got them on assistance. Got them into housing, and they found employment. Farming – or picking, harvesting or whatever – for the season. They went off assistance now. All five of them are working, that's the three kids too. So I don't know if that's such a great success story. They were making enough money. So the mother said, "We don't need your assistance anymore." And I'm like, "Whoops!"

SUSAN: It's sort of judgmental, but the main barrier really is their value system. It probably conflicts with our expectation.

CLARA: And even for the younger generation it's the same. At least from what I'm seeing, from my position.

SUSAN: And they're supported by the churches and the community with some of those beliefs.

MIKE: Also, their work experience is limited to rural work, right? So there's not a lot they can do in the winter.

KELLY: It's really unfortunate because it's a barrier, as I see it. Maybe they don't see it as a barrier. Maybe if you were to address that with a Mexican Mennonite person, a woman, she wouldn't think she has those barriers. That in itself is a barrier – from our perspective.

LUANN: So they may not think it's a barrier because they may think it's okay to do field work for the rest of their lives?

SUSAN: And stay at home and take care of their children.

MIKE: And have a child every year.

SUSAN: Definitely. And not value education. For Ontario Works anyway, my goal is to get people to go to work. Right? Which these people do, sometimes more than we'd like them to do.

MIKE: But our goal is get them to go to work making more than minimum wage. Making enough money to stay independent of Ontario Works. And that's our goal.

LUANN: And if you make minimum wage, can you stay independent of Ontario Works?

MIKE: Probably not. But our goal also is to identify and remove the barriers that are preventing them from getting off assistance.

The evaluation of a successful outcome depends upon making repeated judgments against rather imprecise end goals. Furthermore, the evaluation of outcomes is the sole responsibility of service providers, as they alone define the desired outcomes, and determine when and how they are met. The needs and wishes of those being "served" are made irrelevant – even disparaged – throughout the service delivery process.

In the case of Dietsche (im)migrants, the desired outcomes most often referenced or implied by practitioners had to do with evidence of individual and family compliance to "Canadian" norms in all aspects of daily life. Risk or need is addressed by discarding traditional practices, dress, language, even beliefs and ideals. For example, human service workers claimed personal success for various behaviour changes of Dietsche clients, including regular attendance at school or training programs, non-agricultural employment, having fewer children, speaking English, and donning "Canadian" clothing. Ed, a long-time educator, revealed that the goal of intervention is to erase all remnants of non-conformity, to make *them* like *us*.

> ED: When I worked in a small town where there are a lot of Mennonites, we had an ESL teacher and we would translate things. We would bring people in and speak to them, and so on. So that's what we did. But there would be children with Mennonite last names who spoke English without an accent, as well as you and I, and succeeded very well in school. But their parents may have spent time here [in Canada], or their grandparents may have come here. And then we would get them going back and forth. I had one student who applied to university. Now he's broken that –
> ANDREA: Cycle.
> ED: Cycle. And now he'll go on. And his children won't be any different than any other children in the education system, because he values it and he's shown he has. [English service providers]

Clients are taught to perform, to go through the motions, even though the unlikelihood of making the mark is tacitly apparent to both the service provider and the recipient. Individuals, as outcomes, are thus classified as complete and successful, or not.

Symbolic power is essential to evaluating the outcomes of practice. Human service workers, through their official accounts of what people have done and what people are, dispense symbolic value and thus establish legitimacy *and* illegitimacy for all those engaged in the left hand of the market-state social field. Symbolic capital is produced and distributed through the valuation of the social, cultural, and even economic capital held by target populations.[12] Symbolic capital, "which is the form that the various species of capital assume when they are perceived and recognized as legitimate" (Bourdieu, 1989, 17), is responsible for the extent to which material, social, and cultural holdings for individuals and groups can be exchanged or converted. In other words, symbolic capital is necessary to protect the functional value of all other forms of capital.

Symbolic power, subjective exclusion, and "site effects"

The symbolic work of risk assessment, case management, and outcomes evaluation is particularly effective in the processes of social exclusion, as it is symbolic capital that determines social and economic trajectories for individuals and groups. People get stuck in social places and physical spaces of deprivation, and symbolic violence – the depreciation of all individual and group holdings – is the means through which upward mobility is stopped short. The undermining, or spoiling, of economic, social, and cultural capital is *subjective exclusion*, and it is the result of and rationalization for all forms of social exclusion.

A primary way in which symbolic capital is denied to individuals and groups is through the misrecognition and sabotage of the cultural capital they hold. Cultural capital, as a symbolic resource, is embodied capital, in that the personal characteristics of the bearer make all the difference. Through attributing or withholding value to a wide range of everyday practices, such as food preferences and fashion taste, the practical effectiveness or quality of all assets held is determined. Cultural power thus works to situate people according to their embodied cultural expressions. Without cultural recognition or resources, or the economic and social means to acquire them in the market-state field, individuals and groups have limited capacity for their own cultural reproduction. For Dietsche (im)migrants who are classified as clients, many of the means of preserving their heritage are taken from them, as the very practices that sustain their way of life are those that reinforce their social exclusion in all its forms and thus restrict their access to all species of capital in the market-state social field.

Bourdieu (1990b) claims that cultural capital may be the only form of accumulation that is possible when economic capital is not recognized (118). And yet, as is evident for Dietsche families, once the processes of economic, spatial, and sociopolitical exclusion have been sustained by a particular group of people over a period of time, it is likely that individual, embodied forms of cultural capital remain unrecognized, and the usual conversion strategies are denied to all members of the group. For instance, when asked to reflect on the ways in which they are viewed and represented in their local communities, Mennonite immigrant service providers – all of whom are educated, credentialled individuals – gave testimony on the sweeping force of subjective exclusion:

> Where do I start? Lack of intelligence is a big one. Lack of social skills. We don't know how to read and write. Low education. It goes on and on. It could be anything. [Jake]
>
> Abuse. Alcoholism. Incest is a big one. When I went to college, one of my fellow students said, "Oh, you're Mennonite. Well, then you must have had sex with your dad." I was like, "What?!" She said, "Well, that's

how they teach their daughters about sexuality." Ahh, no. I never had sex with my dad. [Marie]

When we had our baby, somebody mentioned it at work. And somebody mentioned it to one of the other workers from the hospital, that we had a baby. And we just got talking. And she found out that I was a Mennonite somehow. And she said, "So, how are you gonna discipline him?" Like, right away there was that stereotype that I was going to beat my son. And he had just been born! Right away, she wanted to know. I just said, "Well, you have a totally wrong understanding of who I am." And she said, "Oh, well, well, I didn't mean it like that." And I just left it at that. [Jake]

Well, to this day, I regret sometimes not reporting a doctor that once examined me when I was pregnant with my oldest daughter. I was eight months pregnant. And I had high blood pressure. I had a lot of complications. And so, my family doctor wasn't there, and there was another doctor. And he examined me. And I said, "When do you think I'll have this baby?" Because I was really not feeling good. And he says, "Well, you should know that by now. Isn't this about your sixth or eighth child?" And I said, "Excuse me?" And I started bawling. And I said, "For your information, this is my first child." Because I was twenty-seven, he automatically assumed, because I had a Mennonite name. [Tina]

If the opinion comes from a doctor, it's usually that we are sick, and unwilling to change, and generally overweight and fat. [Will]

Escape from social spaces of exclusion is made formidable, as the legitimate means available to a person for acquiring any type of capital from such a social location are sharply restricted.

The effects of subjective exclusion in one social field are contagious, so to speak. The devaluation of social capital in the market-state field was shown to result in the de-credentialling or denial of social, cultural, and even economic capital in all other social fields in which individuals participate. This discrediting most often affects women whose relationships with their husbands – who hold the concentration of social capital – have been severed or jeopardized in some way. Nettie, a Dietsche (im)migrant who worked in a private Old Colony school, described her experience of subjective exclusion in her own Dietsche social field after she left her alcoholic husband.

When we first separated, I had no friends. And just to back up a little bit, before we separated, I was already teaching an ESL class once a week. We had gone through our first year, I think. So I was very familiar with these women at that time. But during the time that we separated, for about a year after, none of those women would speak to me. I mean, if we were to meet face to face somewhere, they would say hi. But I never got a phone call or invited to anything that they would have. Let's say, things that I would get invited to before, parties, Tupperware parties, fund-raisers. I was completely left out of them. So from being very, very involved in fund-raisers, in school, and with the group, to completely being shut out. It was hard, but also it was partly what I expected. Staying accepted wasn't something that I thought would happen.

The valuation of classifications and those classified functions as an *exchange* between worker and client. When confronted with clients who demonstrate need of any kind, the service provider, by comparison, more closely approximates the standard, the social archetype. Thus, those who are reliant on the state for any portion or aspect of their well-being provide the means through which service providers accumulate symbolic capital. Similar to the "social alchemy" of gift exchange, the accrual of symbolic profits through delivering programs and services presupposes and reinforces the more advantageous position of the giver or the provider. Thus, "A man possesses in order to give" (Bourdieu, 1990b, 126). Yet the conversion of the economic gift (in the form of social benefits) into symbolic profits for the gift-giver is in no way automatic. Conversion demands "the (sincere) disposition to give things that are more personal, and therefore more precious than goods or money" (ibid., 128). Human service practitioners repeatedly boasted about their giving to the Mennonites from Mexico, describing in detail the extraordinary time, patience, and tolerance demanded in their work with this population. Personal investments, required to make the "gift" adequately generous to exercise protective authority over disadvantaged Others, pay symbolic dividends in the forging of a dependent bond between the helper and the helped.

Even more fundamental to the symbolic economy of social services is the certainty that the "gift" of social assistance can never be returned; so in the act of providing a welfare or disability cheque, in-kind benefits, training, language or parenting programs, or volunteer "opportunities," the state has secured a debt, a lasting obligation. Thus, "he also possesses by giving" (ibid., 126). The exchange of capital that is vital to the order of the social services field is hidden, as the symbolic power of getting and keeping a lasting hold through imposing a moral obligation usually remains unrecognized. The "soft domination"[13] of selectively providing and withholding services and resources is gentle, invisible, and denied.

Subjective exclusion, accomplished through classification practices and subject construction, is complete when *they* are made into the opposite of *us* in the ways that matter most to us, as difference and its meaning are manufactured and ascribed by "the difference that makes the difference" (Corrigan, 1991). Service providers, who necessarily assume the inclinations of the classifying habitus, repeatedly asserted that *they* need to learn how *we* do things here. Dietsche culture and values were described as backward, primitive, and oppressive, implying that our culture and values are singularly progressive, enlightened, and liberating. We cannot be who we are unless they are who we make them to be. For example:

> I really think that that's where it [education] really needs to start – before people arrive here. There has to be more information available. "Don't hit your kids!" would be a really great start [laughter]. [Victoria, English service provider]

It is made clear that *they* hit their children; *we* don't. Similarly, I heard concern for the way women and girls are treated in Dietsche culture. The traditional patriarchal roles and views were contrasted with "our" culture, in which (it was claimed) women are equal to men. *They* don't value women and girls; *we* do. Incest and sexual violence were named as disconcerting problems among Dietsche (im)migrants, but always in the absence of specific evidence and usually without mention of strategies for intervention. References to domestic and sexual abuse were generally used to clearly demarcate them as different from us. The necessary work of the helper habitus is investing social classifications with meaning, which serves to reinforce and extend economic, spatial, social, and subjective *distance*. Dividing practices are integral to classifying work.

Repeatedly, the Dietsche people – as a uniform category – and their culture, beliefs, and values were juxtaposed to an undefined and implied opposite. At times, the contradicting and sanctified culture or group was identified as "North American" or "Canadian." More often, the comparator remained unidentified, formless, and therefore unavailable for examination. Similarly, to stand in contrast to – to collectively embody the difference that serves to mark and classify *them* – requires *us* to assume a precise uniformity that overrides any and all ambiguity. The following discussion among English social service workers reveals the criteria for inclusion that must remain implicit yet unequivocal, malleable yet unyielding, in the making of an excluded kind.

MIKE: Now I'm sure they worked from dusk to dawn, all five of them. And they worked seven days a week.

SUSAN: Oh yeah, oh yeah. What were the ages of the kids, do you know?

MIKE: They were from fifteen – fifteen, ten, and eight.

SUSAN: What about our child labour laws? I think it used to be seventeen, or sixteen?

KELLY: They have them out at eight years old.

MIKE: Now, you can work at McDonald's at fourteen.

KELLY: But part-time.

SUSAN: Yeah, sure. And I worked in tobacco when I was twelve.

NANCY: I was thirteen.

MIKE: I don't know what the law is – [laughter]. Kids delivering newspapers, I guess that's different?

KELLY: But there is that. There is some rule about part-time –

SUSAN: Fourteen, fifteen – that's the legal –

KELLY: They have to have a SIN [Social Insurance Number], and they get that fairly often, I noticed, in that population.

NANCY: They are encouraging everyone to get their own SIN number – all children.

KELLY: Because it always amazes me when they [Dietsche (im)migrants] come up with a SIN card for a child. I don't know, that just seems strange to me.

MIKE: My mother, as soon as we were born, she got us a SIN card.

KELLY: Really?

SUSAN: Really?

MIKE: And I spent my summers in PEI [Prince Edward Island] on a farm, and the whole family worked. We all went out and milked the cows, did the hay, and –

SUSAN: I would like to look at the occurrence of re-applications. And if that family goes off and stays off [social assistance], to me that's truly success. I think a family, when they are able to come and say, you know, "I'm making enough money," they see that as a great success. They've accomplished, you know, being in the workforce. And we've done our jobs. We've referred them to different agencies – and agencies that could assist them. We've got the employment supports in place. So from our perspective, yes, we've helped. We've got them on their own two feet. That's our goal. And I'm sure on the other end of the spectrum, they're seeing it as success because they can say, "Bye. See ya." [Laughter]

Even when practices appear the same or similar, *they* and *we* must be made the same within and categorically opposite between. This is the work of group-making. Mennonite immigrant service providers describe how dichotomizing and homogenizing mechanisms of group-making operate in tandem to produce the classified Other, or subjective exclusion.

> CORNELIUS: Another thing that enters into that too, is the people
> who integrate well are not a problem. They're not really seen as the
> Mennonites. But the ones that have difficulty, that need all the extra
> attention, and even though there's nine out of ten that don't need help
> here, but the one that does, that's who everybody hears about.
> TINA: Yes.
> SUZANNE: Yes.
> CORNELIUS: Because these guys that set up big greenhouses, they didn't
> require a lot of help. They knew how to do things. They're really not
> categorized, and they probably don't even want to be categorized as
> Mennonites anymore.

Subjective exclusion denies the ability for individuals and groups to define the principles of their own identity and interests, as they are stripped of the necessary social tools and resources.

> My sister-in-law is not even Mennonite by birth. Mennonite by choice.
> She's English. She had a baby. And they said, the doctor, on his way out the
> door after the baby was born, "See you in another nine months." Because
> of her last name. She can't speak a lick of German. [Marie, Mennonite
> immigrant service provider]

The social kinds that are made through subjective exclusion are unusually stubborn. Not only is their self-conserving essence hidden, the potential for effective resistance is thwarted in the very correspondence – the *fit* – with the mental structures through which they were produced. Bourdieu et al., (1999, 129) describe the potency of "site effects" this way:

Like a club founded on the active exclusion of undesirable people, the fashionable neighborhood symbolically consecrates its inhabitants by allowing each one to partake of the capital accumulated by the inhabitants as a whole. Likewise, the stigmatized area symbolically degrades its inhabitants, who, in return, symbolically degrade it. Since they don't have all the cards necessary to participate in the various social games, the only thing they share is their common excommunication. Bringing together on a single site a population homogeneous in its dispossession strengthens that dispossession, notably with respect to culture and cultural practices: the pressures exerted at the level of class or school or in public life by the most disadvantaged or those furthest from a "normal" existence pull everything down in a general leveling. They leave no escape other than flight towards other sites (which lack of resources usually renders impossible).[14]

The processes of subjective exclusion are covered over by the presumption that people are positioned in and move through hierarchical social structures according to their inherent and inherited characteristics. Social kinds are accepted, without question, as natural and inevitable. The categorical perspective thus successfully dissolves any contradiction between social structure and personal agency – between determinism and choice – as individuals are customized, made to order. Such custom-made subjects are always perceived to *choose* to behave as expected, in ways suitable to their classification, as the principles through which they are seen and known define the limits of what is seen and give meaning to what is known. Moreover, the active, speaking, knowing subjectivity of those so classified is erased, effectively un-making the subject and preparing it for re-making.

Subjective exclusion then circles back on itself, and it becomes the basis and justification for the dispossession of all species of capital, thus rendering all forms of social exclusion seemingly necessary and fitting. The symbolic violence of subjective exclusion has profound material consequences, as it is the origin and culmination of all forms and processes of social exclusion.

The symbolic economy of marketized human services

Migrations give rise to confrontations of enormous consequence, as they represent a collision between destabilized social fields. Both the Dietsche subfield and the left hand of the market-state suffer from a crisis in the structure and regulations of the social field, and agents struggle to regain a feel for their own game. In this case, a "deficit in legitimacy" (Wacquant, 2001, 402) that has accompanied the marketization of social services is most keenly experienced by the agents of the detached and devalued left hand of the state. For instance, women have long outnumbered men in the "helping professions." In the market-state social field, in which all things masculine are hyper-valorized and profits are accrued from patriarchal imbalances, economic and symbolic rewards for players in the left hand of the market-state are in short supply. The work and workers of social services are further discounted in the "hollowed-out" and, more recently, criminalized social welfare system (Hallsworth & Lea, 2011; MacKinnon, 2012). This depreciation of lifetime accounts of symbolic capital leaves some service providers eager to adopt new acquisition strategies, adjusting to the shifting rules of the game. In such social positions among the "dominated-dominant" (Bourdieu, 1990b, 72; 2000b, 188), the symbolic (and therefore material) rewards of classifying work for service providers are significant and necessary to be appropriately recognized as not-clients, as helpers. As extensions of state structures and policies, human service practitioners maintain their required symbolic holdings through the symbolic dispossession of clients. One Mennonite immigrant service provider described with some precision how symbolic power works in the delivery of social programs:

LUANN: In your work with community agencies, do you ever experience a conflict in how you think a situation should be handled and how they think it should be handled, and what do you do?

WILL: Well – the first case that comes to mind is Children's Aid – really disturbing. Especially since the law changed. They now only have one mandate, and that is to protect the child. Not to work with families. Secondly, they get paid by the number of cases. And – and they have such high staff turnover that they don't ... Some of them are so inexperienced and, and they just want to all cover their behinds from legal suits and, so they don't listen, they – total unwillingness to work with churches, total unwillingness to bend for culture. I mean, let's not kid ourselves. They're enlarging their kingdoms through our community as well. Another example: the more people the Canadian Mental Health Association can put up here, the more it bolsters their statistics and the more money they get.

LUANN: Mental illness is a commodity.

WILL: Yeah. It doesn't all go one way. And as much as we would hope that everything is genuinely, truly compassionate, there are some ulterior motives.

Furthermore, social service bureaucracies are invited – even obliged – to join forces with right-hand authorities to exercise state power through particular forms of social intervention. "The regulation of the working classes by what Pierre Bourdieu (1998) calls 'the left hand' of the state, symbolised by education, public health care, social security, social assistance and social housing, is being *superseded* – in the United States – or *supplemented* – in Western Europe – by regulation through its 'right hand,' that is, the police, courts and prison system, which are becoming increasingly active and intrusive in the lower regions of social space" (Wacquant, 2001, 402).

The *enforcement* of social services – increasingly prevalent and necessary in the residualized and marketized welfare state – is practised through the borrowed tools and re-masculated authority of surveillance and policing, and it requires an unusual intimacy between agents of the left and right hands of the state.[15] Possessing the "informational and human means to exercise a close surveillance of 'problem populations'" (ibid., 407), the enforcement of human services in this particular Canadian context is accomplished primarily through the appropriated potency of the police and the courts. For instance, various practitioners from healthcare, education, and social services meet monthly with local and federal police to discuss problems related to Dietsche (im)migrants in a southern Alberta community. Such teamwork is also widely evident in the complicated delivery of child protection services, necessitating the cooperation of a wide range of interventions from the left and right hands of the state. Social service professionals – themselves made vulnerable by various forms of capital dispossession – are lured by promises of symbolic power.

The spaces of dominated dominance occupied by all those who represent the beleaguered left hand of the state can lead to despair. Such despair was evident in conversations with service providers for the various ministries of the state, who recounted the uncompromising dilemmas they face in their work. They see themselves as "client-focused," but government interests focus on the "taxpayer." Practitioner narratives revealed some inkling that their sincere intentions for the good of their clients are ultimately and inexplicably unfulfilled in the human service system. The manifest goal of many social services is to help clients to exit the system – "to get off the rolls" and "to close files." But service providers noted the futility of such efforts, as many clients return to the same employment and social conditions that forced them into the system in the first place. "Reforms," "amalgamations," "downloading," and "devolution" of the past decade have resulted in escalating demands on local agencies, as they are responsible for increasingly broad mandates, larger geographical regions, and more clients, with diminishing resources. Some professionals commented that the knowledge and expertise gained through years of formal education are of little value in their work, as an entirely new set of skills is required with continual reforms. The cultural and economic profits of higher education have been diluted by the proliferation of diplomas, certificates, and degrees that are of limited practical use yet serve to qualify one for the delivery of social services.

A dominating habitus carries with it anxiety, because social positions and identities of inclusion are based on social positions and identities of exclusion.[16] The dispossession of cultural and symbolic capital – or subjective exclusion – is the initial step in preserving the classifying habitus and the idealized included subject, as the making of an *included* kind is contingent on the making and remaking of an *excluded* kind.

> When we tried to start up the Habitat for Humanity program [for Dietsche (im)migrants] in this area, we met up with a lot of resistance because there is such a large immigrant population here that's not Mennonite based, but European based. It's like, "We came to this country with nothing, and we worked our tails off and now we've got this. Why can't these people just get it together and get working and get educated and, you know, do the same thing?" [Will, Mennonite immigrant service provider]

A typical citizen is thereby reproduced to be at once industrious, self-determining, and self-reliant. Furthermore, the ordinary *immigrant* citizen is every North American settler who emigrated with nothing and, through perseverance, hard work, and commitment became a "self-made man." The immigrant citizen subject is the forefather of the classifying habitus. All material and symbolic gain in the market-state field corresponds with his image.

Social classifications and corresponding stereotypes, as ideologically constructed subjects, serve as collective representations that fulfil political as well as social functions: "in addition to permitting the 'logical integration' of society … classification systems serve to secure and naturalize domination" (Wacquant, 1998b, 225). By means of everyday yet "official" practices that pathologize, vilify, and racialize difference, the identities of whole groups of people are ascribed in the precise and constrained terms of our divided social world. Internal and external realities are at once produced and aligned. A perfect match. Assembled identities justify material deprivation and punitive regulation, and all forms of domination are made right and natural. To return to the main gist of this project, making sense of self-imposed social exclusion is not possible through the dividing schemes of the classifying habitus. "For to impose one's art of living is to impose at the same time principles of visions of the world that legitimize inequality by making the divisions of social space appear rooted in the inclinations of individuals rather than the underlying distribution of capital" (ibid.).

Scholars often assume that human behaviour and actions are determined by *reasons* (mechanical or rational) that can be ascertained by an outside expert observer. Rather than encouraging an understanding of culture and practice, this leads to judgments that are explicitly value laden. Such non-comprehension (Cixous & Calle-Gruber, 1997) is inevitable when principles of everyday practice are recognized only as reasoned intention, purpose, enlightened self-interest, or utility as it appears to an impartial observer, or "one who is perfectly informed" (Bourdieu, 2000b, 140). From this spontaneous assessment, the reasonable response to such seemingly nonsensical practices as those exhibited by Dietsche (im)migrants would be to educate them, with a view not only to helping them to become more knowledgeable, but to adjusting their values and beliefs. This, Bourdieu (2000b) claims, is "misrecognition, or forgetting, of the relation of immanence to a world that is not perceived as a world" (142). Such superficial readings that fail to look beneath the surface or beyond appearances of Dietsche practices and dispositions reveal much more about the symbolic economy of human services, the classifying habitus, and the typically classifying work of assessment, management, and evaluation. A common sense approach to Dietsche clients exposes the categorical perspective and market ideology that supports it, demonstrating its generative and organizational effects in the left hand of the market-state. But the market does not define all social space. To understand expressions of self-imposed social exclusion in the market-state, we must intentionally view everyday practices through the social field and system of capital that defines Dietsche Mennonite tradition and practice. This is the focus of the following two chapters.

Chapter Five

Producing the Economic Habitus

We visited in the small, tidy, and sparsely furnished sitting room, surrounded by the sounds of living in a rented farmhouse shared by three families. Our conversation in English flowed with ease, and my concern for the need for a translator was soon forgotten. The young parents told me they had lived in Canada for more than seven years. They had emigrated from their Mennonite colony in Mexico to rural Ontario. Their three young boys were extraordinarily talkative, curious, and engaging. My exchange with the youngest members of the family alone could have taken us late into the night. The two eldest boys, ages six and seven, attended the local public school, since there was no Old Colony school nearby. Despite their youth, they unreservedly demonstrated fluency in verbal expression and reading – English-language skills that already surpassed those of their parents. They told me they loved school; the youngest could not wait to get there. Later, when I asked their father what sort of life he would like for his sons, he said he hoped they would continue in school until they were thirteen years of age. Then he would like them to work in the fields. Field work. This is the work he does in Canada, following the various harvest seasons from early spring to fall, picking and processing vegetables for farmers until the season ends. Then beginning again each spring. This work approximates the subsistence farming lifestyle of the colony the family left behind. As he patiently listened to and watched them with a smile, it was evident that he was proud of his boys and wanted the best for them. And carrying on their father's life, and his father's life, would be the best. His confident and quick responses to my queries suggested that he did not understand his aspirations for them to be limiting or holding them back in any way. He wanted his sons to stay with his people, their people, to remain in the church and withdrawn from "the world." Even in Canada, far away from the colony of his upbringing, he wanted them to know something of colony life, to maintain their Dietsche identity. To encourage his sons to aspire to be somebody, to stand out, and to become something other than he is would be to push them away – away from what they have been taught, away from God.[1]

The work that Dietsche (im)migrants generally engage in – even prefer, prepare for, and wish for their children – represents a form of self-imposed social exclusion, resulting in the dispossession of all types of capital in the market-state social field. My intention is to show that such dispositions towards work make perfect sense for Dietsche families. Central to this chapter are contradictory meanings of work and their associated symbolic power. Further, I propose that an exploration of conflicting social fields and competing systems of capital provides a focal point through which to understand expressions of self-imposed social exclusion.

I focus our attention in this chapter on the specific symbolic value of *work*, apart from and alongside its material power, in each of the dissimilar and colliding social fields occupied by Dietsche (im)migrants. I begin from the premise that the market is not the *only* game in town. Yet, it *is* dominant, impinging on all, and a very certain material reality results in the places and spaces we inhabit in this field. Those who insist on difference, who are deliberately and persistently committed to non-capitalist systems of capital, are more vulnerable to processes of social exclusion in the left hand of the market-state field. Thus, the market-state system of capital *counts* in the everyday material matters of life. Through the inquiry of meanings of work within competing systems of capital and associated habitus, this chapter offers a specific and reflexive view of an alternative social field: the countercultural system of capital that is the Dietsche social field.[2]

The recognition and evaluation of social exclusion invokes "different or even antagonistic points of view, since points of view depend on the point from which they are taken" (Bourdieu, 1989, 18). My examination of the symbolic power of work is an attempt to view a point in social space (and time) from two distinct points of view. The competing systems of capital that organize the market-state social field and the Dietsche social field result in conflicting visions or world views. I aim towards an articulated challenge to the categorical perspective as the assumed universal and transcendental representation of the social world.

Systems of capital are complex and multifaceted, such that the specific economies intersect and overlap in ways that limit their discrete inquiry, as I have endeavoured to do in this work. A discussion of social fields and their structuring systems of capital is neither particular to one specific instance, nor general to all participating members. While certain characteristics of the Dietsche social field may be peculiar to the Mennonite culture and tradition, many are common to rural, agrarian communities and cultures.[3] Furthermore, the system of capital defining the market-state social field, rooted in the rules and assumptions of neoliberal global capitalism, contradicts the experience of all those who are forced to eke out a living on the margins of labour markets. Consequently, unemployment tallies – essential in determining the extent of social exclusion as an individual kind – are not useful where the informal economy flourishes. When people are compelled to survive by way of any means available to them, and labour markets are closed off to them, the more important criterion marking the excluded kind from within a categorical perspective may be certain methods of making a living. Even in so-called developed countries, where social protection systems exist but are weakened, more and more people are driven to engage in the informal economy, hold several low-paying and part-time jobs at once, and rely on food banks to make ends meet.[4] Cultures and practices that are forged through necessity and a harsh day-to-day struggle for survival are clearly distinctive from those that can afford a more contemplative stance towards the world and the self. "The fundamental proposition that the habitus is a virtue made of necessity is never more clearly illustrated than in the case of the working classes, since necessity includes for them all that is usually meant by the word, that is, an inescapable deprivation of necessary goods. Necessity imposes a taste for necessity which implies a form of adaptation to and consequently acceptance of the necessary, a resignation to the inevitable, a deep-seated disposition" (Bourdieu, 1984, 372).

Habitus is embodied history in that it is internalized as second nature and thus forgotten as history. In this way, habitus "is the active presence of the whole past of which it is the product" (Bourdieu, 1990b, 56). The habitus of necessity, which is associated with alternative social fields and the dispossessed positions occupied by so many people in all regions of the world, finds itself displaced – out of sync – in the market-state field, where attachment to the wage labour force is promoted as the ticket to a better life. Therefore, the dilemmas and struggles resulting from conflicting social fields and competing systems of capital described for Dietsche (im)migrants are most accurately read as a case in point that is more common than peculiar.

Out-of-place livelihoods

The dynamics of social exclusion in global capitalism are evidenced to function together to propel people out of place. In this case, accounts of hardship in Latin America, varying in depth and detail, were offered by all Dietsche (im)migrants. When asked what brought them to Canada, Dietsche reported that their move was motivated by economic reasons – "to make a living." It is no longer possible, for more and more Dietsche, to provide the most basic of necessities for their families in colonies in Latin America.

Some (im)migrants recalled sending children to bed hungry. Others recounted that there was usually "enough to satisfy," but not in the way that there is enough in Canada. According to (im)migrant accounts, the variety of food is extremely limited in Latin American colonies, and most rely on a diet of corn tortillas, rice, and beans. Research narratives conveyed evidence of significant malnutrition for Dietsche women and children, such as iron-deficiency anaemia, low-birth-weight babies, and pica. Dietsche women described the painstaking precision with which one "makes ends meet":

> LUANN: Did you have to borrow food then? At the store?
> HELENA: [Trans.] Often we had to borrow, and often what we earned in one week, we had to count it out. A lot was always needed at the week end, and we had to count it out – for this a little bit, for that a little bit, so that it just reached until the end of the week. And at the end, when the cheque came, everything was gone again. And if it didn't reach, if he [her husband] couldn't earn, then we had to see one more week.

Dietsche respondents and immigrant service providers described Mennonite colony homes of poorer families in Mexico as constructed from "braided wood smeared with mud" and likened them to "shacks" or "henhouses." Most migrating families did not own property in the colony, so they had nothing to sell when they left. As a result, many made the move burdened with overwhelming debt.

> LUANN: Your husband made wells for a living in Mexico, is that right?
> HELENA: [Trans.] Yes, but it didn't go very well because out there, there are so many rocks in the land and the machine couldn't make a well very good because of the stones. You could only dig one metre in a week because of the hard stones in the dirt, and that doesn't earn much.

LUANN: So he wasn't paid for his time.

HELENA: [Trans.] No. Only on how many wells he could dig. He went under. He didn't get out of it what the machines cost him. And then we had debt because of the machines, and we couldn't do enough to pay for them.

LUANN: So, when you came, you had sold your house and paid off all your debts?

HELENA: [Trans.] No, we haven't yet. We still have debt there. We have to find out if we can save here enough, that we can pay it all. But you need money here too, and we have to wait and see if there will be enough.

LUANN: And you have been here only one year.

HELENA: [Trans.] Yes. And maybe it will work yet.

Corroborating the work of Mexican economist Pedro Castro (2004), Dietsche (im)migrants cited at least five interrelated sources of their economic hardship in Mexico. First, and most important, the scarcity of productive agricultural land is preventing Dietsche from expanding their self-sufficient colonies and preserving their agricultural way of life. Large families generate a rapidly growing demand for land. Adding to this problem is a series of economic conditions that make it difficult to save enough money to purchase farmland, including free trade, giving rise to staggeringly low prices for agricultural products; abnormal and extreme weather conditions, resulting in very poor – and sometimes the complete absence of – crop yields; government policies that favour the interests of landowners and international business investors; and corrupt practices within and outside Mennonite colonies.

Dietsche (im)migrants recounted the day-to-day challenges presented by these compounding challenges. For instance, one Dietsche woman described the unyielding limits of Mennonite colony land in Mexico:

HELENA: I was born in Durango. I was fifteen when my parents moved from Durango to Zacatecas.[5]

LUANN: Why did they move?

HELENA: [Trans.] Durango was full, and then they bought a fresh piece of land in Zacatecas.

LUANN: Many families moved to Zacatecas then, yes?

HELENA: [Trans.] Yeah. It is a big land yet. It's still a big piece. It has yet about twenty villages.

LUANN: Is there still room for more, in Zacatecas, or is it full?

HELENA: [Trans.] All is full. And when young people want to get married, everything is full. They hardly know where to go.

LUANN: So how big is a colony? How many people would be in one colony?

HELENA: [Trans.] 7,000.

LUANN: How do you decide when to start another colony, instead of just making a colony bigger?

HELENA: [Trans.] When the land is full, and then, when no more can come, then they – They have cows there. There are cow herders. The common ground is where they send the cattle in the fence, to graze. And then when no more can come, then they divide the common ground into certain pieces and then they build there. And then they can come there and move there. And if that doesn't reach, then they have to do it with acreage land. And then when the land is all full, then they start dividing it.

LUANN: When people move to this common ground that has been divided, do they get their own farm?

HELENA: [Trans.] No. They just have the place with the house, and they just have to go to work.

The repeated division of colony land has resulted in very small parcels. Castro (2004) notes that, in Mexico in general, "it is not unusual to find plots of no more than a half hectare. As any farmer knows, this is not enough to raise a family" (29). However, land ownership in Mexico is sometimes contested and cannot always protect people from poverty or the need to migrate. One Dietsche man, who has worked as a hired farm hand for seven years in Ontario, explained:

LUANN: Did you own land in Mexico?

ISAAK: Still have it. Fifty acres.

LUANN: Do you plan to keep it, even though you're living here, or what do you think?

ISAAK: The thing is, there we don't have papers, like here. You can't sell it without being there. That's the problem. We don't have land paperwork. That's one problem there. My wife's father, before he died, he bought land there from the Mexicans. They never handed that deed in. He died, and over the years – Well, now I don't know what's going on, but they still don't want to hand it in. So before we get that, we can't, we can't sell it.

LUANN: So, who doesn't want to hand it in?

ISAAK: The old owner, the owner before. He's Mexican. That's who he [wife's father] bought it from and they never brought the deed in.

LUANN: But that would have been how many years ago?

ISAAK: I think about ten or fifteen years ago, I'm not sure. They're still working on it. They were working together quite a bit, I think. And they know each other pretty good so they trusted each other. But now, her father died and nobody has the papers that show it was paid for. If that guy ever wants to take it back, there's nobody that can say anything about it. And the thing is, when her father died, her mother gave every kid some of the land. That's why we own it now.

Adding to economic hardship, global climate changes have caused recurrent droughts for several Mennonite colonies.[6] Dietsche (im)migrants also reported that other areas have lost crops to drowning floodwaters. Elisabeth described the devastating effects that even one dry season can have for a family in Mexico:

In Campeche, there the people just grow corn in the summer, and they borrow the money from the bank for buying fertilizer and corn and everything, so that they can get the land ready to plant. And if it gives a good crop, they make money so they can work further. And if it only gives very little, then it sometimes isn't even enough to pay debt. And that's how it was with us. That last year – It was too dry for corn, and it didn't give very much. That's why we came here. People often rent land out there. And then after, they have to give some corn for it, or money or like that. That last year, there was so little, and we had to give more than we had. Now we don't have anything there anymore.

The problems associated with the unequal distribution and shortage of productive land are compounded by the scarcity of work in Mennonite colonies, and Dietsche are forced out of their sacred villages into the secular world around them.

LUANN: So your father worked outside the colony?

AGANETHA: Yes.

LUANN: What was his work?

AGANETHA: I'm not sure what he did. Those were Spanish people he worked for, when he left on Monday and was gone for a whole week. I think sometimes he was working on the fields and repairing tractors.

LUANN: So there wasn't work for him in the colony?

AGANETHA: No. A lot of people work for the Spanish people. [Dietsche (im)migrant]

Yet many (im)migrants reported that finding paid work, or work that pays, has become next to impossible in the Global South. The opening of the Mexican economy to the global market in the past two decades has had tumultuous political and economic effects. Many "in-bond industries" were established but subsequently closed, protections for domestic agricultural production and pricing have been discontinued, and a change in the legal definition of rural property allows "the *ejidos* (a sort of 'common' land for the poorest farmers)" (Castro, 2004, 32) to be bought and sold in the land market. Dietsche (im)migrants observed that economic difficulties for Colony Mennonites (or Dietsche) have been aggravated by Mexico's free trade agreement with the United States and Canada, as the prices for their agricultural products have declined dramatically while their farming expenses – such as the cost of diesel fuel, seeds, feed, and fertilizer – have climbed to unmanageable levels. The cost of farming is therefore prohibitive for many, and wages are often too low in Mexico to decently support a family.

Dietsche (im)migrants repeatedly described Mexico as a "land of lawlessness." If one has sufficient resources, state authorities, such as police and bureaucrats, can be bought. Some expressed a deep fear of the Mexican legal system and law enforcers, as "They try to take your money away." Mennonite colonies are not exempt from corrupt and illicit practices. Accounts of exorbitant interest rates charged by Dietsche businessmen and landowners constitute extortion of those who are most vulnerable. Colony Mennonite farmers were reported as taking advantage of both Mexican government subsidies, such as the "Procampo grants" (Castro, 2004, 30), and the sizeable profits from sharecropping:

LUANN: You said that when someone has land, that they get money from the government?

SUSANA: Yeah.

LUANN: Just because they had land?

SUSANA: [Trans.] Yeah, so they can do the planting on it. And then they rent the land further. But the money they keep. The government gives the money so they can plant on the land, to buy the seed and oil to plant on it, and then they keep the land and rent it out further, and don't give the money to plant. Then we have to earn the money somewhere with milking cows, or somehow get it out of the cows, to buy seed and oil and the costs that come with planting on the land.

LUANN: Oh, and that's not easy.

SUSANA: [Trans.] No, it's so hard that one just can't do it anymore.

LUANN: And then you have to give some back?

SUSANA: [Trans.] And then give the rent back. Two-thirds for us, and one-third would be theirs. We have to give that back, and then bring it to their house, and put it in their barn, just so one can work their land, that one can have feed for one's livestock. Those that want to build there have to have a lot of livestock.

LUANN: Very hard to make a living.

For some, circular migration offers the promise of making ends meet, a little longer, in Mexico. For others, migration is a last hope. And competing systems of capital collide.

In-between nation-place

Experiences of Dietsche (im)migrants confirm that when people are poor, they are more vulnerable to the stresses in life. When money is scarce and the social safety net has gaping holes or does not exist at all, people are cast into despair quickly. This is the steep and slippery descent into economic exclusion, and in and of itself it is vigorous and devastating.[7] It was unequivocally evidenced that colony emigrations are provoked by material need, or the dispossession of economic capital. Thus, colony emigrations share decisive features with expanding south-north and east-west labour migrations.[8]

However, decisions are not always inspired by economics alone, as some practices of Dietsche in Latin America and Dietsche in Canada are manifestly contrary to material capital interests. For example, Castro (2004) observed that many Mennonites in Mexico "rejected agricultural change or diversification of their activities. They instead decided to accept the official subsidies, the short-term easiest way" (ibid., 30). Even though they produce high quality products, such as cheese and apples, they do not compete in international markets where even modest profits are more likely (Castro, 2004). Moreover, decisions regarding migration or settlement in Canada sometimes seem inexplicable, in economic terms or otherwise. For example, in contrast to colony life in Latin America, men and women repeatedly described their lives in Canada to be "comfortable," "safe," and "so much better" in ways that extend beyond the decided material advantage they experienced in Canada. And yet, some return to colonies in Latin America, and others become "back-and-forthers," maintaining prolonged and precarious migratory livelihoods.

> LUANN: What you earn here, is that enough for you?
> EDITH: Yeah.
> LUANN: Do you save a little bit too, or is it just enough?
> EDITH: [Trans.] We can always put some in the bank. We save to live through the winter in Mexico. As long as we have something in Mexico and go back and forth, then we don't know if we want to buy something here. We always have to pay rent.
> LUANN: And do you have animals in Mexico, and do you farm the land?
> EDITH: No. Nothing. We are just there at our house and visit.

Some Dietsche families, who are able, stay in Canada only for the harvest season. Men, women, and older children work long days in the fields and processing plants, then return to Latin America when the work runs out. Avoiding the cold Canadian winter months permits them to live temporarily in relatively inexpensive seasonal housing, increasing the net earnings (often paid in cash) that they take with them, back to their colony life. For others, the migrant lifestyle is not possible, as they are not able to earn enough to afford the costly trips to and from the south, or they no longer have a place to live when they return to the colony.[9] When faced with these financial constraints, some Dietsche stay for years, working to pay off their debt and to acquire some financial security, and then return. It is not uncommon for families in Canada – who struggled to establish steady employment and income, start their own businesses, buy their own homes, and ensure their children acquire skills beyond those of previous generations – to pack up everything into the family vehicle, and drive for a week, back to their colony in the south. Anna, a middle-aged Dietsche woman, portrayed this migratory disposition:

> ANNA: I am from Cuauhtémoc, Chihuahua. We moved to Paraguay when I was eighteen. Then I got married. And after some years, we decided to move back to Mexico to see how it would work. It was harder than we thought. We were too poor to start a living there. After we finished getting Canadian citizenships, we decided to go to Manitoba and try to make a living there.
> LUANN: So you both have Canadian citizenship?
> ANNA: I do not have. I have Landed Immigrant. Then, after about three years, we decided to move back to Paraguay again. That's where both of

our families live. Manitoba was quite a cold country, and they told us that Ontario wasn't quite as cold as in Manitoba, so we decided to try this.

LUANN: And before you moved to Manitoba, you moved from Paraguay back to Mexico, did you?

ANNA: Yeah, to Chihuahua.

LUANN: And how were things there? You found things pretty hard?

ANNA: Yeah. They were. Well, we were used to being poor, so we pretty much got through it well. My husband worked out, and he earned some. So we could have at least enough to make a living.

LUANN: Did you buy land?

ANNA: No, we didn't. We wouldn't have been able to. No.

LUANN: So your husband worked outside the colony then, did he?

ANNA: Yeah, he did. He built houses, for Mexicans mostly. That work paid well. We had quite enough to get by. Not enough to start our own business or buy some land. There wasn't enough to save.

LUANN: So, you were looking for something when you moved to Manitoba. What was it that you were hoping for, or looking for?

ANNA: Better paying work. We thought for a year we would do that. So we could have our own house, or something. We had never experienced that. That wasn't easy.

LUANN: And so how were things in Manitoba for you? How did that work out?

ANNA: Beautifully! I liked it there, very much! Oh, yeah. We lived and rented. Well, we worked hard there. I did sewing in my home. I had two children. Little children at the time. So, I was sewing for the company, at home. I hardly went to work and we had – finally we had enough so we could buy a house. Only an old one. It needed a lot of repair. So, we decided to buy that since my husband knew how to renovate houses. So we bought that, and after four o'clock when he came home from his work, I stopped my work as well, and we'd start working on the house together. So we had to do this also. We did the whole house. We took some walls out and put some walls some where's else. [Laughter] Made it new from the inside and from the outside. We attached a garage, and whatever we needed.

LUANN: Sounds like you enjoyed working on it.

ANNA: Yeah, we enjoyed it, but we were tired after. Because we sometimes worked to twelve o'clock in the evening, you know. Got up early and started working again, you know.

LUANN: So you went back to Paraguay, though? You didn't stay?

ANNA: Yeah. We sold our house. We sold everything we had. And, you
   know, that's the way we do: we sell everything in one week. We sell
   everything we have, and then we move on. [Laughter]
LUANN: But what took you back to Paraguay?
ANNA: Well, it mostly was our children, our families. Both of our families
   were there. And our children didn't know – didn't even know who their
   grandmother and their grandpa was. And so they had forgotten. They
   didn't know what "cousins" meant. They called everybody "grandma"
   and "grandpa" as long as they were a little older. [Laughter]
LUANN: What a hard thing to do, though! To sell everything?
ANNA: Yeah. It is hard. But you know, you kind of get used to it. We have
   done it before. We sold everything here. And when we moved to Mexico,
   we were there almost two years. Then Manitoba, and back to Paraguay.
   We lived in Paraguay almost six years. And now we've been here about
   two years.

Economics cannot adequately explain this "uncontrolled migration"
[Will, Mennonite immigrant service provider] and such seemingly self-
defeating behaviour. Undoubtedly, there is meaning associated with
work – with *making a living* – that goes well beyond the accumulation
of economic capital.

Making a living

Sustained for generations, the ideal of colony life has been reduced
to little more than a "broken dream" for thousands of Dietsche
(im)migrants. Yet I argue that the social field, system of capital, and
habitus associated with the Mennonite/Anabaptist tradition endure
to varying degrees for most Dietsche (im)migrants in Canada. The
enforcement of Canada's human services and the resulting conflict arising from competing systems of capital severely limit opportunities for
giving expression to the Dietsche disposition. Understanding this conflict is key to understanding self-imposed social exclusion. Thus, the
Dietsche social field and habitus, necessarily adapted and transformed
when confronted with the market-state social field in Canada, is essential to this analysis.

   Certain characteristics define the habitus of the Dietsche Mennonite
social field. I propose that the two consequential and intersecting dispositions specific to the embodied history of Dietsche people are a collective *difference and distance* in relation to the social world around them,

and *submission and proximity* to the necessities of the natural world.[10] These inclinations are apparent in the following excerpt from the reflections of church leader *Ältester* Gerhard Wiebe (1827–1900) regarding the decision of the Bergthal Colony (one of the colonies from which Dietsche Mennonites emigrated) to relocate from Russia to Canada in 1874.

> Yes, dear reader, at that time we still were of "one heart and one soul" because all, whether rich or poor, said, even if we don't get the best land, as long as we can get a spot where we can feed ourselves and our children, and above all where we can follow our religion according to God's Word; and above all that we could have our own schools in order to teach the children God's Word and commandments. (Wiebe, 1981, 33)

Throughout generations, Mennonite religious convictions and material necessity have intersected, such that living within the limits of life's basic needs is virtuous, and righteousness is found in submission to circumstance. The realities imposed by a "theology of migration" (T.F. Guenther, 2000), deriving from the Mennonite commitment to nonconformity and discipleship, reveal the extraordinary imperative of the "rules" of this game, as all species of capital – including, and especially, religious capital (a cultural asset) – are appropriated through a habitus of communal difference and submission to the necessary.[11]

Language, education, and work are intertwined in traditional cultures and religions. The various streams of Mennonite religious faith that stem from Anabaptism are rooted in tradition and history, expressed in a way of life. Mennonite religion is also a tradition, a history, and a way of life that is grounded in faith or religious beliefs. Belief and daily life practices cannot be separated. This coherence was demonstrated repeatedly in conversations with Dietsche (im)migrants. For example, translation of concepts of "faith" or "belief" proved to be difficult, if not impossible, and attempts to inquire about them were often met with uncertain and brief responses. Most (im)migrants, however, were very clear about the "right way to live." Emphasis is placed on obedience to acceptable practices and behaviour, rather than on private, individual beliefs. In this way, Dietsche faith is practical and communal.

Cultural and religious expression in books, art, and music is secondary to the work of daily life, as submission to necessity is central to the Dietsche religious conviction. Difference and distance from worldly ways are sustained in the specific living of the mundane and the necessary: traditional dress; the everyday working language of Plautdietsch

(Cox, 2011); and most important, the family work of farming, making a living, within the social, cultural, and religious boundaries of the colony. The everyday practices of work and submission to necessity form the cornerstone of the Mennonite faith tradition, because work is vital for preserving the right way of living.[12] For the Dietsche habitus, living "so that God will be satisfied," or to be a "good church person" is to work on the land. This esteemed life is one of subsistence farming, whereby the family functions as an economic unit. Even though gender roles are usually clearly defined, the division of labour between men and women is somewhat blurred, as every member of the family is expected to contribute to their daily survival, and all work is valued for its part towards the continuance of their way of life. Thus, Dietsche people describe working to have enough. Many (im)migrants seem indifferent to improving their position in the Canadian labour force or aspiring to "make something of themselves." For example, Jacob and Susana, parents of fourteen children, described their hopes for their family, whether in Mexico or Canada:

> JACOB: [Trans.] I would wish that we could work as much that we could live good. Not overly enough, I wouldn't wish.
> SUSANA: Not that we had overly enough. That I wouldn't wish. Just so we always had enough to live.

Dietsche (im)migrants define themselves as a people set apart. As distinct communities, Dietsche Mennonites strive to be on the outside, segregated, distinct, and countercultural. The Mennonite interpretation of the New Testament teaching to be *"in the world, but not of the world"* demands a different way of life: a collective life of discipleship in agrarian, self-sustaining colonies, in which all members abide by the principles of pacifism, simplicity, and mutuality (Hedberg, 2007). To resist the world is "to stay with what we have been taught," which refers largely to strict adherence to tradition, and preserving – with as little change as possible – all aspects of their communal life, including school, church, clothing, language, and work. Change – to "go beyond what I was taught" – is to go the way of the world. This principle is central to the Dietsche migration story. Agatha, a mother of ten living in southern Alberta, described the challenges of the separated life in this way:

> It seems to me, how would you say it, everything is advancing. In the last ten years, how it's changed with all those cell phones and everything!

So much new stuff. And the Dietsche, the children too, they go and get exactly the same things that everyone else has. They have everything – internet, computers – and they're eager to get it. We were always taught that we should not do as the world, we shouldn't have all that. We're supposed to stay away from what the world has. Of course the world will entice us, but we don't have to have it all. We shouldn't spend money on what isn't necessary.

In the largely self-contained Mennonite colonies in Latin America, educating children is shared between the home and the church, and is necessary for their continued existence as a people. The purpose of school, which is not distinct from the church, is to teach children the values and beliefs of colony life. Too much education – education that is not required to live a traditional farming life in the colony – is considered an unnecessary burden (Hedges, 1996). Hence, parents have a significant role in the education of their children. Young women and girls learn the skills of mothering and homemaking. Boys work with their fathers, learning the skills of farming and animal husbandry.

While non-conformity to the ways of the world is necessary for acceptance before God and church leaders, so too is conformity to the ways of the colony. The communal or *collective life* is rooted deeply in Mennonite heritage. Mennonite colonies in Mexico were first established in accordance with principles of equality and mutuality, as each family unit received the same amount of land to farm, and each village had a common pasture. The tradition holds that to be a Mennonite is to be part of the community, a faith community. This ideal is expressed as *Jemeenschaft*,[13] the everyday yet deeply spiritual quality of these family and community relationships that is fundamental to the centuries-old Mennonite faith tradition. One's consciousness, or sense of self, is collective. The community defines the individual, and the individual belongs to the community, as the church seeks to be "of one heart and one soul" (Wiebe, 1981, 33). This collective or shared self-image has to do with staying separate and different from the world, with more emphasis on eternity than the present. "We were taught that the world is not going [to heaven] where we are going."

Further, to be a part of the community, the church, is to yield – to submit – to higher authorities: God, the church, elders, parents, the community, and tradition. One Mennonite author describes this collective identity and yielding as "a master cultural disposition, deeply bred in the Mennonite soul, that governs perceptions, emotions, behaviour, and architecture" (Kraybill, 2001, 30). The roots of this way of thinking can be traced to the Anabaptists of the sixteenth century, who believed that a dedicated heart would "forsake all selfishness. They believed that Christ called them to abandon self-interest and follow his example of suffering, meekness, humility, and service" (ibid.). Such selflessness requires that individuals do not strive to stand out, think independently, or be their own person. Rather, the best is to blend, to conform, and to submit to the group. Not only are ideals of individualism and competition foreign to this way of thinking; they pose a threat. It is best for the needs of the group to be considered above the needs of any one of its members.[14] Dietsche (im)migrants reported that many adults, especially women, are unaccustomed to making decisions for themselves, as it is better to abide by the conventions and rules established by individuals in positions of higher authority.

A yielding disposition accepts what life brings. And life is suffering. An identity as a persecuted people seems to be genetically inscribed. All groups deriving from the Anabaptist martyrs know this identity.[15] There is even a certain virtue associated with suffering, as the "pilgrim people of God" in all times have had to suffer "for living a non-conformed life of discipleship" (T.F. Guenther, 2000, 169). Echoing the songs and poetry of the Old Testament, lamentations of persecution and hardship are often centrally represented in Mennonite music and literature. This identification is in keeping with the values of self-denial, self-sacrifice, and selflessness. Resignation to the realities of life may mean tolerating conditions or illness – especially mental health or emotional difficulties – that can sometimes be ameliorated or treated. Righteousness dwells in the contrite heart, the yielding spirit.

Submission and collective identity are demonstrated most clearly by Dietsche women. A woman knows herself as wife and mother, and her identity is firmly rooted in the family. It is common for a woman to identify herself by her husband's names, first and last. She is known according to her family relationships. Furthermore, the work of a woman, her role in life, defines her. She may occupy a position subordinate to her husband and to God, but she is vital to the preservation of her people. Tina Fehr Kehler (2004) writes about Dietsche women from Mexico: "[They] come from sacred villages – communities that are organized vis-à-vis the church. In Mexico, their life's work was geared to maintaining the church, community; that is raising children, baking bread and growing a garden were important though unrecognized ways in which the community of faith survived. Though women's work in Canada is no longer conducted in and for this sacred village, they continue to prepare the next generation for entry into the larger church" (22).

Many (im)migrant women demonstrated that their children and their role as mother were paramount for them. Preservation of religious tradition depends on women's work of reproduction – cultural, social, religious, and ethnic. A Dietsche woman knows that her primary responsibility in life is to "raise her children right." Virtually every aspect of life (healthcare, housing, work, and language) relates to caring work, raising children in the ways of her people. In this way, women's reproductive work is also fundamentally – and necessarily – material. This is God-ordained work with which they have been entrusted. To separate her from her family, the church, her people, is to strip her of her identity, of her self.

The Dietsche habitus is oriented towards *making a living* through familial agrarian and homemaking work and informal exchange within the boundaries of the colony. Although many men in Mennonite colonies in Latin America take up waged labour opportunities with Dietsche or Mexican employers, the need to do so is consistently described as a last resort and recalled with a sense of loss. As one Mennonite immigrant practitioner noted, "Being your own boss sort-of-thing is deeply, deeply rooted." These particular livelihood practices are core to the Dietsche social field and way of life. Confrontation with the system of capital in the market-state social field works, necessarily, to undermine and oppose the Dietsche system of capital. For Dietsche (im)migrants, participation in any aspect of Canada's human service system requires trading in the practices, inclinations, and even longings associated with the integrated, collective, and separated life for an individualized, commodified, conformed, and compliant life. This is how the economic habitus is produced.

Earning a wage

The economic habitus is oriented towards *earning a wage* and is the basis of employment-based social welfare systems. This is something quite different from – even antithetical to – *making a living*.[16] Research reports from the United States, New Zealand, the United Kingdom, and Europe draw attention to the inadequacy of low-wage, temporary jobs into which social assistance clients are often forced, and the ultimate failure of welfare-to-work programs to help escape the trap of poverty (E.K. Anderson & Van Hoy, 2006; Blalock, Tiller, and Monroe, 2004; J.B. Brown & Lichter, 2004; Davis, 2004). Further, studies show that successful movement from social assistance to employment results in worsened material conditions for some families, owing to factors such as the loss of health benefits, low wages, high employment instability, and childcare expenses (Scott, Edin, London, & Kissane, 2004). Employment activation strategies are accompanied by bare-bones benefits to those meeting very restrictive eligibility rules through punitive practices. In Ontario, for instance, a 22 per cent reduction in welfare rates has translated into a 40 per cent decline in the purchasing power of social assistance since 1995 (E. Lightman, Herd, & Mitchell, 2008). In most Canadian provinces, welfare reforms have combined cuts to both cash and in-kind benefits such as childcare (Cleveland & Hyatt, 2003). As a result, what has been known as "social assistance" in Canada has taken on a character that is neither "social" in its emphasis nor "assistance" in its delivery. The explicit and solitary goal, for example, of the reworked social assistance programs in Ontario – Ontario Works and the Ontario Disability Support Program – is to "help people move to long-term self-sufficiency" (Government of Ontario, 2005). The values and ideals of a marketized social welfare state – the responsibilities of which have been downloaded, to a large extent, to provincial and municipal levels – are articulated in recurring terms and phrases: "practical help in finding a job," "help determine what people need to become employed," "become self-reliant," "move as quickly as possible to a job," "help get skills needed for today's job market," "achieve economic self-sufficiency," and "escape the cycle of financial dependency." Eligibility is based on "immediate" and "temporary financial need" and one's willingness to participate in "employment assistance activities" (ibid.).

The symbolic power of earning a wage manifests itself in a social welfare system – even a whole society – that is organized by the belief that "hard work pays," or at least paid work pays, and the assumption that social inclusion is realized through labour market engagement of any sort. Yet there is mounting evidence that the relationship between social inclusion and labour market attachment is, in fact, variable and complex. In Canada and most advanced capitalist countries of the world, welfare reform has coincided with labour market restructuring in the globalized economy. In the past three decades, workers all across the globe have been confronted by a general deterioration and narrowing in their employment options. Precarious employment – work that is insecure, offers limited protections and benefits, and allows workers minimal autonomy, recourse, or control – is on the rise internationally, with contingent effects that are often shouldered disproportionately by the most marginalized (Goldring & Landolt 2011; Standing, 2011; Vosko, 2010). Research shows that such trends are resulting in deepening poverty and widening income and wealth inequalities that reinforce the social organization of societies based on gender, citizenship, and race (see, e.g., Standing, 2011; Vosko, Preston, & Latham, 2014).

The common sense belief in the ideal of earning a wage is not entirely unfounded, as there is some truth in the conviction that people without jobs are generally worse off than people who are employed. Yet in the contest for scarce resources in the market-state social field, the volume and structure of symbolic capital are valued according to the characteristics of its holder, and the powers of accumulation and reproduction are carefully protected. This shows up in the uneven effects of globalization and labour market restructuring and preferential employment opportunities and income. Specifically, it is apparent that immigrant status, race, country of birth, gender, and family structure *matter* in the competition for economic and social capital in Canadian labour markets. For instance, while more women are participating in the labour force than ever before, a disproportionately high number of them are working in jobs that are insecure, low wage, without benefits, and part time (Vosko, 2006). The prevalence of low-paid work has risen significantly among immigrants, even those with high levels of education, and their earned incomes and overall economic positions have declined in recent years (Mitchell, E. Lightman, & Herd, 2007; Morissette & Picot, 2005). In Canada recent immigrants and racialized groups are more likely to have precarious work and experience unusually high unemployment rates (Block, Galabuzi, & Weiss, 2014; Goldring & Joly 2014). Furthermore, once in precarious employment, workers are unlikely to move into better working situations within five years (Saunders, 2005). The end result, then, in day-to-day terms is that more and more people the world over are and will continue to be working too much or too little, for less pay, in unregulated and short-term jobs, and with irregular work schedules. Globalizing processes have produced a gendered and racialized global labour force that is deeply divided (J. Lewis, 2007; Mills, 2003; Shola Orloff, 2002). For millions of people in all regions of the world, earning a wage has little to do with making a living.

In between earning a wage and making a living

The various spheres of life, or social fields, are hierarchically ordered. In the current ideological context of global neoliberalism, the market and its particular system of capital are not only dominant, but highly autonomous. That is, the market has gained, in the course of its development, an impressive capacity "to insulate itself from external influences and to uphold its own criteria of evaluation over and against those of neighboring or intruding fields" (Wacquant, 1998b, 222). On the surface, the social field of Dietsche (im)migrants and the market-state social field seem to have similar economies regarding work, as a strong work ethic is materially and symbolically profitable in both. Yet the work-related practices of Dietsche in Canada do not pay off in ways that one might expect. I suggest that such incongruity is a necessary result of the specific economic and symbolic capital of work – of *making a living* in the Dietsche social field, and *earning a wage* in the market-state. In many ways, (im)migrants who encounter Canada's human services – and all clients of the social welfare system, I argue – end up *caught* between earning a wage and making a living in the market-state social field.

In the market-state social system, the habitus of recognition and advancement is necessarily inclined towards the principles of capitalism, the cornerstones of which are individualistic enterprise and competition. The economic habitus is both compelled and free to "stand on his own feet and try his luck" (Fromm, 1941, 61). He is the master of his own fate.[17] The impossibility of such a feat is not called into question. Dietsche tendencies towards collective livelihood practices, acceptance, and submission contradict the symbolic currency of ambition, control and self-determination. Repeatedly, service providers dismissed the traditional, communal and non-conforming Dietsche lifestyle as "backward" and "uncivilized," as it challenges the moral imperative of personal flexibility and adaptability in the face of rapid social and economic change in the global economy.

In a fused market-state social field, clients are made to conduct *individualized lives*. Specifically, even remnants of the collective disposition expressed as mutuality and shared responsibility – values and practices that are diametrically opposed to the residual welfare state – must be used up and cast aside. Marketized social welfare programs require one to be lacking resources from all sources, including family or community members, to be eligible for support. For example, an English service provider explained:

> Well, part of Ontario Works – before an applicant comes in and asks for assistance, they're supposed to look at what other supports they have. What other means of income is there for them? And family members would become part of that. We don't really do anything about that, but the expectation is there. It's just like lots of times when somebody's coming on with us, they want something that's called "community start-up," and they want it now. So they want money to move into a place – first and last month's rent, or whatever. Now our legislation stipulates how we're to give those monies out. However, we would say, "Can your family member help you with that down payment on your rent?" Things like that. So they are supposed to be accessing any support they can get. Whether we ever know about it, that's a different story, because they don't usually divulge anything like that to us.

Individual, self-reliant efforts to provide for one's family must repeatedly fail in order to establish and re-establish eligibility. Revealing more coercive approaches, service providers report that clients are penalized for accepting monetary gifts or loans or "pooling family resources."

> SUSAN: So they are very close-knit, and I would say very hard-working. From the dad to the mom to the children, they all seem to work together as a family unit. They work as a family unit.
> NANCY: But, that's kind of a problem, you know. I find with the Mexican [Dietsche] families, they pool their resources very, very much. If the children are working – adult children, or whatever – they may still live in the home. That's quite often seen. And the children are bringing in monies to that family, the parents.
> LOUISE: That particular family, actually, the daughter works and gives all her money to her parents. That poses a problem for us [social assistance], sometimes. Because if we find out about it and it's going into a parent's account, we're going to look at it as income. And if it's an adult child (we call them independent adults if they're making more than a certain amount of money), we're going to charge that as income as well. [English service providers]

The individualism of economism that forms the basis of social services delivery acknowledges and permits only competitive market interests

and exchanges, disallowing and vilifying any evidence of a cooperative "good-faith economy" (Bourdieu, 1990b, 115). As described in the
following dialogue among English service providers, such communal
relationships and personal transactions, common among Dietsche, are
considered suspect and even fraudulent if conducted by a classified class.

SUSAN: I wanted to mention something else, too. They do get the Child Tax
Benefit. I have some families getting almost $1,000 a month, in Child Tax
Benefit. So, they have a fair amount of income sometimes coming in to
that family. And they don't spend that kind of money. I'm sure it's not
going out. I don't know where it's going. Because I don't think they're
known to spend a lot on their children. So, that makes me sometimes
question, are they hiding what they have in bank accounts?

LOUISE: Are they church supporting? I don't know what they do about
tithing.

SUSAN: I don't think they spend a lot in clothing, obviously. They sew. The
women probably make most of the clothing.

MIKE: Yeah. They distribute amongst themselves in the community.

LOUISE: I think a lot of it must go into the church, or helping other family
members. I don't know.

MIKE: Their house might be an issue because if they're working a whole
harvest season, the whole family, and they're making $10,000 a month or
whatever, they still show up at our door after the harvest season is over.
They claim they don't have any savings or investments.

NANCY: And it was my understanding that the whole family works
together and they save enough money to buy a house for the male child
when he gets married. And then they go on to the next male child. And,
you know, they provide a house for all of their children and that's why
they all work together.

LUANN: It is interesting how their work ethic and their culture of looking
after each other, in some cases, work against them. Is that an accurate
observation?

SUSAN: I think it's an accurate observation. [English service providers]

Thus, any material or social cushion afforded by a fraying Dietsche
collective lifestyle is subverted by the market-state system of capital.
The more dispossession marks a person, the greater the potency of the
forces that divide and isolate. The ideal of the self-made man and the
myth of individualized success can be preserved only through the man-
ufacture of dispossessed social groups and their individualized failure.

Critics of welfare-to-work programs claim that employment-based social assistance is designed to "promote a more mobile work force and to order a more work-ready group of welfare clients for low-wage employment" (Prince, 2001, 11). There is ample evidence that residualized human services, understood in the broadest sense, function to maintain a steady supply of educated and skilled (or uneducated and deskilled), healthy and emotionally stable (i.e., reliable and flexible) workers for the desocialized labour market (e.g., Byrne, 2005; Good Gingrich, 2008, 2010a; E. Lightman, Mitchell, & Herd, 2005; Peck, 1999; Vosko, 2002). Market (im)morality serves to define and valuate all things in its own terms, generating *commodified lives*.

In this case, Dietsche work hard. This was not disputed. Yet most services are explicitly geared towards modifying (im)migrant behaviour in order to affect some change in opportunity and preference for work. Circumstances of difference must be read through a specific system of capital, according to the ethic of the economic market. The work preferred by many Dietsche men is farming – working on the land, planting and harvesting crops, and managing livestock. For women, their traditional place is in the home, caring for children and tending to broadly defined domestic responsibilities that often overlap with the work of subsistence farming. Field work and caring work: both have little value in the left *or* right hand of the market-state social field. Employment as a farm labourer is usually seasonal, unregulated, and low paying. Caring labour, when conducted in one's own home for family members, is made invisible and inconsequential. In market terms, such activity is not counted as work at all. Prince (2001) argues, "The guiding principle for reforming social programs is that they support the work ethic and economic productivity" (6). This is clear. However, it is also apparent that only certain kinds of economic productivity count.

MIKE: Some of the mothers have taken their children and are trying to forge a new life for them.

LOUISE: It's a lonely life.

MIKE: Yeah, but I mean, the two daughters, you know, this one mother made sure they completed their high school. One's going on to post-secondary. One's working at Wendy's. At least it's not working in the fields, you know. And we've got the mother into the Salvation Army now, volunteering. She's doing a community placement there, so she's starting to build her life. [English service providers]

The risk of *inappropriate* work standardizes a specific employment relationship and thereby assembles the "normal" employee or waged subject. These ideas about what is typical – assumed norms upon which
labour laws, legislation, and policies are based – reflect an atypical,
selective reality. This is the Standard Employment Relationship, which
ironically is increasingly rare and non-standard (Vosko, 2010).

In the case of Dietsche (im)migrants, the labour market engagement
required by marketized human services in Canada may have little or
nothing to do with making a living. Moreover, the symbolic power of
earning a wage operates to erase and undermine all other activities –
all other *work* – in which people engage in order to make a living and
define themselves as individuals and as a people. Practitioners from
employment programs, social services, school boards, public health,
mental health, and primary healthcare agreed that a principal goal
of their work is to help people get and keep a job. Thus, the value of
work – especially traditional women's work – and its contribution to
the livelihood of the family is discounted, reduced to the wages her
labour earns. In this case, English service providers describe the work
of redirecting Dietsche (im)migrant women (and men) into low-paying
jobs with poor working conditions in precarious sectors of the labour
market.

JEN: We probably should tell them about our sewing project.

KATHLEEN: Oh yeah. That's a good one.

JEN: We have fifty Low German women sewing out of their own homes for
a company in London. And that was a big project that we just got –

KATHLEEN: A very high percentage of those women had never worked
outside of the home.

JEN: They've never worked outside of the home. Most of them with grade
four education.

KATHLEEN: And they have several of these sewing things, and these ladies
are providing the best quality in –

JEN: The company is really happy with them.

KATHLEEN: – the whole company.

LUANN: Is this for hospital garb?

JEN: Sewing scrubs. All the pieces are delivered to them. They just pick
them up, and then they bring their finished product back. They're
making some money and they're right in their own home, and –

KATHLEEN: They can still meet the obligations of their homes. That's right.
That's so empowering to be earning money, and –

JEN: The company got them their machines, and what they're doing is taking the cost of the machines as payroll deductions. So they had to sign a form just saying they would pay back, I forget – it was $25 a pay, or $20 a pay, or something until the machine is paid for. Some even opted to get a better quality machine, because they felt even if this job came to an end, they would still use the machine. A lot of them sew their own children's clothing, and that kind of thing.

KATHLEEN: And the word is spreading! It's really –

JEN: It's spreading. We have a list of about sixty-five women that have signed on to try doing it once we need more.

KATHLEEN: We had started with using anybody who was interested, and all of the Canadian people dropped out. They didn't work out at all!

JEN: These Low German women are so committed, though. If they say [they] are going to do twenty-five hours a week, they will do twenty-five hours a week. Even if they are in their own home. Where some others may say they will do twenty-five, and do five.

KATHLEEN: Or say, "This isn't worth it." But that's because you have other options. For these ladies there isn't another option, so they're saying, "Oh this is great." So, they're doing it.

On the whole, making a living Dietsch-style is associated with illegitimacy and devaluation. For example, Dietsche seasonal agricultural workers are often paid in cash, "under the table," particularly when children help in the fields. Situated in the "informal economy" and shared by all family members, such work then takes on an illicit quality. Similarly, traditional women's work is disallowed for social service clients, as only waged work that is often precarious, low-wage, unregulated, and dead-end counts for anything at all. Not only are Dietsche (im)migrant roles and identities cheapened; they are made dishonourable and ultimately costly. In a social field organized by market ideals, the Dietsche disposition of proximity and submission to necessity marks Dietsche men and women as unworthy and justifies the denial of social and economic gain in both the social service system and the labour market. In this way, the livelihood strategies of (im)migrants function in reverse, earning negative social and economic returns in all social arenas of Canadian society in which they must engage.

In the left hand of the market-state social field, or the human services system in Canada, Dietsche ingenuity and know-how – or habitus – for making a living is most often read on the surface, from a categorical point of view, and strength and resilience are erased and recast as deficiency and deviance. The contradictory conclusions drawn by service providers give evidence of the paradoxical space that is reserved for social services clients. Courage on the part of Dietsche is seen to be defiance. Resourcefulness is read as fraud. Simplicity is converted to simple-mindedness. Thrift is regarded as deceit. Hard work is made into foolishness. The consequences for Dietsche (im)migrants are profound, as self-preservation turns to self-defeat. Neoliberal ideals and idealism transform Dietsche assets – social, cultural, and even economic – into liabilities.

Further reinforcing the order of things, symbolic capital is tightly tied to economic capital, as "the accumulating of material wealth is simply one means among others of accumulating symbolic power – the power to secure recognition of power" (Bourdieu, 1990b, 131). For instance, the experiences of Dietsche (im)migrants in Canada reveal that a scarcity of symbolic capital severely hinders the accrual of material profits, as access to legitimate means of making money – such as steady and decently waged employment – is cut off for most clients of a residual social welfare state. On the other hand, if one has enough economic capital, other forms of capital are unnecessary or may be automatically (albeit temporarily) endowed. Will, a Mennonite immigrant service provider, described the unreliable worth of economic capital – money – when exchanged for a small bit of symbolic capital from a dispossessed position in the market-state social field:

> There are a number of legal aspects. For example, you need a driver's licence to drive here, and you need an insurance certificate to buy a licence plate. And so they will buy travel insurance over in Texas, and present that certificate over here [in Ontario]. And the agencies here will sell them licences with that travel insurance. But recently, somebody was pulled over and hauled to court because of that. He had just finished buying his licence plates on that insurance certificate, and it was totally valid. There was no problem [when he bought the licence plates]. Yet he was charged $6,000 for driving without insurance. And so it seems that whenever they [representatives of the state] can get money, it's valid. But when they [Dietsche] want to use it, it's not valid.

The function of one's assets, even money, is largely dependent on the total worth of assets held. These are the taken-for-granted processes that function to keep people in place in the labour market and therefore in employment-based social welfare systems. For example, Val, an

English service provider, admitted that material gain may not be possible for social assistance clients in a workfare program:

> VAL: Our agenda is reform because the system before just didn't work. What it did, it was a system that caused people to be irresponsible. The more irresponsible you were, the more you qualified for assistance. And now, the Ministry has done an about-turn. Their philosophy is that this is a system that will make people responsible, because if you're now responsible, you get extra perks. If you are responsible and you do an employment participation, we will give you certain – incentives. You know, if you need work boots, we'll pay for them. Those kinds of things. The only problem with that is, because of the economy thriving as well as it has been for the last five years, we are left with the hard-to-serve. Now, the Ministry believes that success is somebody exiting assistance. We believe that somebody is a success if they would go from being a hard-to-serve client who couldn't get up in the morning, get ready, go to work or placement, or anything like that, that they actually do it.
> LUANN: So that they follow through on the expectations that you have for them.
> VAL: Exactly. That is success to us. Yes, we'd like to have a lot of people exit assistance, through employment, so that they could – carry a job, and not have to be on assistance. The only problem with that is, if the government really wants to be serious about it, they have to look at increasing assistance to the next layer, which is the working poor. Because, quite frankly, sometimes it's worse to be the working poor than it is to be on assistance. They do not give enough incentives to that group of people. So, even though we have all these employment incentives here, and we're pushing people to go back to school, to get voluntary experience to put on resumes and to go out and find a job, once they get a job, most of the time we know it's going to be minimum wage. Second of all, are they any better off than they were on assistance? Well, on assistance, they could get drug cards, things like that. What happens when they become the working poor?

Site effects are powerful. Upward social and economic mobility for clients of marketized welfare systems is made highly unlikely, and a downward trajectory is made next to impossible for large holders of material and symbolic capital. Because economic capital is so tightly tied to symbolic capital, the economic profits associated with waged work in highly polarized labour markets (both global and local) are largely dependent on the personal attributes of the worker. This is demonstrated in the racial, gender, and class patterns that circumscribe low-value and high-value waged work. Furthermore, high levels of education and credentials may have little or no financial return in the labour market for some, and, for many, more paid work does not pay more in the overall share of earnings, in purchasing power, or even in disposable income (Aydemir & Skuterud, 2005; Frenette & Morissette, 2003; Good Gingrich, 2010a).[18] In other words, who gets ahead and who falls behind is not accidental. Consequently, the polarized positions for workers in the labour market are precisely and steadfastly replicated – and at once justified and made inevitable – in the marketized welfare state.

Economic migration to Canada, therefore, requires participation in a marketized social welfare system that is ordered according to a singular market ethic of individual interest, competition, and, above all, material profit and market consumption. This is the moral imperative directing policies and programs in the human services system, and it functions to override and undermine all other strategies for making a living. Programs and services focus on overhauling all economic practices – thus a "whole lifestyle or, better, a whole system of solidary beliefs" – to produce the "so-called 'rational' economic agent" (Bourdieu, 2000a, 18). The dispositions demanded by the economic order appear self-evident, universal, ahistorical, and necessary for modern, even human, existence. All contrary economic behaviours, such as those daily life practices defined by collectivity, submission to necessity, and nonconformity, are to be replaced by the economic logic of waged work. This is the production of the economic habitus. In order to get ahead in the market-state field, it is necessary to abide by the rules of the game – conformity of behaviour, if not thought and belief. In the absence of adequate material and social resources to remain invisible, contradictory and competing social fields collide for Dietsche Mennonites, and advancement in one social arena results in dispossession and exclusion in the other. The (im)migrant is "trapped in that 'mongrel' sector of social space betwixt and between social being and nonbeing," and is "out-of-place in the two social systems" that define the (im)migrant's "(non)existence" (Bourdieu & Wacquant, 2000, 178).

Double jeopardy in between

Ironically, it is when women and children encounter the social worker that Dietsche families are confronted with the full force of the market.

The logic of the market draws lines of inclusion and exclusion, directing attitudes and ways of seeing to determine "which groups and needs are deserving and worthy of support, and which are undeserving and the object of exclusion or stigma" (Prince, 2001, 8). But it is important to note that the lines of inclusion and exclusion operative in the labour market and social welfare system are identical, inscribed by the very same principles of vision and patterned after existing objective divisions. Moreover, there is an immediate fit obtained between structure and agent, as the individuals producing and reproducing the system of capital – the rules to get ahead in the social services system *and* the market – are predisposed to precisely reinforce the social divisions from which they have emerged. These agents, endowed with symbolic capital, necessarily reconstitute the social order that advances and valorizes their own assets and position, and that erodes and devalues the volume and structure of capital associated with all subordinate positions. The intervening state, therefore, functioning through social policies and implemented through the network of social services and regulations, is unable, owing to its fundamental structure, to achieve anything other than the enhancement of market inadequacies and the reinvigoration of market contradictions.

The fusion of the state with the market to form a closed social field, operating according to a singular system of capital, thus provokes a devastating contradiction for many of its citizens: when the only legitimate means of meeting income needs is through waged labour in the private realm, and when the public system of redistribution is directed by market rules of appropriation or gain, those who are excluded from the *primary distribution* of resources (the market) are also necessarily excluded from the *secondary distribution* of resources (the social welfare system). In the unified social field, people who occupy dominated social places in the labour market also and necessarily occupy these same subordinate spaces and dispossessed places in the welfare state. It is unlikely for engagement with social services to effect upward mobility, as its organization and order replicates, precisely, that defined by the market. Marketized social policy and commodified social services are thus organized to reinforce downward trajectories, because "those who are deprived of capital are either physically or symbolically held at a distance from goods that are the rarest socially; they are forced to stick with the most undesirable and the least rare persons or goods. The lack of capital intensifies the experience of finitude: it chains one to a place" (Bourdieu et al., 1999, 127). And the force of site effects remains veiled.

The principles of division in the market-state social field are increasingly extreme and absolute, and we see widening economic and social gaps between individuals, groups, and societies. Social and economic divides are systematically fortified and increased through the rules and practices for gaining and exchanging all types of capital. As the global movement of rich and poor people complicates social identities, these divides must often be negotiated from within competing systems of capital in divergent social fields. The habitus is split. But from subordinate and dispossessed positions, the necessary practices for economic, spatial, sociopolitical, and subjective survival inevitably – by design – reproduce double jeopardy, generate double binds, and reinforce social exclusion. Consequently, social and physical spaces defined by division of enormous scope and paradox of great intensity are self-sustained by the very fractures – between and within – that they produce. The contradictory spaces of social exclusion, and the various double binds that arise, must be negotiated by (im)migrants who engage, out of necessity, in the market-state social field. These practices – both adaptive and maladaptive – will be explored in the following chapter.

Chapter Six

The Practical Sense of Self-Imposed Social Exclusion

When the Dietsche "theology of migration" (T.F. Guenther, 2000) gives way to individual economic migration in order to meet the basic needs of everyday life, competing systems of capital collide. The habitus of *difference* and *distance* does not serve as a fruitful response to the pressing lack of food, clothing, and shelter. The cornerstone of the religious colony way of life – the subsistence production of life's basic necessities through physical labour shared by the family – runs up against capitalist ideals of accruing excess money, personal property, and leisure time. In the market-state social field, the hierarchy of lifestyles, misrecognized as the hierarchy of social classes (Wacquant, 2007), is organized by distance from material necessity. Further, need that cannot be met through market participation or personal resources affects a different (but related) sort of confrontation and engagement with the market-state field. Without the material resources necessary to establish themselves as autonomous, self-sufficient, and therefore "integrated" citizens promptly upon their arrival, some Dietsche (im)migrants accept assistance – usually as a last resort – from Canada's social welfare system. Viewed by most (im)migrants as yet another failure on top of the failure of migration, financial need or mandated intervention forces some families to engage with the market-state social field as social service clients.

Migration offers hope for survival, in all respects. Yet migration accounts from Dietsche (im)migrants describe the spaces with which they are confronted as contradictory, as the terms of inclusion in the market-state social field invite exclusion in their own, and the means for capital accumulation in the traditional Mennonite social field are associated with dispossession in the "secular" world around them.

These are the conflicts, the paradoxes of the everyday and ordinary, that must be negotiated in the divides of social exclusion. For Dietsche (im)migrants, navigation of these contradictory spaces often introduces the conceptual and empirical paradox of *voluntary social exclusion*. In this consideration of the Dietsche inclination towards social exclusion, I aim to zero in on paradox and all its uncertainties and irritations.

At the crux of this inquiry into self-imposed social exclusion is the notion of individual and group agency, of choice. This is a contested topic, and whole theories, philosophies and religions, and economic models are built on various explanations of how people make choices, assumptions of individual free will, and principles of self-determination. Typically, agency is understood to be about subjective, individual experience as opposed to material, social realities. Such binaries of thought and language have fed debates and disputes in academic, political, and professional arenas for years: binaries such as micro/macro, subjective/objective, recognition/redistribution, ideas/materiality, individual agency/structural determinism, self/Other, past/present, and status quo/change. It is easy to become trapped in the simplicity of either/or thinking, in the conventional and arbitrary divides that are familiar. Yet accepting these cognitive divides as truth, as inevitable, tends to reinforce social divides, as we are inclined to take up one side or the other.

Bourdieu's reflexive sociology[1] in general, and his concept of habitus in particular, is somewhat radical, as it integrates a particularly prevalent yet false binary: that of the individual versus the social. The concept of habitus is fundamentally both individual *and* relational, recognizing that humans are not determined by their location in a social order, yet choices are bounded or limited by external social conditions, in particular the relevant system of capital. That is, certain material, physical actualities of existence are associated with a social position, and these everyday facts of life condition or guide the inhabitant of that position – out of necessity, as a matter of adaptation and adjustment – with a particular habitus, or space of dispositions. Rather than privileging individual subjectivity and agency or defending a deterministic view of social structures, "Bourdieu substitutes the *constructed relationship between habitus and field(s)*, that is, between 'history incarnate in bodies' as dispositions and 'history objectified in things' in the form of systems of positions" (Wacquant, 2007, 269). Neither habitus nor field – neither individual agency nor social structures – has the capacity, on its own, to determine social action. Our choices and actions are influenced from within, by subjective experience and individual meaning, *and* objective realities structure our choices and actions from without, shaping subjective experience and meaning. To explain any social pattern or event, such as self-imposed social exclusion, we must consider the relationship *between* the individual and the society – "the conditions under which agents and social fields come to encounter and impinge on each other" (Wacquant, 2007, 269).

This chapter continues our exploration of the relationship between Dietsche (im)migrants and Canada's human services. Here, the emphasis is the nature of the encounter, the confrontation between social identities and the divided social order of the market-state social field. I aim to probe the paradoxes of social divides that give rise to double binds and threaten splits between and within. The overall goal for this chapter is to use the ideas of symbolic power and subjective exclusion to understand apparent expressions of self-imposed economic, spatial, and sociopolitical exclusion. Such an inquiry acknowledges that the paradox, even double binds, wrought by social divides cannot be reduced to the personal, to individual experience, despite the fact that they are intensely lived as such. External divides are translated into internal divides in and through the necessary, everyday negotiations of material and social contradictions.

The paradox of (im)migration

Various concepts are used to describe the global mobility of people, resources, knowledge, and ideas. In an important and recent direction in migration scholarship, theories and methodologies of transnationalism are emerging, inspiring related notions such as simultaneity, hybrid identities, trans-state spaces and activities, and translocalism (e.g., Barkan, 2006; de Haas, 2010, 2012; Faist, 2008; Levitt & Glick Schiller, 2004; Tsuda, 2012).[2] Cañás Bottos (2008b), in reference to the Old Colony Mennonite migrations between the most traditional colonies in Latin America, convincingly argues that these anti-modern groups are "transstatal" rather than transnational, because they maintain membership in a network of colonies – a community and a land base – that is spread across state borders and is "bound by a common agreement, and imagined and maintained through various practices such as publishing, travelling, inter-colony migration, visiting and census practices" (227).

In contrast to the intercolonial, intra-Latin America movements that Cañás Bottos describes and emphasizing the heterogeneous nature of Old Colony groups and migrations, I maintain that the northern migratory flow of Dietsche Mennonites is neither "trans-statal" (Cañás Bottos, 2008b) nor transnational, but rather *supranational*. I make this claim based on three key aspects of the Dietsche social field. First, a central tenet of the Mennonite tradition carried forward from their early Anabaptist forebears is that "their primary allegiance was not to the political kingdoms in which they lived, but to the kingdom of God" (Fast, 2011). Second, as is true for the full range of colony Mennonite groups, identity, ethnicity, and sense of belonging are not so much associated with a nation or a state (see Cañás Bottos, 2008a), but have "been constructed and protected to exist *despite* the nation-state" (Good Gingrich & Preibisch, 2010, 1502). Finally, and this gets to the heart of the matter, this unsanctioned, familial migratory pattern is in sharp contrast in practice and meaning to the church-led colony migrations and settlements of Mennonite history. Families migrate independently, apart from the colony, outside of the church. Dietsche (im)migrants break from the colony heritage and relinquish their colony "citizenship" in their migration to Canada, thus calling into question their commitment and capacity to remain "separate from the nations that were promoted by the states where they settled" (Cañás Bottos, 2008b, 228).

Yet, paradoxically, Dietsche (im)migrants in Canada express and demonstrate that, as in their past, migration is about *preserving*, even as it threatens to destroy. For example, obtaining "papers," or Canadian citizenship, is an essential livelihood strategy, as legal status provides an accessible alternative resource base if family provision in the colony becomes impossible. A young couple who had recently migrated to Ontario and were planning for their future explained:

EDITH: Well, we want to have our own land.

HEIN: If we had money, we would have bought land [in Mexico].

EDITH: But we didn't have money, so we couldn't.

INTERVIEWER: Is that a reason you are in Ontario, to try and get money together to buy a farm there?

HEIN: Well, if we had luck like some people, we would say yes. But the hope is a long way, so we can work with our citizenship and then maybe something ... We were poor there and the houses over there are very scarce. And later we might want to come back to Canada if it should not work out in Mexico, that for all those that come after, like the children we would have. If we didn't do it now, then our citizenship would all be for nothing, and then we wouldn't be able to make our children citizens. And through that we came to the decision that we would come here. It is far thinking, but –

There are some Dietsche (im)migrants whose material and social resources permit them to settle in Canada, for a time, without notice. With or without official residency status, income from paid work (most often fieldwork) combined with assets accumulated prior to migration provides enough for them to continue a somewhat separate and distinct lifestyle without need for support from outside the family and Dietsche community. But for most who have been driven north by poverty, the meagre wages and precarious conditions of the employment available to them, especially in the first few months of settling, are not adequate to meet even very basic needs. It is at this point that confrontation occurs. To participate in any aspect of the public sector, including voluntary or mandatory receipt of the thinning services and resources offered by the left hand of the state, is to be situated in the fused market-state social field. The terms and conditions for legitimate apprehension of material and symbolic capital in this field must be accepted, or entrance to even the lowest social positions is denied.

The paradoxes of (im)migration are numerous, impacting every aspect of daily life. Dietsche (im)migrants report that, in their experience of the confrontation between conflicting social fields, the survival they seek – stability of the family, continuance of the church and preservation of their way of life – is threatened by the imposed and rigid divisions between home, school, church, and work in Canada. In Canada, where farm labourers are in demand and the wages are considerably higher than in Latin America, the field work that is readily available is hope – hope for both physical survival and religious survival. But in the fields of rural Canada, making a living becomes earning a wage, and assigned subordinate positions in the labour market and broader society leave (im)migrants vulnerable to exploitation.

Moreover, traditional gender and generational roles are disrupted when waged labour is the only form of recognized work. Many (im)migrant parents expressed appreciation for the economic gains and educational opportunities for their children in Canada. Yet with mandatory public school attendance for children and the decoupling of women's caring work from sustaining work, families are separated in their daily lives. Limited work and social activities for children and teens result in boredom and sometimes misbehaviour, and women share little time and few activities with their husbands and children, which often leaves women isolated. Edith, a forty-four-year-old mother of twelve who returns to Mexico with her family every winter, described the sacrifices that are bound up with the benefits of learning "so much" in Canada. At the ESL program for women she attends, she learned English, but she also came to believe that it is important "that a wife gets the thought that she is also a person, just as someone else." Yet she worries that her daughters are not learning what they need to know to make Dietsche lives for themselves, because "the girls are taught more over there," in Mexico, about how to live right. With some bitterness, she noted that even when her daughters are grown, "their housework is still all mine," because in Canada, they either go to school or go to work.

Further dividing people and practice, church life is split off from everyday life, and families must make decisions for themselves. Outside the closed and integrated colony life, it becomes harder to keep out the world and almost impossible to protect their home and children from worldly influences. Work thus sustains *and* divides; migration preserves *and* destroys. Women and men find themselves in between – in between the sacred and the secular, in between conflicting social fields and systems of capital. Helena described the contradictions of in between, and was clear about her preference, when she is free to make her own decisions:

> I came to Canada for the first time in 1992 and we lived in [rural Ontario]. My husband was working on a chicken crew, and then we moved to [a town further south] and there he worked in grapes and the children attended school. They really liked their teacher, but my husband had had enough and so then in 1994 we returned to Mexico. But he had enough of that soon too, and so two years later we came back. The teachers were really happy that we were back, that the kids were back in school. Everyone was happy. But the children were growing up and when our oldest was in grade eight, then my husband, he didn't want our children to go to high school because then they would lose their Dietsch-ness completely. So then we returned to Mexico and stayed there for three years. Then for five years we came here every summer to work and returned to Mexico for winter at the end of October. For five years. So now my husband died in Mexico, and now I'm back here. And I'm staying.

In daily life, the confrontation of competing and contradictory social fields presents more than a mismatch or clash of values and ways of living life; these are the *double binds* of migratory livelihoods.

Double binds and internal splits

Judith is a mother of ten who, with her husband and children, has engaged in circular migrations between the sacred and the secular: from a colony in Mexico, to rural Ontario, to the Durango Colony in Bolivia, and then to rural Alberta. She described the double binds of economic migration:

> [Trans.] My parents were perhaps two, three, six years old when they moved from Saskatoon – that's where they were born – to Mexico. They taught us that we weren't supposed to return. They had removed us from there, and we weren't supposed to return. But because there wasn't land [in the colony], people just didn't have land, there wasn't work, people were returning anyway. And we often feel bad about that. Our parents instructed us: Don't. You're not supposed to. They taught us that way, but we did anyway. Mostly, we worry about that. We didn't obey, we didn't do as they taught us, but we had to! We also wanted to provide for our family. Our parents died long ago. Did we do right? They told us not to, but we did. It's *confusing*, isn't it?

Double binds arise when the strategies of necessity in one social space are associated with disapproval and rejection in the other. Dietsche (im)migrants experience the double binds of contradictory social spaces in the passing down to one's children a way of living and being and surviving: when all that you are and believe in and have for your children will serve to perpetuate and intensify double binds for them. This is the double bind of inheritance, and it was articulated clearly in the dilemmas parents encounter in raising children Dietsche in Canada. Aganetha, a mother of five young children, reflected on the struggle of making a life for her children that challenges her religious, cultural, and familial roots:

> Right now we are trying to figure out what church to go to, and we know that there will be people that won't like it. And then it's hard to not know exactly what to do if you know that there are people that won't be happy

with it. But you have to do it for your own family. You have to do what's best for your family. You can't go back [to the colony and the Old Colony church] for somebody else, what they want you to do. You have to do what's best for you and for your children.

The Plautdietsch language is a vital expression of an enduring faith-tradition, separation from the world, and cultural identity. An inherited language holds "everything which belongs to the art of living, a wisdom taught by necessity, suffering and humiliation" (Bourdieu, 1984, 394). Parents demonstrated and described deep ambivalence about preserving and transmitting their traditional way of life, especially their traditional language, to their young children. Attending school requires children to learn a language that undermines the structure and relationships of the nuclear and extended family, as well as Dietsche culture and religious heritage. At the same time, Plautdietsch is not useful in the world around them. Moreover, some women, especially, know that preserving the Plautdietsch language and Dietsche culture and religion, which demands separation from the world, leads to intense isolation in Canada (Good Gingrich & Preibisch, 2010). Some Dietsche parents expressed their struggle, even pain, as they watch their children gradually abandon Plautdietsch and thus turn away from the colony way of life. Yet Dietsche parents rely on the English language and cultural skills of their children, and they often spoke proudly of their children's accomplishments in Canada. For instance, Eva, a mother of four, described her desire for her children to speak Plautdietsch to ensure continuity with her family and tradition; while Abe, her husband, prefers they learn English and sever ties with colony life to spare them the pain that he endured.

LUANN: So your children speak English with their friends?
ABE: Yeah.
LUANN: Do they speak Low German?
ABE: A little bit. Not too –
EVA: They do understand more than they – they never really talk in [Low] German.
LUANN: So you don't speak Low German at home to your children?
ABE: We do. Oh, well not – I do not as much. [Laughs]
EVA: We do. I still do, yeah.
LUANN: Would you like them to know Low German? Or doesn't it matter to you?

EVA: Yeah, I would like it. When we go back to Mexico to visit our parents, I would like that they can talk to their grandparents.

We came back to the topic of language a little later in the conversation, and this time, the man of the house spoke with conviction:

ABE: I know that it will be difficult, but I just don't want them to be suffering so much, as I did.

LUANN: So, not knowing how to read?

ABE: No reading. No writing. Then the language. Why the language is so important to me, why I speak English to my children, is because I – we grew up in German, you know – We spoke Low German at home. Church and school was a different language, High German, which we could not understand. And besides, the kids and mom stayed home. Dad spoke Spanish. Mom and the kids could not learn Spanish. And I think now, as I see life, growing old, for me, my kids have to speak in the language that's out –

LUANN: The world around them?

ABE: Yes.

LUANN: And why is that important to you?

ABE: So that they can do business. Just for example, Anna [his oldest daughter]. She wants to be working. She wants to work in an office where they get the 911 calls for the police officers. And she needs high education for that. She has to speak the language. But if I would say, "Anna, you can't speak English, only in school. At home, you speak Low German." She would never get to that point because I held her back.

Mingled with expressions of fresh possibility and "freedom" in Canada were often traces of inner turmoil and fear that comes with teaching your children to leave behind – to choose to reject – all that you are:

ABE: The teachers, they're really telling me I care a lot for my kids. My oldest daughter, she's on top of the school. She's doing very, very well! But that is not easy for me, you know, to teach my kids to get them to that point, you know? It's very, very, very, very difficult. Because I grew up so different. There [in the colony], there is no help from schools, no parents' help, nothing. It's so – should I say – careless. Or should I say they don't know better? Or what – I'm not quite sure what I should say. But sometimes I think that they don't know better. Because they grew up the same way.

LUANN: And you're trying to do things differently for your children –

ABE: Yeah.

LUANN: – than your parents did for you?

ABE: Yeah.

LUANN: That's a hard thing, isn't it?

ABE: Oh, yes. Unreal.

LUANN: To change. To raise your children in a way that's different than you know.

ABE: Sometimes you almost break down. That's how hard it is. And you stand up again, and go ahead. And for me and Eva [his wife], we think the school's the most important thing in life right now.

LUANN: So you really value education and the education that your children are getting?

ABE: Yes. Yes.

In the face of double binds, people come to be divided within themselves. The day-to-day experience of irreconcilable paradox, of coincident gain and loss, "is at the heart of a system of dispositions that is itself contradictory and divided against itself" (Bourdieu et al., 1999, 383). In the fused market-state, even temporary material need that cannot be met through engagement in various private realms, including the market and informal social supports, forces confrontation between contradictory social positions and fields. This confrontation, brought on by failure to sustain the *appearance* of self-sufficiency and autonomy, sets in motion the dividing practices that split the habitus against itself. Double binds can be resolved through complete disengagement from, or full conformity to, the dominating system of capital, the rules of the game. But a split in the habitus is forced when neither strategy of resistance is possible.

For those who experience the double bind of conflicting social fields and spaces, the process of rebuilding dignity (respect for self) and honour (respect from others) – and thus resisting and pacifying shame – involves at least partial "submission to the dominant values and to some of the principles on which the dominant class bases its domination, such as recognition of the hierarchies linked to educational qualifications or to the capacities they are supposed to guarantee" (Bourdieu, 1984, 395). A "cleft habitus" is a "product of the 'conciliation of contraries' which then inclines one to the 'conciliation of contraries'" (Bourdieu, 2007, 103). A divided (im)migrant habitus has adapted – but only in part – to new and often contradictory rules of appropriating capital, and it has ambivalently adopted practices consistent with furthering one's place in the new social field.

People thus come to be divided from others when social distinction is necessary to get ahead. Aganetha described the social strife made necessary in the double bind, as she struggles to preserve extended family relationships on the one hand and her own family and sense of self on the other:

AGANETHA: My children's lives are way different than mine was. I wish I could even, just even be better. If I could just be stronger, and – To be strong for them if they need me, that I can be there for them.

LUANN: Has your mom been supportive of you in making these changes for yourself?

AGANETHA: My mom is okay with it, but not on my husband's side. If they would support [us], it would be a lot easier. Because I think we would have made changes sooner. And he still isn't quite sure. He says he wants what's best for his family but he knows that his parents won't like it and won't be happy with it. And now, he is saying that he's okay with it. He says "I just have to do what's best for my family. I can't hold back anymore." It is hard. Like at home, it's fine [to not wear traditional clothing], but if his parents come around, then it feels like they stare at you and you just feel uncomfortable around them. And if we go to his parents' house, then I put on what I usually do. And I don't know, I always feel different, or I feel like they kind of look at me a different way. But the thing is, the clothes won't bring you to heaven. But if there's nobody to support [me], then it's tough.

LUANN: It's hard to do what you've done. And it takes a lot of courage.

AGANETHA: Oh, yes. Like for me, it's hard to make changes. I grew up in those things, and that's the way I learned. They always say, "Stay on what you have learned." But there are some things – I just don't like the way it was, and I want to make changes. I'm still working on those, and it's not easy.

Reflecting the gaping social divides of Latin American societies surrounding them, Mennonite colonies, especially those that have embraced some measure of modernization and engagement with the world (Fast, 2012), are increasingly fractured in economic, and therefore social, terms. This divide within the colony reveals that the colony disposition offers disparate life chances from opposing social positions within the Dietsche social field, inducing and reinforcing internal conflicts. For example, within the same colony, large and lucrative farms sit across the road from dilapidated shacks: wealth and poverty are uncommonly close neighbours. The unsettling of the Dietsche social field due to growing economic disparity forces confrontation within, between oppositional social positions. From the unusually severe deprivation of dispossessed places in the divided Dietsche social field, a disposition of inward conformity and outward non-conformity is not effective in providing the material necessities of life within the colony in Mexico. Moreover, coherence and continuance of habitus is possible only for the few who possess adequate economic capital, as a habitus of difference and distance is self-defeating in the absence of the basic material assets needed to sustain physical life. Deep social divides within the Dietsche social field generate paradoxical burdens, a habitus that is divided against its self.

A divided, out-of-place habitus is demonstrated most basically in the migratory livelihoods that seek to hold onto the ideal of colony life. Emigration from the colony clearly signals a movement *away* from the Dietsche habitus and the cherished heritage *towards* a different life. To leave the colony is to be lost to the world. In the early years, colony emigrations posed a significant threat to the continuance of the Old Colony church in Mexico, and migration to Canada was often met with excommunication.[3]

Sometimes, when people make a decision [to leave the colony], what they do in Mexico, they give you an *Utschluss*. Then you're not part of the church. An excommunication. Then you can't come back to the church. You're not welcome in the colony anymore. And nobody will do business with you. And besides, you have to go talk to the pastor, to make it right. And if you're sorry for what you have done, then you can come back. When you have an excommunication, if you have an *Utschluss*, then you go to hell. [Aganetha, Dietsche (im)migrant]

Although it was reported that excommunication is rarely applied to families who leave the colony to migrate north, the threat of social death seems to hover over many Dietsche people who try to find their own way, without sanction of the church, in Canada.

Under the burden of economic hardship and widening disparity, intensifying destabilization marks the Dietsche social field, diminishing its autonomy and distinction. More and more people are subject to all forms of social exclusion in every field. From places of dispossession, efforts to accumulate material and symbolic capital in the market-state social field operate to divest the self of material, social and cultural capital in the Dietsche social field, causing divisions between and within.

Helen was a cooperative and eager client. I was told that she made the most of the services that were provided to her. With the help of social workers and health professionals, she was able to make significant changes in her life. She had a quick mind, and learned to speak English well enough to communicate to the cashiers in the grocery store and even teachers at school. She was learning to read, for the first time in her life. She was receptive to information and advice about birth control and made the unusual decision to have only three children. While she still always wore a skirt and a head covering, she stopped sewing traditional dresses for herself. She made sure that as her children reached school age, they would regularly attend the local public school – even when the cruelty of other children left them fearful, begging to stay home. And most important, she left her controlling and abusive husband and with her children found a place to live. To meet the job preparation requirements of Ontario Works, she attended an education and ESL program for Dietsche women three days a week.

I met Helen when I was visiting this program in preparation for conducting my research. In her high-heeled boots, denim skirt, and long hair left flowing down her back, her place in the group was not readily apparent, as her appearance was more similar to the English teachers than the Dietsche students. My role that day was to teach a class on child nutrition, and I needed a translator. Helen was a somewhat shy but willing volunteer. It was clear that her language skills were well beyond those of most of the other women attending the program. She approached me after the class, an extraordinarily daring gesture for a Dietsche woman. And we chatted.

I asked the group leaders about her at the end of the day. I was interested in interviewing Helen, because she stood out as an unusual woman in her community. I learned that, like most Dietsche women who leave their abusive husbands, she was an outcast among her own people. Women and men alike refused to speak with her. Especially among more traditional groups, men regard single women as free for the taking. When she feared for her own safety and the safety of her children, she had gone into hiding. She moved. She changed and delisted her phone number. The teachers and social workers at the program reported that they were pleased, however, as she and her children seemed to be managing quite well. With the occasional use of the food bank, she was able to get by on social assistance. It was noted that she was appearing

more self-assured, making "good" decisions, acquiring new skills and knowl-
edge, and demonstrating increasing independence and autonomy. Unlike
many Dietsche women caught in the horrors of domestic violence, Helen had
been unusually responsive to and compliant with the interventions of service
providers. She had done everything right.

I returned a few months later. When I asked if I might contact Helen to
request her participation in my research, I was told that she had disappeared.
No one had heard from her for weeks. Shortly after my earlier visit when I
had first met Helen, she had stopped attending ESL classes, which meant she
could no longer collect benefit cheques from Ontario Works, her only source
of income. Even the Plautdietsch-speaking service providers, who had worked
with the family since they had arrived in Canada, did not know what had
become of her and her children. Some assumed she had returned to Mexico:
to her colony, to her husband, and to the desperation that had driven her to
Canada in the first place.[4]

Out-of-place shame

The cleft habitus is vulnerable to shame. In the contradictory spaces
of social divides, shame arises in the recognition (or misrecognition)
of one's place as devalued and dominated and in assuming one's self
to be "naturally," yet paradoxically, placed out of place, dispossessed
and shameful. Shame is "that self-defeating emotion that arises when
the dominated come to perceive themselves through the eyes of the
dominant, that is, are made to experience their own ways of thinking,
feeling, and behaving as degraded and degrading" (Wacquant, 2004,
393). Along with other "bodily emotions" such as humiliation, timidity,
anxiety, guilt, anger, and "impotent rage," shame is "triggered by the
magic of symbolic power" (Bourdieu, 2004, 341) and the dispossession
of symbolic capital. The magic of symbolic power lies in its disguise,
so that it is not recognized or known as power or violence at all. Social
exclusion generates in-between spaces, a "magical frontier between
the dominant and the dominated" (ibid.). Such in-between spaces are
magical because all manner of illusion looms large here, and faith in
myth appears necessary. Paradoxically, it is through the practicality
of shame that the "dominated, often unwittingly, sometimes unwill-
ingly, contribute to their own domination by tacitly accepting the limits
imposed" (ibid.). The struggle of shame, of handing over the definition

of one's self to the dominating other, can be heard in the following dialogue with a young Dietsche couple:

LUANN: What didn't you like about English classes?

EVA: I don't know.

ABE: Well, we found it very funny, you know. There are two ladies in the Mennonite church here, that teach stuff, you know. They had, with their seven ladies and seven men there, and all sitting around one table, and they took their pictures of corn and tomatoes. And you had to say, "This is corn." [Laughter] You had to tell each other that, you know, back and forth. And we thought it was very silly, you know? But that's where we started. We didn't know how to say it, "corn" and "bread" and – And all that kind of stuff. But that's how we started out. We felt like children. Very much!

EVA: Like for us. Once we are married, and we are parents, then to go to school, that's not something we are used to in Mexico. That's very different.

ABE: They treated us very nicely and very kindly. But we thought, you know, we are Mennonites coming from Mexico. They thought we were just kids, you know, children. It was not fun. But now we see what came out of that, you know. Now we see more than a while back.

LUANN: Right. So they were kind, but it felt like they didn't respect you as –

ABE: As an adult.

LUANN: But then later, you did take more English classes?

EVA: Yeah, and then we had it in a Mennonite church. There were a few ladies who came a few hours a day. And we had there some classes. More through the week.

LUANN: Did those times feel different than the classes before? Did you feel that you were treated differently, or was it much the same?

EVA: I don't know. But I think we were more used to it. I think we were really more used to that. We had been here a little bit longer and we got used to it a bit more.

ABE: And they were there for a very big reason. It was just the very beginning that we felt that it was a really a slap at us. We felt it that Canadian people don't – they thought we didn't know anything. They just treat us – they treat us the way of kids, you know. But that very soon changed.

LUANN: It changed?

> ABE: Very soon! Very soon, because we learned then – see, it's not for
> everybody the same, you know? Some people they – it takes them longer
> to accept that. But for me and my wife, it was very soon that we thought,
> "Oh, that's important for us. She is treating us right." She is, yeah. She
> wants to help us.
> LUANN: So you tried to understand it in a more positive way?
> ABE: Yeah.

Shame reveals an internal split, a division within and against one's
self that operates to reproduce dividing practices, enacting a replica of
the external reality. Likewise, shame is etched in physical space, and it
shows itself in what Wacquant (2000) calls "territorial stigmatization."
Competition and conflict come to define those spaces, as people are pit-
ted against one another for their survival and escape. Any sense of "us,"
expressions of communal bonds, and forms of mutuality are weakened.
This, in turn, "fuels a retreat into the sphere of privatized consumption
and strategies of distancing ('I am not one of them') that further undermine local solidarities" (ibid., 114). From these in-between spaces, the
rejection of self and others who occupy dominated places is inevitable.
A Mennonite immigrant service provider described the struggle for
subjective distance that occurs within groups:

> WILL: Oh, you know what happens. A kid is picked on one year. Next year
> there's a new kid that gets picked on, and the one that was picked on last
> year wants to assert himself and doesn't want to be picked on, so turns
> and picks on the newcomer. "You blow out somebody else's candle and
> mine glows a little brighter" kind of mentality is here among us as well.
> LUANN: Like an adult form of bullying.
> WILL: Yes. Yes.

Shame, a recurring theme in the narratives and demeanour of
Dietsche (im)migrants, gives testimony to the force of the market-state
social field and its social order as it grows in those who have absorbed
the social archetype as the personified principles of inclusion and exclusion, good and bad. To borrow Bourdieu's language, dispossession of
capital in a foreign social field automatically negates any "home advantage," because the attempt at play, and subsequent placement out-of-
place, is, in effect, leaving "home." From positions of dispossession
in the market-state social field, shame is expression of a fundamental
belief in the myth of the idealized included subject. Yet the (im)migrant

necessarily carries the habitus of their "native world," giving rise to an out-of-place habitus at "home" *and* "abroad," or "there" and "here." This is a double shame, or "shame twice over" (Bourdieu et al., 1999, 572). There is shame in being "here," as

> there is always someone to ... make you say to yourself ... you don't have to be here, you're not wanted here, it's not your place ... The second shame is over there; it's having left there ... it's having emigrated. Because whether you like it or not, even when everyone hides it, hides it from themselves, even when no one wants to know anything about it, *emigrating always remains an error, a fault.* You do everything to get forgiven, and to pardon this necessary "fault," this useful "fault," this "fault" you don't want and which no one wants to be a "fault." That's the emigrant's "shame," and he is, like it or not, [the] "shame" of himself, the "shame" of his people. (Bourdieu et al., 1999, 572; emphasis in original)[5]

The indignity of symbolic violence operates at the most basic level of human existence. The means for physical, material survival cannot be differentiated from cultural and religious survival, because abiding by the rules and expectations of the dominant system can leave people cut off, severed from the practices they know, whether physical, cultural, or religious, in order to make a living. Mennonite immigrant service providers explained:

> SUZANNE: Very often those who went to Canada, when they came back [to Mexico], they were sort of looked down upon as the ones who hadn't quite made it out there. When you came back, your inferiority complex was – You were looked down on even more, because you were one of the ones who couldn't make it out there. You couldn't make it without coming back.
> CORNELIUS: Yeah, people go through real trauma that way. They're not really accepted here. They're not accepted there anymore.
> SUZANNE: They really don't have an identity anymore, so to speak. They're not one. They're not the other.
> MARIE: Fringe. Real fringe.

Shame can be brought on swiftly and unexpectedly when confronted with a foreign system of capital. In such circumstances, a misreading of the rules of the game is inevitable, thereby giving rise to the sudden and self-conscious realization that one's self is a "fish out of water." An

abrupt stripping of symbolic capital necessarily accompanies this placement out of place.[6] Caught in the contest between physical survival on
the one hand, and cultural/religious survival on the other, family relationships, roles, beliefs, and values are brought into question.

Turning away from self

The internalized double bind, or shame, seeks resolution, as the appearance of coherence is available in disavowing – splitting self and rejecting, disowning, as if they never existed – one's past, one's people, one's
self. The double bind may be resolved by turning away from *"staying
with what we have been taught,"* precisely opposing the essence of the
Dietsche disposition that has sustained a cultural and religious tradition for generations. But their tradition is also a way of life that has
let them down. A deep sense of disappointment in her heritage, perhaps even betrayal by her own people, was apparent throughout Justina's narrative as she described the life she has made for herself. She
migrated to Canada with her family when she was a young girl. She
has not returned to Mexico for visits and has little or no contact with
family in Mexico. She has discarded traditional dress and chose to conduct her interview in English. It appeared that there was little of value
in the colony for her: no land, no family connections, no language, no
traditions. In Canada, Justina unequivocally demonstrated a desire to
assimilate to English ways, preferring to live in town rather than the
country, expressing distaste for farm work, freely engaging with the
local community, expressing strong opinions and a sense of personal
entitlement, and choosing not to pass on the Plautdietsch language and
traditions to her children. She has adopted a more fundamentalist and
evangelical religiosity and values this above extended family relations.
Justina no longer engages in any form of migratory practice, and has
adopted new religious thought and ritual, unreserved secular engagement, and a non-traditional individual assertiveness.

Perhaps giving evidence of repeated collisions with market forces
over the years, some Dietsche (im)migrants have rejected their heritage of a collective, practical religious tradition and have sought symbolic profits by appropriating the personal and private belief-based
religion of evangelical denominations. A "modern" religiosity has also
been thrust upon them, as Mennonite missionaries from less traditional
groups have toiled to "revive" the Old Colony church in Mexico through
preaching and teaching a more zealous religion that emphasizes the

assurance of individual salvation only by way of a "personal relationship with Jesus Christ" (Quiring, 2003). Many in Mexico and in Canada have accepted an individualized Christianity, thus opposing the traditional expression of faith through a communal commitment to a traditional lifestyle (B.L. Guenther, 2004).

For some (im)migrants, the negotiation of contradictory rules of the game and the incompatible but necessary practices to get ahead are too difficult to endure over time, and they gradually discard practices of the colony; to the extent possible, they adopt one life over the other. Yet the double bind persists, because to reject the inheritance is to be left, in the moment, without an inheritance to bequeath. For example, it is both despite and because of Abe's resolve to have his children surpass him that he ambivalently reverts to his colony inheritance.

> ABE: Sometimes we feel a little bit left out. [Laughs] Because, you know why? We feel lonely sometimes, because we grew up as Mennonites, and totally different than here, you know. And now we have to see a different people, and they don't really understand our – what we speak. It's very hard. Some people cannot understand. That hurts. That hurts. And how to deal with that stuff? We think different than they do. But sometimes it's almost breaking down. Yeah, in that spot there. [He holds his fist to his chest.]
>
> LUANN: So it's hard not having people who understand your struggles, the things that are hard for you. If there were Low German people in this area, would they understand?
>
> ABE: Not really, because there are no Low German people who are the way that we are.
>
> EVA.: They're still in the Old Colony [church]. They're different. They don't really –
>
> ABE: Sometimes I try to speak to some Low German. They say to me, "I see what you're saying, but you have to come back to the Old Colony church. Then you'll feel better." And that is not it. They really try to get us back. I said, "What's the point?"
>
> LUANN: So you feel left out of the Low German people, and left out of the English-speaking people. Is that right?
>
> ABE: That's right. You have very lovely people around, and they want to try and do the best for us as what they can. But sometimes they're – because our language is not quite there yet, the English. And most of these people didn't go through what we went through as we grew up, and all of that. And we are different. And the only reason why we do this, go through

this hard life is to be there for the kids. Many, many, many, many, many times I think I want to be in a different place than I am right now. But I will do this, because I want the best for my kids.

LUANN: Where would you like to be, if you could have the best for your children and be where you want to be? Where would that be?

ABE: I would go back to Mexico.

LUANN: Would you?

ABE: Yeah, just to show our parents we love them. But I do see, if we would go back, my children won't get their education. Never. Never.

LUANN: No. So what would take you back there, if you could?

ABE: Our parents. We miss our parents a lot. That's for sure.

LUANN: So, it's hard being here when they don't want you to be here. Is that right?

ABE: That's right. That especially.

LUANN: You've gone against them in what they want. Yeah?

ABE: And I feel when I speak to them about something, I feel if I would have an accident here or something like that, they would say, "Oh, you shouldn't be there. That's why this happened." And we would have to hear all that kind of stuff, probably.

LUANN: So, you'd like to do what they want you to do. You'd like to please them. Is that right?

ABE: Not really any more. I would like to show them the way – because they don't know us as well anymore. Because I would like to show them respect, better than I did before. And just to show them that even if we do things different, we still love them. We still love them. And even if we think different than they do, then we will show them more our love that we have.

LUANN: So you'd like to show them that there's another way?

ABE: Yeah. There's another way to live than they do.

To believe in inclusion from spaces of exclusion is to believe in conflicting systems of valuation and perceiving and living and being, both at the same time, all of the time – which is, of course, impossible. It is to be forced to choose without really choosing, vacillating in between. It is to be caught in the nothing of *entredeux* (Cixous & Calle-Gruber, 1997).[7]

Some Dietsche reconcile the conflict by striving for higher ground in the dominant social field and turning against members of their own group. Such efforts were expressed in boastful accounts of self-importance or claims of distance and difference from common negative stereotypes. These expressions of self-promotion were usually accompanied, ironically, by disparagement of Dietsche people and their cultural and religious tradition. For example, one Dietsche father admitted to feeling embarrassed that he is unable to read. Later in our conversation, he described overcoming his struggle with alcoholism, a struggle that continues for his father and several other men in his family. Yet he repeatedly referred to "Mexican Mennonites" in the third person, describing "them" as illiterate people who "drink a lot." Wacquant (1998b) notes the "struggle between classes (and class fractions), as each tries to gain control over the classificatory schemata that command the power to conserve or change reality by preserving or altering the representation of reality" (225). This struggle between manufactured kinds occurs within groups when occupants of subordinate social fields or positions must borrow dominant principles of judgment and exercise them against themselves in order to improve their dominated position in the preferred social field: "Thus the dominated have only two options: loyalty to self and the group (always liable to relapse into shame), or the individual effort to assimilate the dominant ideal which is the antithesis of the very ambition of collectively regaining control over social identity" (Bourdieu, 1984, 384).

The most remarkable example of self-contempt was demonstrated by a potential participant in the failed and prolonged process of setting an interview time. Several service providers had referred me to this individual, whose reputation as an interpreter for the courts is both notable and notorious. She is Dietsch, but has married an English man who works as a public servant. She was recognized by some as a traitor and by others as a champion of her own people. Several Mennonite immigrant service providers commented that they knew her best for her translation inaccuracies – or manipulations – to bring about a certain outcome in the courtroom. It was suggested that she and her husband collaborated as an unusual "law and order" tag team that was exceptionally effective in criminalizing Dietsche (im)migrants. While she successfully dodged every scheduled interview, our numerous phone conversations revealed that she held Dietsche (im)migrants in considerable contempt, yet her position and work in the market-state field prohibited complete erasure of her Dietsche identity. I concluded that my request for her participation in my study with Dietsche Mennonites posed a threat to the fragile coherence of her social world and the position she has come to occupy. For members of subordinate and racialized groups, co-optation and betrayal cannot be separated (Adams, 1999). When the internal divide cannot be negotiated or tolerated, self-alienation – the cutting off of one part – is necessary to appear whole to others and to one's self (Chambon, 2005).

Internalization of the idealized included subject, the social archetype, initiates self-condemnation and self-contempt, and alienation from self and others serves as a defensive response to the heavy and enduring shame of in-between spaces. The splitting off and disavowal of the contemptible self affords momentary escape from the torment of double binds.

In the market-state field, choice, individual freedom, and autonomy serve as symbolic power, readily transferable into material assets. Yet, paradoxically, compliance with the presumed ideal is necessity. Conformity – believing in the illusion – is made necessary by material and symbolic deprivation. The system of capital that defines and divides the market-state social field opposes itself at its very foundation, as "there is nothing independent about everyone acting in the same way, making apparent 'free choices' among a highly restricted range of human and social options" (Chambon, 2005). This is the paradox – the inherent and consequential self-contradiction – that produces the double binds of everyday living in dominated spaces.

The divided habitus and self-imposed social exclusion

It is through a careful and sustained consideration of paradox and double binds that we find the means for making sense – practical sense – of self-imposed social exclusion. Self-imposed economic, spatial, and sociopolitical exclusion is, by its very nature, never simply *choice*. Rather, self-imposed social exclusion is *necessity*. This necessity is rooted in the double binds of dispossession in the divided market-state social field.

The necessity arising from divided social spaces and their double binds is instructive in clearly distinguishing between self-imposed social exclusion and self-exclusion as non-participation. Social exclusion, by definition, involves the objective and material processes and outcomes of economic, spatial, and sociopolitical exclusion. Apparent expressions of self-imposed social exclusion, therefore, always result in the material and social decline in observable ways for the individual or group. When disengagement is seemingly chosen – intentionally taking up a place outside – but the inclination does not incur material or social costs, this is something different altogether. As a specific example, the disposition to remain separate and distinct does not result in significant material or social losses for all Dietsche (im)migrant families. Instances of self-exclusion – rather than self-imposed social exclusion – were evident among a few newcomer families who migrated with ample material resources and were able to avoid engagement with Canada's social welfare system. Resistance is possible only for those individuals and groups whose material and social resources are adequate to fend off the double binds of dispossessed social spaces. To the contrary, once divested of material and symbolic assets, self-imposed social exclusion is triggered by compliance, by taking up the practices necessary to get ahead, or following the rules of the game; but owing to structural double binds that leave little room for choice, these very same strategies of survival lead directly or indirectly to the further devaluing and deprivation of economic, social, and cultural capital in the social fields in which people are engaged. In this way, self-imposed social exclusion presents itself as *compulsion* – unavoidable, and paradoxically practical.

The coherence of despair

Suzanne and Cornelius, two Mennonite immigrant practitioners, described the catch-22 of subjective exclusion, shame, and self-imposed social exclusion. In Canada, many Dietsche, men and women alike, know themselves to be dominated and determined – by a rather capricious God, church leaders, their fathers, and state authorities and agency professionals. For some, hopelessness sets in. Once the effects of social exclusion – of dispossession – have settled, the conditions of mobility are well beyond reach, even beyond imagination. Self-imposed social exclusion may be – but is certainly not always – an expression of despair: the habitus given into all forms of social exclusion, but most especially the symbolic violence of subjective exclusion. Despair is adaptation.[8]

> CORNELIUS: I think it's ahh – A lot of the people, probably 90 per cent of the people that come here, come with a great big inferiority complex –
> SUZANNE: Yes.
> CORNELIUS: – already from home.
> SUZANNE: Yes.
> CORNELIUS: Because they are the people that were kind of marginalized there. They couldn't afford to buy farms anymore. They tried to stay there as long as they could. The church leaders told them, [Trans.] "We will help you. You can't move back to Canada." Until they finally found out that they just couldn't. They had too much debt to pay, or whatever

it was, and they came to Canada. Most, a big percentage of our people, when they come here, they come here with borrowed money. Their self-esteem is way down there. And then of course, here, they come among people that have an education, and it gets worse. [Mennonite immigrant service providers]

The symbolic violence of subjective exclusion, most commonly exercised in laws, policies, and official state practices as "the naming and classifying that creates the things named," is "the *violence which is exercised upon a social agent with his or her complicity*" (Bourdieu & Wacquant, 2004, 272–3; emphasis in original). Complicity is practical, as symbolic violence against one's self turns shame to honour. The weight of shame – in both social worlds – is lifted by spoiling one's own assets. People come to know themselves to be *deserving*, accepting the existing social order as inevitable and right. This is to say that people come to know their place, "which leads one to exclude oneself from the goods, persons, places and so forth from which one is excluded … Dominated agents … tend to attribute to themselves what the distribution attributes to them refusing what they are refused … adjusting their expectations to their chances, defining themselves as the established order defines them, reproducing in their verdict on themselves the verdict the economy pronounces on them, in a word, condemning themselves to what is in any case their lot" (Bourdieu, 1984, 471).

The double binds of the spaces of subjective exclusion are repressed, kept hidden, because without the symbolic capital required to define and claim one's self, people yield to the principles that order the market-state social field and their assigned classification and place. A coherent self is possible here, but it is externally ascribed, representing both annihilation and alienation of self. Habitus and self find coherence in wretchedness. This is, after all, the disposition of necessity, the "habits-of-mine" that are fitting to the most dominated and dispossessed spaces in a divided social field. The classified habitus – coherent and necessarily compliant, and possessing only the type and volume of capital permitted – is more likely to give into a low position and dominated lot in life than any other habitus.

For some (im)migrant men and women who lack the necessary resources, whether emotional or material, to preserve meaningful connections with colony life, double binds provoke shame and despair, apparent in a demeanour of apathy, defeat, and hopelessness. For example, both Lisa (a forty-three-year-old mother of ten) and Anna

(a forty-year-old mother of four) maintain outward attempts to preserve their cultural distinctiveness through their traditional dress,
language, and deferential disposition. Yet, in their daily lives, neither
demonstrates inclinations and practices consistent with the sacred *or*
the secular. Poverty inhibits their relationships with extended family
and has destroyed the dream of the close family farming life inside the
tight boundaries of the colony. Although Dietsche women are typically
meticulous housekeepers and attentive mothers, Lisa portrayed mainly
indifference to these concerns, as well as to her husband's alcoholism.
For her, the material, social, and emotional gains of migration seemed
minimal. Anna, who had lost her two youngest children to child
welfare services and appeared to be in an abusive relationship, presented herself in a way that suggested she was alienated from herself,
her children, and the world around her. These women remain caught
in contradiction, betwixt and between, in conflicted and dominated
positions in both social fields in which they participate. In this way,
they are forever both, and neither, "e-migrant" and/or "im-migrant"
(Bourdieu & Wacquant, 2000).

The despair that accompanies such resignation to external principles
of identification, to being defined and dispossessed by others, serves
to confirm the reproduction capacities of the classifying habitus. For
human service practitioners who occupy positions of dominance –
albeit often positions of dominated dominance – in the market-state
field, individual and collective practices of self-creation and self-
identification are necessary for the preservation of their assets and
associated social positions and identities. The objectification of subjective exclusion, or its expression in the bodies of the classified habitus,
"guarantees the permanence and cumulativity of material and symbolic acquisitions which can then subsist without agents having to
recreate them continuously and in their entirety by deliberate action"
(Bourdieu, 1990b, 130). In other words, symbolic processes and power
generate multiple versions of complementary sets of habitus, and thus
people. And symbolic power is magical in that its very products are
self-generating and self-reinforcing.

Improvisation and divided habitus

The habitus, as "a spontaneity without consciousness or will" (Bourdieu, 1990b, 56), has the capacity to improvise under changing conditions. This ability to acquire dispositions, for the body to "take the

world seriously," demonstrates a necessary incorporation of the structures of the social world when "faced with the risk of emotion, lesion, suffering, sometimes death" (ibid., 140). Yet there are certain limits to the adaptive capacity of the habitus, particularly in conditions of profound and sudden change. In such critical circumstances, people are prone to define "the world in terms of a set of relations which no longer apply" (Fowler, 2000, 13). Dispositions may become "out of line with the field and with the 'collective expectations'" that make up all that is normal (Bourdieu, 2000b, 160). In situations of sudden confrontation between conflicting social fields, or when limited resources restrict improvisation, habitus is often not adapted to its situation or coherent. The improvisational capacity of the Dietsche habitus is doubly constrained when "uncontrolled" economic migrations force sudden confrontation between incompatible social fields from low positions in both. The double binds of the dispossessed social spaces of social exclusion often coincide with a destabilized habitus, torn by conflict and internal division, generating suffering.

> LUANN: Do you have a lot of family there, back in Mexico?
> JACOB: [Trans.] Parents and brothers and sisters, yes. They are almost all there.
> TRANSLATOR: Was it hard then, that you thought you would let go of them?
> JACOB: [Trans.] Yeah, that is hard. But finally we cannot stay where we just can't make it any more. What are we supposed to do? It was too hard. It just always gave debt. I've always just worked for debt and I was tired of it. And it gave envy. One was always supposed to make it with rented land. A big envy. Then I said we would just go to another land where we could make it by working. That was our drive. We wanted to see what we could do here.

For some, especially Dietsche who are poor and without a claim to Canadian citizenship, improvisation is severely narrowly bounded. The traditional Mennonite way of living, which demands extraordinary know-how and good fortune in the expanding and deepening global economy, is not productive for everyone. Some seek land and the possibility of a livelihood further south, in the more conservative colonies in Bolivia, Belize, and other regions of Latin America. Many find at least equal measure of hardship and desperation in these colonies.

Others, like so many people the world over, have no choice but to turn to the informal economy of the streets and in particular to its "most dynamic sector," the trafficking and selling of drugs (Bourdieu et al., 1999, 135). On the surface, drug smuggling by individuals from this deeply religious and traditional "sect" – as Dietsche are sometimes identified – seems ironic, attracting widespread curious and critical attention (e.g., CBC, 1992; Mitrovica & Bourette, 2004). At the same time, Dietsche (im)migrants know only too well the desperate conditions of many in Mexican society that leave a whole variety of illicit and illegal practices largely unchecked.[9]

The apparent inconsistencies in Dietsche inclinations may be understood as a mal-adaptation of habitus. Giving evidence to the burgeoning grey market or under-the-table economy that is present at all levels and in all sectors of societies all over the world, it is not unusual for Dietsche workers to be paid in cash for their labour by their employers in Mexico and in Canada. Participation in the various configurations and activities of "informal finance" (Aliber, 2002) in the "shadow economy" (Schneider & Enste, 2003) constitutes a means of making a living that is consonant with the entrepreneurialism, family autonomy, and precariousness of subsistence farming. The practice of striking a business deal that will generate some immediate income, for example, is part of the farming know-how, or disposition. In this way, economic exchanges in the informal economy require minimal improvisation of the Dietsche habitus. The legitimacy of such activity, however, is usually determined by the volume of material and symbolic assets of the individuals involved in the exchange.[10] Without significant economic, social, and cultural capital, engagement in informal economies – whether technically legal or not and by even a few members of the group – initiates broad-spectrum suspicion and indictment of all Dietsche (im)migrants. As the rules of the game evolve, provoked by threats to survival, dispositions become dysfunctional, and efforts to sustain them often lead to deeper failure, even to self-destruction. From a categorical vantage point, social exclusion in material, social, and subjective terms for those who insist on illicit activity is viewed as not only self-imposed, but deserved.[11]

Integrated ambiguity

For Dietsche (im)migrants, social and/or economic pressures force confrontation with the market-state and distance from the colony. Many aim to remain largely invisible in the contradictory spaces of the market-state field. Invisibility provides protection from the classificatory practices of the state, but exposes (im)migrants to exploitation in formal and informal markets. Whereas cultural and religious survival is available in invisibility, physical survival is often not possible for families who find themselves alone, isolated – sometimes owing to rejection – from a larger Dietsche community. Unseen labour (im)migrants are extraordinarily vulnerable, and thus the livelihoods of off-the-record economic migration are intensely precarious. In the face of economic hardship, the symbolic power necessary to resist subjective exclusion and to define self as a people is no longer available to certain Dietsche (im)migrants. In such circumstances (i.e., in the double binds of social exclusion), the double binds of social exclusion, efforts towards coherence of habitus – the consistent and complete abiding by a single system of capital, perfectly inclined towards a narrow social position within the dominating social field – force internal splitting and the continual disavowal of one's incompatibilities. Absolute coherence of self is illusion.

The divided habitus and split self are vulnerable to shame, self-contempt, and despair. Yet such suffering is not inevitable. To the contrary, a divided habitus allows for the containment of paradox. When there is enough to satisfy physical and social needs, the out-of-place habitus adapts, or improvises, through integrating ambiguity; through incorporating an extended range of everyday practices and inclinations as diverse, even contradictory, "habits-of-mine." Incoherence of habitus is an expression of congruence to multiple positions and the divided self (Chambon, 2005). Some (im)migrants, for example, with adequate material and social resources engage with the secular only to the extent that it preserves the sacred. Even though they may be separated by significant geographic distance, familial and church networks of Dietsche (im)migrants extend across rural regions of Canada and beyond, providing informal systems of support: a "transnational village" that is "far-flung over vast distances" and "consists of tens of thousands of individuals who have never met" (Loewen, 2013b, 230). Close ties with this "imagined pan-American" Mennonite village afford a sure and valued position in Dietsche "face-to-face communities" within the "'closed' and rural places" of Canada (ibid., 231), more economic, social, and religious autonomy, and less engagement with the worldly ways of the secular society around them. Consistent with a Mennonite faith heritage, a collective difference and distance guards against shame and protects dignity.

Aiming to recall religious colony life in Latin America, some extended families and small groups form informal yet intentional communities in rural Canada. For example, the most assertive expression of integrated ambiguity – of resisting subjective exclusion through claiming self – was presented in the refusal to participate in the research process. In this instance, a group of seven Old Colony families withdrew their invitation to me and my husband just a few hours before the scheduled appointment for two focus group interviews, one with the men and the other with the women. One member of the group offered an explanation. They were familiar with Larry Towell's (2000) coffee-table book entitled *The Mennonites*, which displayed photographs of Dietsche, some of whom were their family and friends. Although Towell lived among Dietsche Mennonite families in Mexico and Ontario for extended periods of time and took some care in telling their story accurately and respectfully, many Mennonites (Dietsche and others) consider the book offensive. The pictures tell a one-sided story of poverty, weakness, and misery. Their concern was that, as an English outsider wanting to "research" them, I would also misrepresent them and cast them in a singularly negative light. As the only explicit denial of my request for an interview, I consider the characteristics of this small group to be significant and relevant. The informal group consisted of seven religiously conservative families. Most were relative newcomers, having lived in Canada for a few months to several years. All had a familial tie to other members of the group. They had formed a closed community that met once a week for a meal and "fellowship." Their engagement in the broader society was kept minimal through their reliance on one another. This small group had and claimed the symbolic power to cut their coats according to their own cloth – to preserve a collective separation from the "world," shielding them from the effects of dispossession and dividing practices in the market-state field. In such instances, self-imposed social exclusion approaches self-exclusion, or voluntary non-participation, as the economic, social, and cultural costs are reduced when difference and distance are exercised from a space of adequate assets.

Another way in which integrated ambiguity is expressed is through practices that apply a countercultural system of valuation to the conditions of one's own life and the world in general. For example, in a workshop discussion about the challenges that women face in maintaining transnational livelihoods, Canadian service providers struggled to understand Dietsche (im)migrants who seem to expect and desire so little. An English practitioner, making reference to examples of entrepreneurialism among (im)migrant men, enquired whether there are any instances of women organizing to launch their own business venture. Margaretha, a young Dietsche (im)migrant woman, responded. She explained that it is quite common for women to gather together to work – not to make money, but to sew quilts and other household necessities for families in need in other parts of the world. She described a shared perception of their place in the world that was consistent with the narratives of other Dietsche women. They have enough, and they accept responsibility to share with others who have less. Subjective exclusion through classification as a people who are lacking is resolutely rejected through counting themselves among the privileged. In the everyday and the ordinary of women's work, they enact a global consciousness and obligation that at once exposes and opposes the narcissism of market logic. The Dietsche disposition is inclined towards shared responsibility rather than competition, mutuality rather than individual infinite gain. Further, the practices of Dietsche women demonstrate their recognition that it takes more than money – more than earning a wage – to make a living, to make a life. In this way, subordinate social fields not only are confronted by the market-state, but also confront and challenge this prevailing system of capital. In social spaces of *enough* in a subordinate social field, resources are just adequate to support multiple positions and integrated incoherence. In ways that are perhaps small yet significant, the divided habitus of integrated ambiguity generates strategies of subversion in the market-state field.

For all of us, integrated ambiguity and a habitus that is necessarily divided are accurate to social reality and to self. In this way, integrated ambiguity is truth, if truth is congruence with what is. A divided habitus and integrated ambiguous self makes it clear that inhabitants of social space are not *determined* by its order, and the specific vision of division that sustains the divides of the market-state social field is resisted and interrupted in various ways. For example, not all occupy the position of official representative for the left hand of the state in the same way. Some social workers, health professionals, teachers, and employment counsellors gave expression to a complicated, ambiguous identity. It was in the following exceptional and lengthy interview that the struggle of a divided self and habitus was most poignant. In this discussion between women who provide various kinds of services for Dietsche families, the conflict experienced by Sarah, the only Mennonite immigrant in the group, was apparent in her words, tone, and behaviour:

STEPHANIE: And girls are not as acceptable as boys to a family. That's still huge.

LUANN: So boys are valued more?

STEPHANIE: They can be, yeah.

SANDY: I think so.

SARAH: Certainly the roles of a boy are very different than those of girls.

LUANN: And more valued?

SARAH: Well, there's more prestige in a boy who will grow into a man that does the business for the family, who earns the money, who drives the car, who makes the decisions ...

STEPHANIE: [Laughs. Whispers.]

LUANN: What was that?

STEPHANIE: Our North American value system begs to differ!

RACHEL: Yeah, and maybe we need to keep part of that in mind. Not to judge their system by our system.

SARAH: Or just remember that we are [emotion in voice].

I understood it to be significant that Sarah – who was repeatedly interrupted by the other participants, particularly her co-worker, Stephanie – was the first to excuse herself from this animated discussion, leaving at least forty-five minutes before the conversation came to the first of many conclusions. Throughout the interview, I observed that she was not able to find a place, as Dietsche values and beliefs are spoiled for her, and yet she could not integrate the conflicting perceptions and practices necessary to the classifying habitus. As a legitimate occupant in both the Dietsche and the market-state social fields, she must believe in both, but cannot believe in either. In the absence of concern for daily survival, the paradoxes of contradictory social spaces do not produce the double binds associated with lower social positions, those more emphatically marked by dispossession. Yet the struggle of containing a divided self and sustaining an incoherent habitus is evidenced to be consequential nonetheless.

I considered the few expressions of disagreement among practitioners to be worthy of careful examination, as the dissenting voices achieved a degree of social distance from other service providers and gave evidence of some ambivalence in the classifying habitus. In particular, responses from one non-Mennonite service provider were consistently and notably distinct, conveying his efforts towards respect and understanding. Sometimes directly refuting the assessments of (im)migrants offered by his colleagues, he provided explanation rather

than judgment, interpretation instead of classification. The personal
characteristics of this respondent permit such acts of resistance. He is
white, male, and highly credentialled as a lawyer; he therefore has relatively easy access to all kinds of material and symbolic capital in the
market-state social field. From a social position endowed with profits
significantly greater than are typically afforded agents of the left hand
of the market-state, expression of a divided habitus may be less likely
but also more practical. While those who stand on higher ground in
the market-state field are necessarily inclined towards conservation
and reproduction of the field's system of capital, the penalties resulting
from exerting a contradictory system of capital, expressed in the rejection of official classifications in this case, are more readily withstood.

Further evidence that the classifying habitus is variously embodied was provided by several Mennonite service providers who speak
Plautdietsch. Even though none of these practitioners has ever lived
in a colony, and their social trajectories were markedly different from
those of Dietsche (im)migrants, they communicated a genuine sense
of identification and social proximity with their Dietsche clients.
These respondents, demonstrating a disposition of ease and familiarity on the margins of mainstream and an integrated divided habitus,
tended towards a more protective disposition in relation to Dietsche
(im)migrants. The integration of a divided self and habitus is supported and enabled by economic, social, and cultural assets in any
social field.

Integration of a divided habitus and ambiguous self is made possible through keeping some distance – in standing back, apart – from
the double binds of contradictory social spaces. Greater coherence of
incoherence is found in the ambiguous space *between* social divides. For
Dietsche (im)migrants in Canada, protection from double binds is available through a tenacious distance from the market-state and proximity
to the colony and, to the extent possible, preserving assets in their own
alternative social field. This is critical, as the range of viable responses
to the double binds of divided social spaces corresponds with the positions people occupy in subordinate social fields and the volume and
composition of capital they possess in those fields. That is to say that in
the midst of confrontation, an agent's position in their "native world"
can predict, to a large extent, their position and trajectory in the market-
state social field.

Self-imposed social exclusion is the necessary means for the appropriation of capital – for survival – in the places in between the various

social fields in which many Dietsche (im)migrants inevitably participate. From spaces *entredeux* – in between tradition and rapid change,
steadfastness and destabilization, the sacred and the secular – a disposition of self-imposed social exclusion makes perfect and necessary
sense. In this way, and for some against all odds, an integrated ambiguous self is protected.

> LUANN: How long would you like your boys to go to school?
> ISAAK: I don't know.
> LUANN: Have you thought about that?
> ISAAK: No, not really.
> LUANN: It's not unusual in Canada, you know, for people to go to school
> until they're adults, even. Would you like your children to do that?
> ISAAK: Maybe not. We – we've been talking a little bit about it. And we said
> maybe until six or seven, was it? Eight or nine grades?
> LUANN: Grade eight or nine? That would be enough?
> ISAAK: I think so.
> LUANN: What kind of work would you imagine them having when they
> grow up?
> ISAAK: Field work.
> LUANN: Farming?
> ISAAK: Yeah, work like that.

Self-imposed social exclusion, made necessary in double binds, is
expression of a habitus that is both and at once divided and adapted.
The divided habitus holds the possibility of sustaining a coherent yet
necessarily ambiguous self that integrates the contradictions of paradoxical social spaces. People – particularly members of groups who
wish to maintain distance and difference – "are endlessly occupied in
the negotiation of their own identity" (Bourdieu, 1989, 21). And it is
this struggle that often appears, from a categorical point of view, to be
self-inflicted and chosen hardship. People may necessarily "choose" –
without choosing – economic, spatial, and sociopolitical exclusion in
the market-state field to defend against symbolic violence and subjective exclusion. In the midst of confrontation and forced engagement in
competing social fields and conflicting systems of capital, self-imposed
social exclusion is necessary practice in the struggle towards self-
preservation, the struggle to protect material and symbolic capital, to
define self, and thus to resist subjective exclusion. Self-imposed social
exclusion is survival. It is necessary and practical sense.

Chapter Seven

Social Inclusion: Ideas and Practices of Reconciliation

The Dietsche (im)migrant experience in Canada is far from uniform, in part owing to the material assets held by a family or community. For example, in the rural expanses of Alberta, some Dietsche families own homes and operate their own businesses. These families in particular demonstrate the ability to remain out of sight. Therefore, their engagement with human services is generally quite limited and is more commonly self-initiated. Adding to the multiplicity among Dietsche (im)migrants, Canadian immigration trends of Dietsche families are shifting in response to changes in sociopolitical conditions in Mexico and in Canada. For instance, as drug-related violence has escalated in Mexico, colony Mennonites who are more well-to-do have been targeted and seek safety to the north. Some migrate to fulfil Canada's one-year residency requirements, thus ensuring their access to citizenship, and are not necessarily facing pressing economic need. Still others return to the land of their ancestors for their babies to be born on Canadian soil and then make their way back to their southern colony with their newly expanded family of Canadian citizens. Moreover, Dietsche narratives revealed that the northern migration requires significant resources for families, and the most destitute tend to be left with few options in their struggle to survive in a southern colony. Since the standards for judging entitlement are borrowed from the market in Canada's human services, families that demonstrate economic independence may be granted some measure of symbolic power and thus the right to self-determination regarding certain aspects of life. Money buys a certain degree of autonomy, and therefore dignity, for individuals and groups.

When Dietsche difference is caught in official lines of sight in Canada's human service system, dynamics of social exclusion are set in motion. A state that functions according to the principles and values of the "free" market is sustained through forcing and enforcing conformity to a presumed idealized standard. Difference is assessed and addressed against a mythical social archetype who is dependent on the repeated construction of a whole host of opposite subjects and subjectivities. The paired practices of stereotyping for "archetyping," or group-making, are foundational to market social relations. Despite the overt emphasis on conformity to dominant norms, human services that are organized to meet market objectives rely on practices and procedures of subjective exclusion that work to assemble, accentuate, and devalue – and thus profit from – all manner of difference. This is the symbolic violence of subjective exclusion, which provides the justification for economic, spatial, and social divides.

Social exclusion is, essentially, *conflict* that is at once interpersonal and systemic, manifesting itself in fractured relationships between individuals, groups, communities, societies, and nations. Effective responses to social exclusion challenge the ideas as well as the social systems that generate and regenerate these social divides. Social *inclusion*, then, must interrupt the processes and outcomes of social exclusion and must move individuals, groups, and societies towards the reconciliation of economic, social, and subjective divides.

To practise social inclusion in the everyday and ordinary is to make room for difference. Rudimentary, yet radical.[1] News stories remind us daily that the world has a great deal of trouble with difference. Together, political rhetoric, news feeds, advertising, and entertainment – which are increasingly of one voice – encourage us to view difference with suspicion, even fear. Whether originating from "the west" or "the rest," from up-groups or down-groups, fear feeds global market interests (Harcourt, 2011) and ravages human relationships. Fear constructs the Other as non-human and therefore unworthy of the basic human rights we ordinarily afford one another. This contrived divide – the expanse forged between myself and those I consider to be less than human – is symbolic violence in the extreme and provokes all other forms of violence. To challenge social exclusion is not to change the Other; it is to change ourselves.

The nonsense of common sense social inclusion

In a small suburban community just outside the city of Artiodact, a giraffe had a new home built to his family's specifications. It was a wonderful house for giraffes, with soaring ceilings and tall doorways. High windows ensured maximum light and good views while protecting the family's privacy. Narrow hallways saved valuable space without compromising convenience. So well done was the house that it won the national Giraffe Home of the Year Award. The home's owners were understandably proud.

One day the giraffe, working in his state-of-the-art woodworking shop in the basement, happened to look out the window. Coming down the street was an elephant. "I know him," he thought. "We worked together on a PTA committee. He's an excellent woodworker too. I think I'll ask him in to see my new shop. Maybe we can even work together on some projects." So the giraffe reached his head out the window and invited the elephant in. The elephant was delighted; he had liked working with the giraffe and looked forward to knowing him better. Besides, he knew about the woodworking shop and wanted to see it. So he walked up to the basement door and waited for it to open. "Come in; come in," the giraffe said. But immediately they encountered a problem. While the elephant could get his head in the door, he could go no farther. "It's a good thing we made this door expandable to accommodate my wood shop equipment," the giraffe said. "Give me a minute while I take care of our problem." He removed some bolts and panels to allow the elephant in.

The acquaintances were happily exchanging woodworking stories when the giraffe's wife leaned her head down the basement stairs and called out to her husband: "Telephone, dear; it's your boss." "I'd better take that upstairs in the den," the giraffe told the elephant. "Please make yourself at home; this may take a while." The elephant looked around, saw a half-finished project on the lathe table in the far corner, and decided to explore it further. As he moved through the doorway that led to that area of the shop, however, he heard an ominous scrunch. He backed out, scratching his head. "Maybe I'll join the giraffe upstairs," he thought. But as he started up the stairs, he heard them begin to crack. He jumped off and fell against the wall. It too began to crumble. As he sat there dishevelled and dismayed, the giraffe came down the stairs. "What on earth is happening here?" the giraffe asked in amazement. "I was trying to make myself at home," the elephant said. The giraffe looked around. "Okay, I see the problem. The doorway is too narrow. We'll have to make you smaller. There's an aerobics studio near here. If you take some classes there, we could get you down to size."

"Maybe," the elephant said, looking unconvinced. "And the stairs are too weak to carry your weight," the giraffe continued. "If you'd go to ballet class at night, I'm sure we could get you light on your feet. I really hope you'll do it. I like having you here."

"Perhaps," the elephant said. "But to tell you the truth, I'm not sure that a house designed for a giraffe will ever really work for an elephant, not unless there are some major changes."[2]

This simple (and somewhat silly) fable illustrates the nonsense of the common sense approach to social inclusion. Social inclusion is commonly equated with *participation* in various social arenas, and interventions focus on increasing individual capacity for meaningful incorporation. This ideal of social inclusion implies a "centre" or series of "centres" whereby mandatory insertion or voluntary engagement moves an individual from social exclusion to inclusion. But this common sense idea of social inclusion is not for everyone. To the contrary, integration of the Other into the valued "centre" of the divided social space of the market-state social field is impossible, as it is the exclusion of all that contradicts dominant norms and values that forms its very essence. For instance, an abundance of research shows that meaningful inclusion is not universally available through participation in the labour market, access to social services, or engagement in mainstream society, as these structures and social relations are exclusionary by design (Walcott, 2014). The excluded can never become the included, as the necessary ideal "is never to have been the Other" (Marmur, 2002, 4).

Social inclusion in the market-state social field is reserved for a few, as the value of all resources depends on its uneven distribution and accessibility. Thus, social inclusion through market logic is contingent on social exclusion because if everybody has it, it is no longer of any value. In the context of competitive individualism, universality provokes steep inflation, as units of capital are worth less and less. Neoliberal social inclusion hinges on keeping all forms of capital scarce in order to preserve their differential value, as this is what makes social inclusion possible. Like a circular argument, the end is always the same as the beginning because all ideas, values, and practices are inclined towards preserving and reinforcing the existing social order. For example, neoliberal analyses of productivity, growth, and well-being are based on measures that can determine only how well capitalism feeds and supports itself, not how well it feeds and supports the lives of people. Some have argued that the best that is offered through insertion or participation in these divided centres for individuals and groups made marginal is "unfavourable inclusion" (Sen, 2000b) or "subordinate and disadvantaged insertion" (Munck, 2005, 72). This is exclusion through inclusion, which, I argue, is not social inclusion at all. Rather, it is the essence and potency of social exclusion.

The processes of social exclusion produce devalued and dispossessed positions and identities in the market-state social field that, in turn, serve as negative comparators, as personal and social "bad objects."[3] Official procedures and everyday practices that categorize, medicalize, pathologize, and criminalize produce the value differential required to generate profits. Once drawn inside the game, or the field of struggle, devalued and dispossessed individuals and groups and even nations can be exploited to increase the one-way flow of material and symbolic assets and reinforce the rules of the game. The economic utility of an "included" devalued comparator is apparent in the popularity of unpaid internships for young adults, temporary foreign worker programs, and multinational free trade agreements. Just as "trading places with the slaver does not do away with slavery" (Murphy, 1999, 30), neither can adjusting a few excluded individuals to approximate a presumed ideal of inclusion challenge the material and symbolic exchanges that resulted in such to begin with. Consequently, the common sense vision of social inclusion is an illusion. A viable vision of social inclusion, therefore, must make a clean break from market logic and principles.

Welfare reforms of the past two decades have resulted in the commodification of social benefits, and the privatization and commercialization of welfare administration. Increasingly, human services of every sort – public and private alike – operate according to sound business principles rather than an ethic of service. With the rise of market fundamentalism, the merits of this widespread trend are rarely questioned. Yet a consequential contradiction exists. The character of a "free" market economy is based on the premise that the business of business is business, "not just in fact but as a virtue" (Mikler, 2009, 1). In the words of US economist Milton Friedman and his wife Rose Friedman, "there is one and only one social responsibility of business – to use resources and engage in activities designed to increase its profits" (1962, 133), which is achieved in part by restricting the accessibility of a product to preserve its market value. This is, of course, exactly contrary to the manifest goals of social services, healthcare, and public education systems that claim to offer a service or good that is equally accessible to all. Public goods cannot be readily converted into market commodities, because their universal quality makes them worthless in a profit-generating system.

A market-driven social welfare system delivers public services and social benefits through the exclusionary and competitive logic of the market. A double bind of sorts is produced. Official procedures to determine eligibility and judge worthiness must be engineered in the absence of the natural sorting mechanisms of the market. Thus, the market-based social welfare system is necessarily punitive, exclusive, and divisive. Moreover, the goods and services provided through privatized human service systems cannot be the same in quality as those available through the market. The product line offered by the commercialized welfare state is necessarily substandard and stripped-down in comparison with the goods and services sold for profit, because the value of a market commodity corresponds to its *difference* from that which is more readily and widely available. The profitability of a cheaper, more accessible product is protected through reducing the cost of production or service provision and thus undercutting its appeal. A two-tiered product line of social rights and public goods generates profits through two mechanisms: first, a negative comparator increases the value of the "real" product, enhancing its scarcity factor; second, the desirability of the universal product immediately and dramatically declines, so that even those who cannot afford full price will aspire to the more expensive product, as the symbolic power associated with public goods and services is negative. Various examples of two-tiered systems are emerging in Canada's evolving human services. Welfare-to-work programs, for instance, cannot offer free access to *real* jobs, or the government workfare initiatives will undercut the private sector with whom it contracts to provide these services. In Canada, we see the rise of food banks rather than income security, workfare employment "readiness" programs instead of education, and walk-in emergency medical clinics in place of continuity of healthcare.

Not only are marketized human services costly to enforce, they are largely ineffective in mitigating market failings. Monetary interventions address only on-the-surface outcomes of economic divides and ignore the processes that produce them. Money has no utility outside of the market. Thus, the redistribution of resources within a marketized social welfare system relies solely on market mechanisms, requiring all necessities of life to be met through market engagement. This is, in effect, enforced market dependency for those who can least afford it. Prevailing approaches for the redistribution of money, such as minimum wage standards, taxation schemes, and even guaranteed basic income programs are limited in impact and will be increasingly costly over time, as assisted market engagement subjects all to the same system of capital – the same rules of the game – that generated economic divides in the first place. Not only are all other means of making a living devalued by such strategies, but they are actively denied. On their own, market-based initiatives for addressing social exclusion will, necessarily and over time, further alienate those who are poor and will, inevitably, exacerbate economic and social divides. Moreover, addressing social exclusion through people-change measures is ultimately futile and a waste of public resources.

Entitlements of citizenship and human rights that are protected through market mechanisms are unavoidably transformed into something different. The market-state system of capital replaces social rights with individual moral obligation and supersedes collective responsibility with individual personal gain. Individualized rights and freedoms are necessarily corrupted by their falseness, their impossibility, as human rights have no meaning outside a social context, apart from the collective in which they are realized. The public, in all its various iterations – especially the social welfare state – must be disentangled from the very logic that scorns, discredits, and weakens it.

The practical ambiguity of social inclusion

A reconciling point of view recognizes that the categorical vision of things is a lie: social inclusion as a desired condition is not possible, and social exclusion as a kind of person does not exist. Yet social inclusion and social exclusion as social kinds and conditions do show up to the extent that they are *made*. Practices of social inclusion in human services, in our workplaces, and in our communities and families begin with the subversion of ideas and ideals that pit us against – and place us over – one another. The truth of the social world – and ourselves – is in paradox. Specifically, for example, Dietsche hardship *is* self-inflicted and is also imposed by a society and human service system that devalues and undermines the Dietsche view of the world and way of living. Moreover, each of us is both socially determined and free to choose: a victim of social and personal circumstance and an agent of our own making. Neither wretchedness nor greatness, yet containing both.[4] To think about and practise social inclusion as the reconciliation of divides, then, is to hold paradox – both/and as well as neither and all of ours together with room for mine and yours. And the dynamics of social exclusion are interrupted by making space in our minds and in our social contexts for wildly diverse – even contradictory – perspectives and ways of being in this world. This is the practical ambiguity of social inclusion.

The endeavour of envisioning socially inclusive policy and service solutions emerges from and returns to *social* ideals: a commitment to social rights and shared responsibility through public dialogue and collective action. Such social goals are necessarily rooted in a deep awareness of our common fate – that we all live the conflict and violence wrought by the economic, spatial, sociopolitical, and subjective divides of social exclusion; that, in time, the protections afforded through large volumes of capital will prove to be less and less effective and meaningful in the everyday realities of life. When we pay attention, we can see that the fate of our natural world is already reaching across our idea divides defined by national/foreign, local/global, masculine/feminine, private/public, economic/social. The safeguarding of the distance between "us" and "them" will, inevitably, require more and more – more material and symbolic power and, therefore, more violence. Social inclusion moves us towards one another.

Social inclusion requires an ambiguous view of the state. As is common to many social divides, the split between the left hand and the right hand of the state is false, contrived. A practical perspective regards social policies and service delivery to be simultaneously economic and social in nature and economic decisions to be fundamentally and irrefutably social. In a practical sense, the fiscal concerns and responsibilities of the right hand are nothing if they are not social. Economic decisions are at the root of much local and global social and ecological strife. The split in the state serves to maintain symbolic power through maximizing social distance between up-groups and down-groups, between large and small holders of capital. Symbolic power is invested in a technocratic and market style of governance, and government budgets, social policies, laws, and regulations conserve the scarcity of both public and private resources, thus protecting social divides. A system of capital that is in favour of those who possess it is reinforced. The divided state as a system of practices is merely a microcosm of the economic, spatial, sociopolitical, and subjective divides of the larger social world. Policies and practices of social inclusion depend on a reconciled state, an integrated system of mechanisms to protect social and ecological interests – our common fate.

The practical ambiguity of social inclusion distinguishes between capitalism as an economic system, and capitalism as an ideology. A necessary companion to our capitalist economic structure, in which markets function as the primary system for resource distribution, is a secondary system for resource distribution that has the capacity to address market limitations and failings (E. Lightman, 2003). Left unchecked, the seemingly boundless excesses of the market feed its own blind faith and unreasoned repetitions (Sen, 2000a), giving rise to ideological, social, moral, theological, and ecological fundamentalism; and fundamentalism breeds an endless cycle of fear and violence. Socially inclusive policies and practices oppose two fundamental and interrelated myths of neoliberal market ideology: money is everything, and the market is free. That is, social inclusion challenges the blind belief that money is the only means to sustain life and well-being, and it responds to the failure of the market to provide basic material, social, and cultural entitlements for everyone.

Practices of social inclusion in social policy and human services

Social inclusion demands a reasoned, counter-ideological approach to policy formulation and social service delivery, and it includes analysis and action at global, local, and interpersonal levels. Social policies concerned with poverty and marginalization must reflect what we *know* rather than what is commonly believed. For example, underlying punitive welfare-to-work policies is the presumption that poor people are prone to "milk the system" through legitimate or deceptive means, while research has consistently demonstrated that most claimants prefer the dignity of work. Furthermore, policy efforts geared towards the alleviation of the outcomes of social exclusion must begin to address the debilitated condition of the labour market, as its increasingly polarized and destabilized character severely diminishes its capacity to provide the material, social, and symbolic resources most often associated with paid work. The practical ambiguity of the state may be realized through the strategic alliance between the market and the state – to explore, for example, the potential of social business, whereby we apply the power of the market to achieve social goals and ecological profits rather than individual monetary gain. Government interventions need not choose between economic growth and social advancement, and care for the common good is not against the pursuit of individual interests.

Social inclusion has everything to do with money, while recognizing that money is ultimately unnecessary in the necessary practices of making a living. The market is inherently greedy in this way, as all things must go through it. To the contrary, many of the everyday activities in which people engage – most especially the typical work of women and subsistence livelihood practices of traditional cultures – have nothing at all to do with making money. Social policies and human services that promote social inclusion re-evaluate practices of work, and afford legitimacy to a wide range of human activity beyond making and spending money. Meaningful global and local anti-poverty strategies invoke an expanded understanding of materiality. Redistribution towards social inclusion involves a range of material resources with practical value. These are the resources of necessity, the social rights and public goods to which all people are entitled. The materiality of redistribution incorporates economic, social, and cultural capital – assets that have significant conversion value – thus permitting legitimate avenues for further appropriation of all forms of capital.

Preserving its social and dynamic qualities, the practical reality of social inclusion concerns asset holdings *and* access, taking into consideration both immediate status and life chances within the social order of things. Therefore, and most significantly, redistribution towards social inclusion attends to symbolic capital. This requires the redistribution of recognition and the recognition of redistribution – recognition that goes beyond rhetoric and political correctness. In this way, distribution and recognition cannot be separated, and they depend on one another. The redistribution of symbolic capital manifests in material terms: in redirected social and economic trajectories of individuals and groups; and in the reconciliation of economic, spatial, sociopolitical, and subjective divides. A practical and practice perspective recognizes social exclusion to be the expression of reiterative interactions between ideological and material dimensions, and effective responses promote socio-economic life chances that are more even through the legitimization of multiple social fields and the actualization of a market-mediating system of capital.

Effective responses to social exclusion depend on policies, programs, and services that protect social rights and public goods; that actively promote engagement of widely diverse groups and sectors of society in civic processes; and that facilitate communities of material mutuality and local governance. The delivery of social services across racial, ethnic, class, religious, and cultural divides begins with the premise that patterns of behaviour make perfect sense in the particular historical and social contexts in which they are structured. This "practical sense" is incomprehensible through the objectifying distance of screening, assessing, diagnosing, and incarcerating, which extracts and disconnects taken-for-granted practices and habits from the systems of capital that make them necessary.

Social inclusion as integrative practice recognizes and honours the multiplicity of social fields and subfields and systems of capital – with their own internal order and modes of functioning – in which people move and live. From a practical point of view, difference is not to be tolerated; it is to be regarded as strength, meaning, and value. It follows, then, that social inclusion in the interpersonal is, by definition, a mutual exchange or sharing, and the unilateral prescription or ascription of lifestyle and identity are not compatible with inclusive ideals. In fact, current procedures of the market-state that force conformity are precisely counterproductive to the aims they claim to seek to accomplish, revealing a common underlying discrepancy between manifest and latent goals of policy formulation. Socially inclusive policies and services support and reward engagement in alternative social fields besides the market-state, encouraging practices of acquiring material and symbolic capital in those fields, which protects against economic exclusion in all fields. Inclusive practices actively invite and make space for "participation in all walks of public life by members of racialized communities" (Saloojee, 2003, 17). Through an alternative system of capital, social services have the potential to construct a social space that mediates the effects of the market, intentionally positioning multiple political subjects – lone mothers, Black youth, Dietsche (im)migrants, Indigenous peoples – as entitled citizens.

In the same way that social exclusion concerns the *whole* of society, so too must any imagination for, and realization of, social inclusion. Social divides cannot be effectively addressed through even the most altruistic and earnest of targeted interventions, because social exclusion does not concern only the excluded – just as racism is not only about people of colour, homophobia does not affect only non-heterosexuals, and sexism is not only a women's issue. The categorical perspective, regardless of associated moral sensitivities or political leanings, is necessarily decontexutalized and "a-historicized," and it triggers mechanisms to sort the victims from the villains. To the contrary, a practical and integrative point of view recognizes that the histories and current realities of racism, slavery, and colonialism – of war, poverty, and ecological destruction – these are *our* histories and current realities. These tragic stories are ours to deal with now, to respond to together. While the state, as an integrated entity, is the primary defender of social rights and public goods, government structures and processes alone are incapable of effecting shared responsibility for our common future. Contrary to ideological positions, social inclusion is not all up to the state, or not at all up to the state. Today, more than ever, most of us occupy multiple places in our ongoing histories, and our positions in various and vigorous social relations of power are complicated, ambiguous social spaces. Social and economic systems of global capitalism that are at once oppressive and promising, social relations defined by racism and patriarchy – these are the contexts in which we *all* live today, the histories that we are collectively shaping. We all are responsible.

Policies and practices of social inclusion, then, recognize the violences of poverty and social exclusion to be the chronic failure of human relationships. The cognitive structures that define social structures – structures that comprise local and global communities – generate interpersonal practices and systemic processes that constitute recurring violations of our human responsibility to one another. The fact that social suffering continues, that our responses are so persistently ineffective, suggest that the shared attitudes and beliefs with which we approach our relationships with one another are ultimately indifferent to and condoning of that suffering. "Unreasoned pessimism, masquerading as composure based on realism and common sense, can serve to 'justify' disastrous inaction and an abdication of public responsibility" (Sen, 2000a, 34). Poverty and social exclusion are examples of conflict and failed relationships – relationships in need of transformation, of reconciliation. This is social healing.

Lederach & Lederach (2010) note that the term *reconciliation* "has increasingly become a buzzword for politicians wishing to end wars they no longer seem interested in supporting. The political arena in particular seems to treat the word as synonymous with some form of enmity accommodation, a coexistence necessary to control the bitterness of entrenched division in favour of a reasoned peace" (3). I use the word here to signal two points of consensus that Lederach & Lederach (2010) identify from the varied and contested literature: "reconciliation begins from and solidifies around a relational focus" (4); and "reconciliation is best understood as a process involving some sort of movement as in a developmental progression" (5). Reconciliation is relational and dynamic. So too must be meaningful responses to the relational and dynamic realities of social exclusion. In practical terms, this means that social policies and services that promote social inclusion must facilitate *encounters*, "places for the estranged to meet, exchange, engage and even embrace" (ibid., 4).[5] As global and local markets relentlessly feed and profit from divides defined by race, gender, "dis-ability," and age, there is an urgent need for all stages of social policy and human services – from design to delivery to evaluation – to take place at the local level with broad citizenship involvement, particularly of those who are the "targets" of policy and "clients" of services. Inclusionary practices must strive to "close social distances and promote physical proximity" (Saloojee, 2003, 17). Social inclusion as social healing is located, situated in place, in local communities and in interpersonal relationships.

Practices of social inclusion with Dietsche (im)migrants

To practise social inclusion with Dietsche (im)migrants (and other groups who strive to preserve a culture and way of life that contradicts dominant norms) is to recognize the work and value of *story* – stories we tell about ourselves, others, and our relationships with one another.[6] Much of the work we do in human services – formulating social policies, designing social services, and conducting assessments, for example – is storytelling. These are stories of the way things are and the way things ought to be. Stories construct – and reconstruct – realities. Practices of social inclusion in human services hinge on *listening* to rather than *telling* stories and on "inquiring into the work that they do, and experimenting with how these stories might be reshaped in order to transform relationships" (Winslade & Monk, 2008, 2).

What's the story?

"When relationships are placed at the centre of programs, services, and interventions, risk assessment is turned on its head: rather than applying professional expertise to determine what (or who) the problem is, we ask of all those concerned, 'What's the story?'" (Ball, Caldwell, & Pranis, 2010, 19). Diagnosing and classifying is traded in for listening and learning, to understand the harm that has been done and the needs of every single one involved (Zehr, 2002).

The Dietsche story is centred on work and church. Deep meaning is bound up in the livelihood practices of the family, in making a living. Work is life, family life, and all of life is religious. For too many

Dietsche, theirs is a story of fractured church and family relationships and rejection by their own. For some Dietsche men, the pain resulting from the loss of place and authority in the community and family leads to alcoholism and abuse. Women suffer "*Narfentrubbel*," or nerve problems and "headaches," often diagnosed as depression, in the face of isolation and threats to her identity as a mother – perceived and real. To go against the church, even if mandated by social services or required by the laws of the land, provokes internal divides and renews the trauma of being cut off from one's self. Especially in the Dietsche tradition defined by a collective identity and interdependent way of life, harm is a communal experience, and parsing the victims from offenders has little meaning in the day-to-day life of families and communities. The assessment of harm and needs requires holding paradox in order to recognize obligations and harness resources of the group as a collective as well as each individual.

What can we do together?

Although some Dietsche colonies, communities, families, and individuals are fractured and even dysfunctional, that is not the whole story. Practices of social inclusion call forth and rely on the strengths and assets on all sides, not only those of the social welfare state and its representatives. Interventions that devalue and undermine traditional ways not only deepen social exclusion for Dietsche clients, they work against the purposes of human services. Case management, which requires the endless work of monitoring and regulating behaviour, is turned towards pooling resources and sharing responsibilities, to see what we can do together.

Notwithstanding that the social organization and relationships of Dietsche communities and families are imperfect (as they are for all groups, especially groups made marginal), the collaborative work of finding solutions together depends on looking for what is working well. For Dietsche (im)migrants, for example, research narratives highlight the strength and resilience of many women like Susana, who hold their homes and families together in the face of poverty, alcoholism, rejection from the church, and separation from extended family – when nothing is as it should be. Furthermore, children and youth are rooted in families, a community, and a heritage. Such rootedness, providing a collective identity, is tenuous or absent for many young people in the possessive individualism of a market society. Traditional Dietsche ways give children, women and men a place to belong, even though that place is imperfect.

Key to working across cultures and world views is understanding and working within the social organization and leadership structures of the group. Any attempts from outside professionals to introduce change in closed communities, including traditional Mennonite groups, must go through the established authority structures of the community (Good Gingrich & E. Lightman, 2004; E. Lightman & Shor, 2002). Formal and informal community leaders are vital to nurturing collaborative working relationships with individual members of the group.

What new story do we want to co-create?

When social inclusion is the goal, the outcome is not the end; it is only the beginning – the beginning of new understandings, new relationships, and a new story. Standard practices of outcomes evaluation, or valuation, that are geared towards justifying imposed interventions and accounting for the spending of public resources are made irrelevant, as outcomes are mutually agreed upon rather than imposed, and obligations for achieving them are shared. The terms of success are determined by the process of working through difficult situations or conflict together, through creating inclusive conversations and spaces of openness "where otherwise unimagined outcomes might become possible" (Ball et al., 2010, 12). The objectives of human service engagement with Dietsche (im)migrants and other groups who live by countercultural, anti-capitalist world views must take into account that "our" way – the "Canadian" way – is not necessarily better, or right, or even normal, and it does not work for everyone, maybe not even for "us."

Practices of social inclusion in the everyday

To practise social inclusion in the everyday is to make room for difference in ourselves. Resistance of the organizing ideology of market neoliberalism begins with the personal and the interpersonal – with relationships between individuals who are personally invested in the social spaces we occupy. The world in which we are bound up is *in* us, in the form of habitus, such that our practices – in our professional and private lives – are constituted by and serve to reconstitute the social order we inhabit. It must not be overlooked, therefore, that the classifying habitus is "home" for many of us, as are the variously classified habitus for the populations we study, serve, and encounter. Thus, we "get sucked into reproducing exclusionary discourses" and practices (Dominelli, 2004, 38). Just as none of us can claim to view and understand the social world from a place outside or above it all, we all participate in the making of our social realities. Hence, there is no neutral act, as every human practice works to either confirm or unsettle the social fields in which we engage.

The social spaces through which agents move and aspire are not simply divided between dominant and subordinate. Contradiction defines the positions occupied by the human service practitioner and all others who represent the disavowed left hand of the market-state, as the classifying habitus is, of necessity, a system of dispositions that itself is contradictory and divided against itself. These are positions defined by coinciding dominance and domination. As such, the habitus of the representative of the left hand may be divided, inclined at once towards conservation and subversion. This internal contradiction may cause despair, turmoil, and perpetual indecision – divides within that replicate divides between. Yet when ambiguity is held within a coherent and divided self of all those intentionally engaged with the social world, dominated dominance – the in-between spaces and dispositions – offers opportunity.

It may be that the incoherence of in-between place and space, a divided habitus, is well suited to the project of social inclusion through the reconciliation of social divides. The divided habitus as point of view is inclined towards ambiguity and recognizes the contrived essence of social archetypes and stereotypes and the falseness of cognitive divides. Practical ambiguity is an analytical point of view that contradicts conventional and conserving visions of divisions and generates alternative mental structures or social metaphors. The social authority afforded social scientists and social service workers – while far from absolute – is symbolic capital, the power of constitution. The coherent incoherence, or integrated ambiguity, of dominated dominance holds the power – the political power – to "transform current classifications in matters of gender, nation, region, age, and social status, and this through the words used to designate or to describe individuals, groups or institutions" (Bourdieu, 1989, 23). To step into one's authority while remaining ever mindful of its limits and offences is to "keep one foot in and one foot out, [to be] an exile and an insider for whom home [is] always a form of homelessness" (Giroux, 2004, 150).

Everyday practices of social inclusion involve turning towards the Face of the one who is my Other – to accept that we are all "things of the same kind," yet to hold the uniqueness of each One. In our sameness, we all are vulnerable to and responsible for the physical and social environments that we generate through our everyday practices and ordinary interactions. Reconciliation of social divides at an interpersonal level requires recognition that if the Other can be discarded and dismissed, so can I.

To practise social inclusion in the everyday is to honour and develop the ambiguity that defines each one of us. This is to restore to humanity those who have been defined outside. More important, to approach the Other and "to *receive* from the Other, beyond the capacity of the I" (Levinas, 1969, 51) is also to bring curiosity and acceptance to the parts of the self that have been severed and disavowed, thereby reconciling internal splits. To practise social inclusion is to be tenaciously subversive: to protect and perform the countercultural systems of values and beliefs – the economies – that we know, that are *in* us, to challenge the polarizing forces of the market and, at the very least, to remind ourselves that the market is not all there is.

The reconciling practices of Dietsche (im)migrants

A critical self-conscious approach to social policy, human services, and our everyday begins with the recognition that the basis of social exclusion is difference, and individuals and groups who have been defined outside have something to teach us about another way to live. In the context of the fused market-state, the collective and apparent "choice" for social exclusion reveals a contradictory social field and a conflicting system of capital. Thus, social inclusion as the reconciliation of social divides is informed and advanced by groups such as Dietsche (im)migrants – by communities that practise, in the everyday, ideas and ideals that challenge and mediate the excesses of the market. For example, the Anabaptist/Mennonite faith tradition of Dietsche (im)migrants is essentially practical, rejecting the tight constraints of commodified meanings of work. Work is both the means and the end to making and protecting a way of life. Daily work, therefore, is about much more than money and involves much more than that which can be measured in market terms. Moreover, Dietsche meanings of work challenge North American associations with individual status and identity. Ideally, the Dietsche family works together, and is collectively financially independent and socially integrated into the colony. Research data suggest that outside the colony, in the context of the Canadian labour market, the meaning of work takes on heightened significance and urgency. The colony ideal, to the extent that Dietsche families ever held it or carry it with them through migration, has been severely compromised. Ironically, the work that is of low value and limited opportunity by Canadian standards is precisely the work that is the most accessible and promising expression of Dietsche culture, faith, and collective identity in the Canadian landscape. Especially in spaces and places in between, work is hope.

Most Mennonite groups today strive to remain committed to the collective, to a shared identity that compels each one to assume responsibility for others as well as one's self. Rooted in a radical Reformation theology, the ideal of "the priesthood of all believers" assigns responsibility to all for the collective well-being within the context of intentional relationships and community. Particularly traditional Mennonite groups, such as Dietsche (im)migrants, practise mutual aid in ways that are both informal and spontaneous as well as formal and structured (Peters, 1988). Giving evidence to the former, daily practices of shared responsibility and mutuality are most clearly demonstrated in family units. For example, research data indicated that it is common practice for all family members, even children, to share responsibility for the family's well-being, financially and otherwise. Teenagers and unmarried young adult children consider their employment earnings to be family income – to pay the rent, buy food, or cover tuition costs for younger siblings to attend an Old Colony school – and seemingly never entertain the possibility of keeping their wages for their own use or savings. Mutual aid is also central to the structure and function of the Old Colony church in Latin America and in Canada. The identified role of church deacons, for instance, is to look after the material needs of families in the congregation (Peters, 1985). Old Colony congregations typically allot a portion of the church's finances, which are constituted entirely by members' donations or tithing, to a mutual aid fund that deacons draw from for families in need.[7] The "reconstituted Old Colony church" in Canada, first initiated in 1958 in Ontario (Loewen, 2013b, 169), has had an important role in the lives of families who are making their way outside the colony. Many (im)migrants affiliate with Old Colony congregations upon their arrival in Canada (Janzen, 1998). Going beyond material needs, the Old Colony church has assumed leadership in addressing social issues, such as domestic violence and abuse, among Dietsche in Ontario (Unger, 1991). In rural Ontario leaders from local Dietsche churches, including the Old Colony church and four other "Anabaptist" church groups, have formed Mennonite Community Services, which provides employment and settlement services and assistance with immigration and citizenship documentation (http://www.mcson.org/). This commitment to mutual aid and service is consistent with a high value placed on living simply, to ensure that everyone has enough. Money is invested not in things, but in family and community relationships.[8] At least in principle, the ravages of greed are resisted.

The Dietsche religious disposition is one of deference to powers beyond our own and an ever-present awareness that we are not in control of all things. A close relationship with the land and the environment – especially for Dietsche groups that continue a traditional and agrarian lifestyle in Latin American colonies – has reinforced a yielding spirit. And at its best, the tradition holds to an enduring belief in non-violent resistance and peaceful relationships with others, including and especially those who suffer the violence of conflict, war, and poverty.

Anabaptist/Mennonite faith principles, imperfectly exhibited by the Dietsche people in ordinary and extraordinary ways, can motivate informed and innovative responses to the social divides of social exclusion. This is not to claim that alternative systems of capital are inevitably and inherently virtuous. Rather, expressions of non-conformity, of dissent, merit our respectful and inquiring attention. Simply stated, the practical practice of self-imposed social exclusion is necessary to the idea and social reality of social inclusion.

Notes

1 Life in Mexico was hard in terms of money [Margaretha's field notes].
2 The preferred way of life is to farm rather than work for wages, even if the employer is in the colony. To find employment outside the colony is often an offence worthy of reprimand by church leaders.
3 I use *Dietsch/Dietsche* to identify the population throughout the book. The meaning and rationale for my use of this term are discussed in chapter one.
4 Some Mennonite migrants from Latin America were born to a Canadian parent, which, for the past four decades, has entitled them to a claim to Canadian citizenship. Although the criteria for citizenship have tightened in recent years, many still undertake the complicated process of acquiring Canadian citizenship. The citizenship laws and process are described in some depth in chapter two.
5 They hired a driver. Families often hire a driver for the first few trips until they know their way around the border crossings and routes. Susana knows a certain Mr Wall, who goes back and forth between Mexico and Canada. He charges to drive people to Mexico and returns with items to sell to Mennonites in Canada (such as candies, chocolate, material for dresses, bowls traditional to Mexico, knickknacks, sombreros, boots, shoes, medicines like antidepressants). Drives to and from Mexico may also be traded for services or goods rather than cash payment [Margaretha's field notes].
6 It is widely known that some translators offer more assistance than others when it comes to completing the test.
7 Canada Child Tax Benefit.

8 Mennonite Central Committee (MCC). This church organization and its relationship to Mennonite migrant population are described in some detail in chapter one.

9 Health professionals, lawyers, settlement workers, student organizations and all provincial premiers across Canada have been protesting the government's funding cuts to the Interim Federal Health Program (IFHP) since they were first implemented in 2012. Besides denying health coverage to some newcomers, the cuts have also resulted in "increased costs to local hospitals and provincial governments while sowing confusion within the health care system" (http://www.doctorsforrefugeecare.ca/). Despite the Federal Court ruling in July 2014 that the changes to healthcare were unconstitutional, even "cruel and unusual," the federal government is appealing this decision. Doctors for Refugee Care launched a National Day of Action on 15 June 2015 to call on the federal government to rescind their court appeal (which had cost $1.4 million to date) (Bateman, 2015). Revealing a similar irregularity in Canada's "universal" public health care program, the auditor general released a highly critical review of Aboriginal access to health care in Canada in the spring of 2015 (Blanchfield, 2015). Trudeau's Liberal government restored full coverage under the IFHP in April 2016.

10 Susana and her husband have ensured that all their children have Mexican rather than Bolivian citizenship or legal status.

11 Seguro Popular is a public healthcare system provided by the Mexican federal government, and it operates alongside well-established free market health delivery institutions and private practitioners. Dietsche participants offered mixed reviews on the quality of care provided through this system. The beneficiary's contribution is based on the socio-economic status of the family and is waived for families in the two lowest income deciles (Gutiérrez, 2014, 5).

12 Susana is describing her desire for her children to get married and to help them have a good start in married life. Since she and her husband are unable to pass down land to their children, as is the ideal, she would like to be able to provide traditional wedding gifts from parents to help set up a household.

1. Social Exclusion in a World on the Move

1 From the author's field notes, interview with Len (pseudonym), a Mennonite healthcare professional, February 2001.

2 Scholars are adopting increasingly strong language to describe the unprecedented reach and force of the market, despite its repeated and

dramatic failures, in everyday life. For example, renowned sociologists, economists, and historians analyse the "tyranny of the market" (Bourdieu, 1998, 2003), the "terror of neoliberalism" (Giroux, 2004), and the workings of "market fundamentalism" (Block & Somers, 2014; Stiglitz, 2009).

3 When referring to Mennonite groups, I use the term "conservative" to reference those who maintain a more traditional lifestyle, preserving or conserving daily life practices, resisting engagement with and accommodation to the dominant culture. Accordingly, the term "progressive" refers to greater accommodation to dominant social norms and integration into mainstream society.

4 For popular media depictions of Mennonite migrants in Canada, see, for example: Browne (2015), CBC (1992), Cannon (2000a, 2000b), Mitrovica & Bourette (2004), and Towell (1999, 2000).

5 Specifically, for instance, the Social Development Secretariat of the Government of Mexico City reports that the richest 10 per cent of the country has an income 45 times higher than the poorest 10 per cent. Furthermore, "20 multimillionaires have wealth equivalent to 6% of the Gross National Product, with an income estimated at around 14 thousand times greater than the population average" (Yanes, 2008, 1).

6 For example, legal categories for people who migrate to make a living range from refugee, asylum seeker, guest worker or temporary foreign worker, and various classes of immigrant. Unofficial and "illegalized" classifications of those engaged in transnational livelihoods include undocumented workers, trafficked individuals, and human smugglers.

7 For various estimates of internal and international migrants worldwide, see United Nations Department of Economic and Social Affairs (UNDESA, 2016), the International Organization for Migration (IOM, 2014), and the Organisation for Economic Co-operation and Development (OECD) Migration Databases (http://www.oecd.org/els/mig/oecdmigrationdatabases.htm). Confusion regarding the numbers of migrants abounds, primarily owing to the different ways in which migrant workers are defined and thus counted and the absence of reliable international migration data. Most estimates agree, however, on the following: the absolute number of international migrants has increased in recent decades; since the 1970s there has been an overall increase in people moving from lower- and middle-income countries to high-income countries; and net migration is expected to account for most of the population growth in high-income countries.

8 In the following chapters, I take some care to define and illustrate "neoliberalism" as it is activated in contemporary social life.

 9 Poverty in this case is a relative measure, defined as living with less than 50 per cent of the median income (OECD 2008).

10 Particularly in Europe, the language of social exclusion has permeated policy and academic debates on poverty for close to two decades (e.g., European Commission, 2012; Eurostat, 2000, 2007; Shucksmith, Shucksmith, & Watt, 2006; Social Exclusion Unit, 2001, 2006).

11 See also international development efforts aimed at reducing social exclusion, such as the Department for International Development (2005).

12 For example, the European Union committed itself in 2010 to reduce by 20 million the number of people at risk of poverty or social exclusion by 2020, initiating the development of broader, more refined measures for country comparisons (European Commission, 2012). A unique application of the term was adopted by the Chronic Poverty Research Centre (CPRC), a ten-year program funded by the UK Department for International Development that concluded in 2011. The CPRC's work on Adverse Incorporation and Social Exclusion explored "the relationship between risk and vulnerability, patronage politics, and chronic poverty; and the way in which inequalities within global economic value chains maintain poverty" (Hickey, 2012).

13 In July 2013 Prime Minister Stephen Harper announced the reorganization and rebranding of HRSDC to Employment and Social Development Canada (see http://www.canadiansocialresearch.net/hrsdc.htm). Reflecting a significant shift in focus and priorities, in November 2015 Prime Minister Justin Trudeau redefined this ministry as Families, Children and Social Development.

14 For a discussion of this law against poverty, see Noël (2002).

15 See the following for theoretical development of the concept of social exclusion: Good Gingrich (2003a, 2003b, 2006); Kennedy (2005); Martin (2004); Nevile (2007); Reimer (2004); Richmond & Saloojee (2005); and Sen (2000b).

16 The symbolic power of common sense will be discussed in more depth in chapter 4.

17 The presumption – or judgment – that social exclusion of all forms is very often self-imposed will be discussed at some length in the following chapters.

18 These provisions, known as the eternal *Privilegium*, permitted the development of administrative and agricultural techniques that have become central to Mennonite institutions and their economic and cultural life. The *Privilegium* became a standard set of conditions used in seeking a new homeland in future migrations (see F.H. Epp, 1974).

19 The largest group of Mennonites to migrate from Russia to Canada was
    the Old Colony, named thus because it originated in the first – or oldest –
    Mennonite colony established in Ukraine in the late eighteenth century,
    the colony of Chortitza. Mennonite emigrants from the old Chortitza
    colony and its daughter colony, Fürstenland, came to be a rather unified
    group in Canada. Four other smaller and slightly less traditional sub-
    denominations emerged to form distinct communities in Canada. The
    smallest of these variously traditional groups was the Kleine Gemeinde
    from the Molotschna colony in Russia. The Sommerfelder, the Chortitzer,
    and the Saskatchewan Bergthaler split from the larger Bergthaler church
    as a result of conflict over public education in Manitoba in the 1890s.
    These sub-denominations, along with the Old Colony church, took a stand
    against public education in Canada (Loewen, 2013b; Sawatzky, 1971).
20 For classic histories of Mennonites in general, see Smith (1957) and Dyck
    (1993). See Friesen (1989), Loewen (1993), and Urry (2007) for portrayals of
    Mennonite life in Russia. Ens (1994), F.H. Epp (1974), and Redekop (1969)
    provide historical accounts of Old Colony Mennonites in Canada before
    their migration to Mexico in 1922.
21 For details of the cherished *Privilegium*, signed by then President Alvaro
    Obregón, see Krahn & Sawatzky (1990).
22 As in Russia over 100 years ago and later in the Canadian prairies,
    traditional Old Colony Mennonites continue to defend themselves against
    the threat of "worldly" intrusion from their Mennonite kin.
23 Various designations for this particular group of Mennonites have been
    applied in academic literature. For example, recognizing a long-standing
    gap in Mennonite studies on the recent migrations to Canada of "some
    50,000 Canadian-descendent Low German-speaking Mennonites from
    Latin America" (Loewen 2004, 7), the chair of Mennonite Studies at the
    University of Winnipeg hosted a conference in 2002 entitled *The Return of
    the Kanadier*. The term "Kanadier" was adopted to "denote the Manitoba
    and Saskatchewan Mennonites who left for Mexico and Paraguay in
    the 1920s " (Loewen 2004, 7). However, the label had a short shelf life
    in Mennonite scholarship, as researchers noted its historic inaccuracy,
    and migrants returning to Canada have never used the word to identify
    themselves (Loewen 2004). Moreover, the name carries with it pejorative
    connotations, as it originated to distinguish and distance the 1920s wave
    of Mennonite emigrants from Russia to Canada from those who pioneered
    the migration route in 1874 (Urry 1999). Popular media and research alike
    tend to incorrectly impose the term "Mexican Mennonites" (e.g., Kulig &
    McCaslin 1998; Treaster, Hawley, Paschal, Molgaard, & St Romain, 2006),

a designation that is offensive to many Dietsche (im)migrants in Canada. Aiming for greater precision, more recent work denotes the dialect spoken by the population (Good Gingrich & Preibisch 2010; Kulig, Wall, Hill, & Babcock, 2008; Kulig, Babcock, Wall, & Hill, 2009). Yet the designation "Low German" or "Plautdietsch" is not adequate to distinguish this population from other Low German-speaking Dutch-Russian Mennonites in Canada, whose heritage does not include the defining Mexican sojourn of 1922. Carefully attending to church distinctions among Dutch-Russian Mennonite groups, a current and expanding Mennonite scholarship concentrates on the traditional "horse-and-buggy" Mennonites in Latin America. However, these works focus on the most anti-modern and conservative of Old Colony Mennonites, and those migrating to Canada are arguably the more progressive among Mennonite *Gemeinschaft* (church family). For scholarship on the religious and social formations of horse-and-buggy Mennonites in Latin America, see, for example, Cañás Bottos (2008a, 2009), Hedberg (2007), Loewen (2013b), and a special issue of the *Journal of Mennonite Studies* (2013) entitled "Anti-modern pathways: 'horse and buggy' Mennonites in Canada, Belize and Latin America." See also Fast (2004) for a detailed analysis of the affects of migration to Ontario for a horse-and-buggy Mennonite woman.

24 A word on the use of *Dietsch* and *Dietsche*. Unlike English, Plautdietsch is a language in which word endings are dependent on gender and number. For the sake of consistency, in most cases the adjectival form *Dietsche* is used throughout this book because it is the most commonly used adjectival form in Plautdietsch (used for all feminine, all plural, and some neuter adjectives) (Thiessen, 2003). However, on occasion *Dietsch* is used to indicate essence, as in we are *Dietsch* (we are German), as opposed to we are *Dietsche* (we are Germans) (Fast, 2016).

25 Relevant research includes my doctoral research conducted in 2003–5 (Good Gingrich, 2006) and two studies conducted with co-investigator Dr Kerry Preibisch and funded by the Social Sciences and Humanities Research Council (SSHRC) of Canada, entitled "Rural women making change" (P.I. Dr Belinda Leach, 2005–10) and "Theorizing choice and voluntary social exclusion" (P.I. Dr Luann Good Gingrich, 2009–13). Dr Kerry Preibisch was recognized internationally for her activist research focused on globalized agricultural and food systems and the people who labour in these systems, particularly migrant farm workers. Our collaborative and comparative research was aimed at investigating the conceptual and empirical paradox of voluntary social exclusion through qualitative research with three distinct categories of migrant women from

Mexico and Guatemala who work in low-wage jobs in Canada's agri-food industry: participants of the Temporary Foreign Worker Program, specifically the Seasonal Agricultural Worker Program and the Low-skilled Worker Program; and Dietsche women from Mexico who move outside of regulated programs, often as dual citizens. Kerry died of cancer in January 2016 at the height of her career and in the prime of her life. The comparative analysis of our research remains unfinished, as is true for so much of Kerry's work and life.

26 I note that central to the story that follows is the analysis or examination of the essence of what is commonly recognized to be "Canadian culture." Thus, I use the term here primarily for its familiarity.

27 I wish to express my deepest gratitude to five women who have been invaluable interpreters, research associates, and companions in this work: Marge Unger, Susan Shantz, Anna Peters, Margaretha Peters, and Dr Kerry Fast.

28 Although MCC receives some government funds through grants, its primary financial support is from individuals and Mennonite churches in Canada.

29 Schmidt, Zimmerman Umble, & Reschly (2002) describe the complexities and contradictions of the insider/outsider position by way of introduction to the issues addressed by the various authors in their edited volume entitled *Strangers at home: Amish and Mennonite women in history*.

30 A total of fifty-six individual or couple interviews, ranging in length from one to two hours, were conducted. Follow-up life history interviews, which were usually about two hours in length, were conducted with four Dietsche women. A total of eight focus groups, each including four to eight service providers, were conducted.

31 Yet I want to be clear that the theoretical layer of Bourdieu's work and the writing are mine.

32 A number of recent publications report on a variety of research projects with Dietsche (im)migrants in Ontario, Manitoba, Alberta, and the United States. See, for example, Crocker (2013), D'Ambrosio, Tiessen, & Simpson (2012), Kulig et al. (2009), Kulig & Fan (2013), Treaster et al. (2006), and Turner (2014). In the latter years of my research with this population, I encountered growing resistance from Dietsche leaders as more researchers found their way into their communities. Particularly in southern Alberta, key informants reported rather widespread distrust of researchers, and cited experiences of disrespectful and inappropriate intrusion in private matters (such as sexuality and practices related to death and dying) and misrepresentation. In the spring of 2011 my research associate, Kerry

Fast, and I began working with Dietsche community leaders in Ontario to design and conduct a small project that would document stories of migration for Dietsche communities in Canada and Latin America. Despite the full support of Dietsche leaders, we met with much resistance from (im)migrants, owing to growing distrust of researchers. We did not continue with the project.

2. Mennonite Migrations and a Common Sense Point of View

1 With only a few notable exceptions, practitioners referred to Dietsche as "Mennonites." I came to understand this fundamental misrepresentation to indicate primarily ignorance of various and diverse Mennonite groups. On occasion, however, I perceived this inaccurate identification to suggest carelessness, especially given the infrequency with which Dietsche (im)migrants use the term "Mennonite" to refer to themselves. For the sake of clarity and respect, I use the term Dietsche throughout this discussion of service provider accounts of their work with the population unless I am directly quoting a service provider who used the term "Mennonite."

2 Indeed, appeals to common sense have served as the basis of political campaigns at all levels of Canadian government in the past decade or two. For example, Mike Harris's "Common Sense Revolution" formed the election platform and subsequent agenda of policy reform and fiscal withdrawal that earned his Progressive Conservative government a large majority in the province of Ontario in 1995. Use of the term "common sense" suggests a value-free universal truth that requires no verification with facts, as anyone with any common sense accepts this inevitable truth. To the contrary, scholars note that common sense both reflects and necessitates specific ideological goals, standards, and procedures. For example, political references to common sense often denote the "neoliberalization" of policies and practices that is especially pervasive in the transfer of American-style punitive approaches to social insecurity (e.g., DeKeseredy, 2009; Wacquant, 2009).

3 Initiated in 1973, Canada's first temporary migrant worker program – the Non-Immigrant Employment Authorization Program (NIEAP) – set the template for the numerous programs that are now jointly offered through the federal Labour Department (now Employment and Social Development Canada [ESDC]) and Citizenship and Immigration Canada (CIC). Canada's Temporary Foreign Worker Program (TFWP) requires noncitizens to apply for work permits as well as request changes in their employment or immigration status, from outside the country. Entry is

afforded only to those with a work permit that assigns them to a particular employer and stipulates their occupation, residence, and length and terms of employment. The workers are bound by all terms of the employment contract for the duration of their stay, including the specific job and wages and, when the contract expires, workers are returned to their respective home countries. Application for re-entry can be made only from abroad. The federal government has made many changes to the terms of the TFWP, responding to public concern and criticism that arose in the spring of 2014. For example, new federal government initiatives have recently been added and expanded to the Seasonal Agricultural Worker Program (SAWP), the largest and most long-standing of these programs. A series of employer-driven changes, begun in 2002, aims to ease and expedite the hiring of migrant workers through the Stream for Lower-skilled Occupations, formerly called the National Occupational Classification (NOC) skill levels C and D, more commonly known as the Low-skilled Worker Program. CIC has introduced major reforms to the TFWP in recent years. A consequential change for workers in the Stream for Low-wage Positions was introduced on 1 April 2011. A regulatory amendment established a four-year cumulative duration limit that a TFW (excluding SAWP workers) can work in Canada, with a minimum of four years living outside the country before reapplication. For a complete description of the "overhauling" of Canada's TFWP (which is ongoing), see http://www.esdc.gc.ca/eng/jobs/foreign_workers/reform/index.shtml.

4 The number of private Old Colony schools has been growing, reaching an estimated total of eight in Ontario and three in Alberta.

5 To describe physical and sexual abuse as a "characteristic" of a whole "population" may seem odd and quite provocative. I chose these words carefully, to more accurately reflect the ways in which service providers discussed the issue.

6 To my knowledge, studies examining incest among Mennonite colonies in Latin America or Dietsche (im)migrants in Canada do not exist. It may well be that this is a serious issue for colony Mennonites. However, as Len acknowledged, our understanding of the severity and incidence of incest in this population compared with the larger population is based on impression and hearsay rather than fact.

7 I found this assertion that Dietsche (im)migrants lack basic life skills, made by a Mennonite who shared their ancestry and history but had never lived in Mexico, to be perplexing and even amusing. Most English service providers, who are likely to be less familiar with Dietsche culture and values, recognized the unusual resourcefulness of this population.

Dietsche Mennonites generally know how to grow and prepare their own food, sew their own clothes, maintain their own vehicles and machinery, and survive on very little.

8 Persecution is central to Mennonite history and has become part of a shared identity. This subject will be discussed in more depth in chapter five. It is interesting here that the Dietsche identification as persecuted was recognized, with some irritation, by an English service provider whose knowledge of Mennonite history and culture was likely to be superficial.

9 The 1947 Citizenship Law states: "a child born abroad, either of a Canadian father in wedlock or of a Canadian mother out of wedlock, could be registered as a Canadian citizen before the child's second birthday, or in such an extended period as the Minister might authorize in special cases" (Janzen, 2004b, 13). Canadian officials agreed to use the flexibility allowed in the law to register people born between 1947 and 1977 – the years the law was in effect – and who were much older than two years but otherwise met the criteria. Therefore, applicants had to verify that at least one parent was Canadian. In accordance with the previous citizenship law, if that parent was born outside Canada before 1947, then documentation proving the parent was born in wedlock to a Canadian father was required. Obtaining such records from Mexican state officials was a lengthy and costly endeavour for many, as most Mennonite weddings in Mexico were performed in the church but not registered with the state.

10 A Mennonite service provider reported that many Mennonite people in Latin America desire Canadian citizenship for purposes of travel and as a kind of "insurance" against economic despair. When the male partner is the Canadian citizen, a US travel visa is usually granted to him and his spouse. Families in which the woman has citizenship are often forced to fly directly from Mexico to Canada, as it is more difficult for a man to acquire a travel visa through his wife's citizenship.

11 Personal communication with MCC service provider, May 2005. Section 8 of the current legislation demands that an application for retention of citizenship is required for all those Canadian citizens who were born outside of Canada after 14 February 1977 to a Canadian parent who was also born abroad and whose parent did not register for Canadian citizenship until after 1977. These individuals "will lose their citizenship rights if they do not, before turning twenty-eight years of age, spend one year in Canada and then apply for 'Retention of Canadian Citizenship'" (Janzen, 2004a). MCC personnel note that an increasing number of migrations are motivated by the need to fulfil these residency requirements, as the first of those born after 1977 turned twenty-eight in 2005.

More recently, in January 2007, a federal government decision placed an expiry notice on certificates issued to people who came under this provision. As a result, even people who have lived in Canada for decades are at risk of losing their citizenship if they fail to go through the retention process (Mennonite Central Committee, 2007).

12 See, for example, "Health care needs of Mennonite women living in Elgin County" conducted by the Elgin-St Thomas Health Unit (Armstrong & Coleman, 2001); "A survey of the opinions of Aylmer residents regarding the services provided by the Aylmer police" (Sim, 2000).

13 Job creation efforts included a sewing cooperative for women, started in 1990, and business advice for men. For further details of these projects, see Janzen (1998).

14 This agency is unique in a number of ways. It is funded by federal and provincial governments (e.g., CIC, Community Action Plan for Children (CAPC), and Ontario Citizenship), non-government organizations such as the United Way, and local Dietsche and other Mennonite churches. It is the only agency specific to the Dietsche population in Canada. Most of the services provided focus on employment and settlement.

15 For extensive information related to the population and MCC's work with them, see http://mcccanada.ca/office/ON/.

16 Several Dietsche (im)migrants described Mexico as a place of "lawlessness." It is not my intention to unfairly represent the state of law enforcement and social order in a diverse society such as Mexico. I use the term here to indicate what I understand to be the perception of many (im)migrants who have experienced violence inside or outside their colonies in Mexico.

17 Most if not all social assistance or welfare programs in democratic social welfare states across the globe have been replaced by some version of workfare, or welfare-to-work programs, whereby the receipt of benefits is contingent on mandated employment-related activity.

18 A particular instance of the application of the categorical point of view is presented in chapter one.

19 To maintain theoretical consistency, I use Bourdieu's concept of self-consciousness. Additionally, I have found Paulo Freire's notion of critical consciousness to inform the practice of reflexivity that is central to my analysis of social exclusion and inclusion. Thus, I adopt the term "critical self-consciousness" to reference the influence of these diverse yet complementary works in my thinking on reflexivity in research and social work practice. For helpful discussions of critical consciousness, see, for example, Freire (1974, 1998), Kincheloe & McLaren (2011), and Montero (2009).

3. Market Logic and the Order of Social Space

1 The following discussion is based on Wacquant's (1987, 69) concise review of Bourdieu's four species of capital. I have extended Bourdieu's concepts of capital production and exchange to develop a conceptual model of social exclusion, as he did not apply his theory of social structures in this way. I have made every effort to preserve the integrity of Bourdieu's concepts and approach.

2 The unusual power of symbolic capital is its ability to convert the arbitrary to the inevitable and to impose common sense or presumed truths. Symbolic power will be further discussed in chapters four, five, and six.

3 See Bourdieu (1998), Davies (2005), Doern, Maslove, & Prince (2013), Hertz (2001), Madanipour, Cars, & Allen (2000), Prince (2001), Sassen (1998), Shucksmith, Shucksmith, & Watt (2006), and van Reenen (2001).

4 See, for example, Brenner et al. (2010), Coburn (2000, 138), Keil (2002), and Martin (2004).

5 It is worth noting here that I am not saying anything new. A host of scholars, from a wide range of fields of study all across the globe and for many years, have reflected on the reality and implications of the reconfiguration of social life – individuals, families, and social institutions – in terms of the market (e.g., Arribas-Ayllon, 2005; Bourdieu, 1998; Clarke & Newman, 1997; Feldberg & Vipond, 1999; Peck, 2001; Peck & Tickell, 2002; Rose, 1999; Shamir, 2008).

6 In Ontario, where most service provider interviews took place, the social service system is a welfare-to-work program, Ontario Works, instituted through welfare reform in 1997. The symbolic economy of such market-based social services will be discussed in some depth in chapter five.

7 For elaboration of the market moral imperative and examples of its expressions in social policy and human services, see, for example, Gonzalez (2005), E. Lightman & Riches (2000), McKenzie & Wharf (2010), Mullaly (2007), Peck & Tickell (2002), Prince (2001), and Riches (2001).

8 This dual focus on dispossession and devaluation, or outcomes and process, is important, as social exclusion is distinguished from static concepts such as poverty by measures that incorporate both.

9 Symbolic power is the lifeblood of the processes and practices of subjective exclusion and will be discussed at some length in subsequent chapters.

10 The procedure of means-testing usually does not consider liabilities, or debt, such that only the "credit" side of personal wealth is assessed. Consequently, assessed "means" or resources are often erroneously exaggerated.

11 The role of the informal economy in this particular case of social exclusion will be pursued in more depth in chapter six.

12 See, for example, Baker Collins (2002).

13 According to the National Occupancy Standard, an acceptable number of bedrooms means one bedroom for each: cohabiting adult couple, unattached household member eighteen years of age or older, same-sex pair of children under age eighteen, opposite-sex pair of siblings under age five, and additional boy and/or girl in the family (R. Lewis & Jakubec, 2004). It is also noted that the criteria determining affordability are arbitrary, and the 30 per cent figure cited here is disputed by some to be unrealistically low (E. Lightman, 2005).

14 In this case, a bunkhouse refers to seasonal barracks-type housing usually provided for temporary visa workers on large farms.

15 At the time of this interview, farm labourers hired through the Seasonal Agricultural Worker Program or the Low-skilled Worker Program (as it was named at the time) were permitted to stay only nine months at a time. The programs were expanded in 2007, and temporary visas for these workers have been extended to twenty-four months, provided they are employed by the same employer for the duration of the contract.

16 Cultural competence, in all its forms, functions as cultural capital only in the "objective relations set up between the system of economic production and the system producing the producers" (Bourdieu, 1990b, 124). Specifically, for example, economic producers, including workers and (increasingly) traders and financiers, are systematically generated by the relationship between the educational system and the family. These objective systems of relations, which function "both as a source of inculcation and as a market" (ibid., 1984, 65), are integral to the market-state social field, as the practices and procedures used in the production of producers regulate the appropriation of all species of capital in the market-state field.

17 As noted by Jewish philosopher and theologian Abraham Joshua Heschel, "The opposite of love is not wrath; it is indifference."

18 I was unable to find support for this practice of denying access to ESL for Dietsche children who have been in Canada for more than two years, despite consulting Ontario's ESL *Policies and Procedures* (Government of Ontario, 2007) and a veteran educator.

19 The establishment of Dietsche private religious schools, ranging from more conservative to liberal, is expanding. These private schools provide education for Dietsche children in Ontario, Manitoba, and Alberta.

20 Interviews with Dietsche families revealed that the Old Colony schools do not charge consistent fees. One Mennonite immigrant service provider

explained that most Old Colony schools designate a certain percentage of their enrolment for students whose parents cannot afford to pay for their children. This loss is calculated into the tuition fees charged to other parents.

21 In December 2005 the Ontario government increased the age for mandatory school attendance to eighteen.

22 An explanation for such regional differences in the experiences of Dietsche (im)migrants is offered in the analysis of the following chapters.

23 The 1 million households excluded from their 2004 report on housing conditions in Canada were composed of farm households; all Native households, on and off reserves; and households reporting shelter cost-to-income ratios over 100 per cent and incomes of zero (R. Lewis & Jakubec, 2004).

24 See, for example, Emerson, Honey, Madden, & Llewellyn (2009) and Pisati, Whelan, Lucchini, & Maître (2010).

25 Studies that measure social exclusion through self-ratings include, for example, European Commission (2012), Mannila & Reuter (2009), and Whelan & Maître (2008).

26 See Das (2009), Popp & Schels (2008), and Reutter, Stewart, Veenstra, Love, Raphael, & Makwarimba (2009).

27 Related and useful concepts that have informed my understanding of subjective exclusion are "unfavourable inclusion" (Sen, 2000b) and "adverse incorporation" into the state, market, or civil society (see, e.g., Hickey, 2012; Hickey & du Toit, 2007). Although these concepts highlight the role of social and political factors in social exclusion, exploitation, and chronic poverty, the everydayness and necessity of practices of subjective exclusion are overlooked in these analyses.

28 In a rather absurd example, the fluctuating price of garbage according to the strength of regional and global markets determines the possibility of survival for the thousands of waste-pickers who toil in Mumbai's airport area. Here, among the 8,000 tons of garbage produced by Mumbai daily, scavenging and garbage-sorting is a new form of self-employment, brought about by India's economic miracle (Boo, 2012). While such work might be considered a simple case of "adverse participation" (Sen, 2000b), the closure of options and the procedures through which livelihoods and lives are actively transformed by the global market system of capital described in Boo's account are revealed to be much more complex and cogent.

29 The identity of this service provider is unique, as she remained a participating member of the Dietsche (im)migrant community, serving as a principal in an Old Colony school. She also worked as a service provider for a local non-profit social service agency.

4. Everyday Practices of Social Exclusion

1 For a thorough discussion of Bourdieu's concepts of social fields, systems of capital, and habitus, see Bourdieu (1990b, 54), Parsons (1997), and Wacquant (1998b, 221).

2 As a case in point, in the 1980s Canada was one of the most successful countries in the OECD to reduce (or limit) the gap between rich and poor through government taxes and transfers. By the early 2000s, major reforms in the country's social welfare and taxation systems had resulted in Canada's redistributive capacity to plummet to the worst among OECD member countries, joining the United States and Switzerland as the countries with the smallest redistribution impact (Banting & Myles, 2015).

3 This is not to say, however, that the classifying habit is born of malicious intent or hardness of heart. To the contrary, I understand the assertions of concern and desire to make a positive difference in the lives of clients to be sincere. Furthermore, this consideration of the helper habitus is not a comment on the subjective intentions or desires of workers or clients. More to the point, I aim to show that the classifying habit of the helper habitus is *necessity*. In the examination of the daily practices and procedures of helping, I am not suggesting subjective feelings or personal desires. People's motives and intentions are not the focus of this analysis. Rather, the matter at hand is the structured social relations and system of capital in which human services work occurs.

4 Adapted from Bourdieu (1989, 22).

5 Efforts to develop tools that will accurately assess social risk and predict harm continue unabated despite repeated failure. At the time of this writing, for instance, 200 to 300 adoption cases have been put on hold by the Ontario Association of Children's Aid Societies. In each case, children were removed from their birth families at least partly because of drug tests from the discredited Motherisk Drug Testing Laboratory at Toronto's Hospital for Sick Children (Ballingall & Monsebraaten, 2016). In December 2015 a retired appeal court justice concluded that Motherisk's drug and alcohol hair-testing processes used in child custody and criminal proceedings were "inadequate and unreliable" (Gallant & Mendelson, 2015). The report prompted the creation of a provincial commission that will review potentially thousands of individual cases from the lab.

6 I consider the economic habitus and the requirements of neoliberalized social inclusion in some depth in chapter five.

7 See chapter three for a definition and discussion of the residual model of social welfare.

8 Owing to difficulties in counting the number of Dietsche in any given region, no one offered an estimation of the percentage of the population on some type of social assistance. Service providers from one social assistance office reported that 10–30 per cent of their caseloads are made up of Mennonites.

9 The SDMT, or Service Delivery Model Technology, is a specialized provincial computer application. It is described as "the mainstay of the Ontario Works program. It not only maintains records of the Ontario Works clients, but also provides tools that help the case managers in a variety of ways to ensure the ongoing eligibility of their clients" (Pekaruk, 2004, 15).

10 Examples of "deskilling," as the technocratization of human services is called by Swift & Callahan (2009), are ubiquitous. A poignant example is the child protection worker who observed that clinical practice "has become such a tick-box profession" (172). In my research, human service workers often reported being overburdened with paperwork.

11 A search on the World Wide Web indicates that outcomes-based models have been adopted for budgeting by universities, quality improvement in the delivery of healthcare, determining a cost-effective public drug coverage plan in British Colombia, designing securities legislation to enforce measures against market misconduct, developing communities to improve child and family well-being, the delivery of foreign aid by NGOs and donor governments, the scoring of points in hockey games going into overtime, the research and delivery of human services, and the assessment of learning as a measure of accountability in education systems all over the world. Specifically, for instance, the Faculty of Social Work at the University of Toronto initiated a Research Institute for Evidence-Based Social Work, a collaboration between the university, the Ministry of Children and Youth Services, and service providers that at the time of its launch was anticipated to "revolutionize" the practice of social work (E. Smith, 2005).

12 Wacquant (1998a) describes the decisive role of state structures and policies in "organizational desertification" through the retrenchment of public authority, the appropriation of "welfare" as an apparatus of surveillance, the degradation of public education and failing public health, and the political devaluation of public social capital for targeted groups.

13 Bourdieu describes how strategies of "soft domination" are applied: "The habitus and the field maintain a relationship of mutual attraction, and the illusion [*illusio*] is determined from the inside, from impulses that push

towards a self-investment in the object; but it is also determined from the outside, starting with a particular universe of objects offered socially for investment. By virtue of the specific principle of division (*nomos*) that typifies it, the space of possibilities characteristic of each field – religious, political or scientific – functions like a structured ensemble of offers and appeals, bids and solicitations, and prohibitions as well … Through the system of regulated satisfactions that it proposes, this space of possibilities imposes a particular mode on desire, which is then converted into a specific illusion" (1999, 512).

14 See Bourdieu et al. (1999, 123–9) for a more complete discussion of "site effects" and how they function.

15 For a compelling and intensely detailed account of the regulatory and punitive measures required to maintain the illusion of free markets and the myth of natural order, see Harcourt (2011).

16 See Fromm (1941) for an analysis of the social psychology associated with the new individualized freedom experienced by the powerful moneyed class of Renaissance capitalism. Fromm writes, "It seems that the new freedom brought two things to them: an increased feeling of strength and at the same time an increased isolation, doubt, scepticism, and – resulting from all these – anxiety" (48).

5. Producing the Economic Habitus

1 From field notes and transcript of Interview 18 with Isaak and Margaretha, a young Dietsche (im)migrant couple.

2 Social fields and systems of capital develop and evolve across time, so that they are imbued with elaborate histories. I suggest that there is a particular and discrete Mennonite structure of symbolic assets that is common to the multiple and indiscrete social fields and subfields deriving from the Anabaptist-Mennonite heritage and faith tradition. It is this Mennonite system of capital, as it is played out in the specific Dietsche social field and as articulated and demonstrated through research, that I will explore in some depth. However, it is important to note that not all Dietsche people or service providers adhere to the principles or ideas associated with their respective social fields in the same way. So I am not claiming, for example, that all Mennonites believe the same things or exhibit these qualities. In fact, some Dietsche people in Canada no longer identify themselves as Mennonite at all, and some aspects of their heritage appear to be little more than faded memory. I have attempted to provide a "mapping" of the complex and multi-faceted Dietsche social field and its associated system

of capital based on a collaborative interpretation of all life experiences shared with me.

3 For instance, Bourdieu's (1990b) in-depth analysis of peasant life and rituals of the Kabyle people in northern Algeria is instructive in understanding the Dietsche system of capital and associated habitus. See also E.P. Thompson's (1967) classic discussion of pre-industrial work life in "Time, work-discipline, and industrial capitalism."

4 For accounts of people in Canada who "cobble together" a living, see, for example, Good Gingrich (2008, 2010a).

5 In this instance Durango and Zacatecas refer to colonies rather than Mexican states.

6 Dragging on for close to two decades in some regions, more than half of Mexico has experienced extreme drought conditions – some say the worst on record (Rosenberg & Torres, 2012). The drought has destroyed millions of acres of cropland, left livestock to starve to death, dried up streams, and cleared some towns as people flee (Guerrero, 2012).

7 To reiterate, the economic factors of social exclusion are clearly worthy of the considerable attention they receive in the literature. At the same time, I argue that these factors alone do not accurately represent the forces of social exclusion.

8 For an analysis of migratory global flows and their distinctions and similarities, see Collyer, Düvell, & de Haas (2012).

9 Contrary to Castro's (2004) statement that it is "mainly the poor ones" (34) who return annually to Mexico, my research provides consistent evidence that the migrant lifestyle is a luxury afforded only to those who are not so desperate. Those who can sustain temporary migration are advantaged with the rather unusual circumstance of being debt-free and owning some property in Mexico. The significance of this for Dietsche families will be discussed further in the concluding section of this chapter.

10 Bourdieu (1984) contrasts the taste (or disposition) for distinction and the taste for necessity. The taste for distinction, referring to art or food or livelihood practices, "implies freedom from economic necessity, [and] the ability to keep necessity at arm's length … The submission to necessity by those less endowed with cultural and economic capital corresponds, on the other hand, to a more functional and pragmatic aesthetic based on the schemes of everyday life" (Johnson, 1993, 24).

11 Mennonite groups have not always been content with such austerity. The gradual weakening of the Mennonite resolve to pragmatism in the nineteenth century gave rise to one of the most enduring divides among Mennonites in their near 500-year history. When some Mennonite

colonies in Russia began to allow higher education, music, and literature to permeate their borders, others felt the threat of the encroaching world from their own people. Groups desiring greater distance and difference stood firm in the face of demands from the Russian state and pressure from the brotherhood. Mennonites who accommodated some measure of change remained in Russia and flourished – economically, socially, and culturally – until they were driven from their homeland following half a century of remarkable prosperity. The thousands of Mennonites who fled Stalin's Terror in the 1920s left behind substantial material wealth, scores of hectares of fertile land, progressive schools and hospitals, and respected financial and political institutions. In contrast to their Dutch-Russian *Frintschoft* (kinship) and the Swiss *Freindschaft*, who fled "worldly influences" years or generations earlier, brutal persecution and divine deliverance – rather than devout difference, distance, and submission – came to define their Mennonite identity. Settling primarily in western regions of Canada and the United States in the 1920s and later as refugees after the second world war (M. Epp, 2000), these Dutch-Russian Mennonites demonstrate a distinct disposition towards unreserved engagement with the world and bold confidence in their educated and cultured heritage. Many who settled in North America in this most recent emigration from Russia are renowned for their economic success, cultural distinction, and esteemed social networks, reminiscent of the lives of their parents and grandparents in Russian colonies. Giving evidence to its inadequate autonomy and influence, the hierarchical order of various Mennonite subfields has come to reinforce the dominant market-state system of capital, and the traditional symbolic power of difference, distance, and proximity to necessity – or simple living – has in many ways, for most Mennonites, been reversed.

12 "Work and hope," derived from the Latin expression *Fac et spera* (Do/ work and hope), became an Amish and Mennonite motto associated with a range of Anabaptist ideals, such as pacifism, respect for the land, faith in spiritual rather than material security, and eternal salvation (Kasdorf, 1995). The motto, with an image of "a little man with a shovel tilling the soil," occupied a prominent place on the title page of all German versions of *Martyrs' Mirror* printed in North America until 1990 (ibid.).

13 The full meaning of the Plautdietsch word *Jemeenschaft* is not easily captured in a single English word. The notion of "fellowship" comes close in its reference to a spiritual dimension of community relationships, to something greater than the "everyday." Yet in Plautdietsch, it is also an everyday word to describe meaningful interaction between people, such as

a good visit with a friend. It signifies the quality of an interaction and the connection enjoyed through relating with each other (Fast, 2011).

14 In an interview for a previous study with Old Order Mennonite informal helpers, one respondent recalled his sense of alarm and foreboding when the Human Rights Act was introduced in Canada in 1985. He described the underlying difficulty in determining whose individual rights and freedoms take precedence when they are contradictory. For him, the common good must always supersede the rights of any one individual (Good Gingrich & E. Lightman, 2004).

15 It is said that the only book cherished by Mennonites more than the Bible is the *Martyrs' Mirror*. Indeed, this book occupies a prominent place in the libraries of many Mennonite homes and churches. Consisting of a rather gruesome and lengthy report, it details the martyred deaths of hundreds of Anabaptists in the sixteenth century.

16 The arbitrariness (and often absurdity) associated with waged labour as the ideal (or perhaps only) livelihood strategy is difficult to recognize without awareness of an alternative. Bourdieu (2000a) poignantly describes the overhauling of a life that is sometimes necessary to earn a wage rather than make a living, thus producing the economic habitus. Making a living Dietsch-style, as described in this chapter, has shown convergence with pervasive market ideals and practices over the past fifty or sixty years. Yet the Dietsche system of capital (which is not always realized in practice) remains countercultural in many respects and poses a challenge to market ethos.

17 Indeed, self-determination (or a related notion) is widely assumed to be a universal value and human objective. To name only one example, according to the United Nations Development Programme (UNDP, 2010), a critical measure of a country's success is assessing whether people "have the opportunity to be educated and whether they are free to use their knowledge and talents to shape their own destinies" (ibid., iv). Especially in western cultures, such notions are often taken up in individualistic rather than collective terms.

18 Research evidence, beyond the case example of Dietsche (im)migrants, abounds. I cite only a few examples here. When accounting for educational attainment and credentials, hourly wages for black males in the United States are 61–74 per cent of those for white males (Darity & Hamilton, 2012). Applying their Economic Exclusion Index to Canada's Survey of Labour and Income Dynamics, Naomi Lightman and Luann Good Gingrich (2012) found that individuals identifying as a visible minority were found to be 22 per cent more likely to have poor economic outcomes,

and visible minority status presents the greatest disadvantage for young new immigrant women. Using data from Canada, Australia, the European Union, and the United States from 1980 to 2006, Leah Vosko (2010) convincingly demonstrates that significantly more women than men, and more immigrants and migrants than citizens, occupy precarious jobs, including part-time, temporary, self-employed, and low-paying work.

6. The Practical Sense of Self-Imposed Social Exclusion

1 Bourdieu identifies and incorporates two stages of reflexivity – methodological and epistemic. *Methodological reflexivity* demands the "relentless self-questioning of method itself in the very movement whereby it is implemented" (Wacquant, 1998b, 219). The construction of the object – the focus of our attention – cannot be defined in one stroke or moment, but is accomplished through the very process of inquiry, necessarily changing shape and acquiring new meaning as the observed material and social realities inform understanding, or theory. *Epistemic reflexivity* exposes the falseness of presumed objectivity – the absurdity of claiming a "bird's-eye-view." In this case, epistemic reflexivity strives to use an awareness of subjectivity as a structured set of necessary dispositions to understand practices and strategies that are put to work in the social relations that comprise the delivery of social services.

2 For thorough reviews of the theoretical and empirical developments in the study of transnational migration and associated gaps in the research, see Faist (2004) and Levitt & Jaworsky (2007).

3 Loewen (2013b) notes that the church leadership in Mexico "disapproved strongly of a return to the land the Mennonites had left in the 1920s, and consequent excommunications were not uncommon" (168). Yet the practice of shunning had fallen out of fashion by 1979, as livelihood practices became increasingly impossible in southern colonies, and more families began to look northward for greater opportunities (264).

4 From the author's field notes.

5 This is an excerpt from an interview with an Algerian immigrant worker in Paris, recorded by Abdelmalek Sayad in a chapter entitled "The Curse," in Bourdieu et al. (1999).

6 For a stunning personal account of symbolic violence in the contradictory spaces in between a conservative Mennonite woman's world and the rather rigid academic field of play, see Dutcher (2004).

7 Hélène Cixous uses the word *entredeux* "to designate a true in-between – between a life which is ending and a life which is beginning ... These

are the innumerable moments that touch us with bereavements of all
sorts" (Cixous & Calle-Gruber, 1997, 9–10). We experience an *entredeux*
when we are confronted, often violently so, by situations for which
we are absolutely unprepared. In those moments "we are thrown into
strangeness" and we find ourselves "abroad at home" (ibid.).

8 Habitus may adapt, over time, to the essential necessity of hopelessness –
when dispossession of all types of capital is severe, and the struggle for
assets is constrained within very narrow limits. The economies of social
positions defined primarily by dispossession of material and symbolic
capital function to sustain the most basic level of physical survival.
Whereas the necessity of self-imposed social exclusion is a constant, the
particulars of that necessity are not, because the structural and relational
paradoxes of dispossessed social spaces are varied and variable.

9 A study released by Mexico's statistics and geography institute in August
2012 reported that Mexico's drug-related homicide rate rose for the fourth
year in a row in 2011. Up by 5.6 per cent compared with the previous year,
homicides totalled 27,199, or 24 per 100,000 people. This is an increase
from 8 homicides per 100,000 in 2007. It is frequently noted that the drug-
related death rate has steadily increased since December 2006, when
President Calderón declared a "war on drugs" and made the decision to
deploy the military to fight drug-trafficking gangs (Fausset, 2012).

10 For example – and there are many – the "Sponsorship Scandal" is a
manifestation of "under-the-table" exchanges between high-ranking
politicians in the Canadian federal government and select individuals in
the finance and business sectors. The program ran from 1996 to 2004. It
is striking that the illicit – even illegal – nature of such economic activity
continued to be debated for years, revealing the discretionary judgment of
the various legitimate means of appropriating capital for large holders of
capital.

11 Here I suggest a moment to take a breath, and I offer a brief summary of
the ground covered so far, as we are at a critical point. Our consideration
of self-imposed social exclusion culminates in the ideas of integrated
ambiguity and divided habitus – ideas that are both complicated and
crucial to understanding. Social classifications organize perceptions of the
social world and, through symbolic power, organize whole societies and
the world itself. The classificatory schemes of market logic – pervasive
and taken for granted – are based on simple binaries, such as masculine/
feminine, strong/weak, deserving/undeserving, and included/excluded.
As is the case in "archaic societies where they often work through dualist
oppositions" (Bourdieu, 1989, 22), the categorical point of view is based

on *mis*representation and perpetuates *mis*apprehension of individual and social realities. Divided social spaces are thus, necessarily, also paradoxical, as the contradictions through which they are organized are severely limited in their adequacy. The absolutism of the categorical perspective is mostly erroneous, and carries only enough evident "truth" to sustain itself.

Such paradoxical spaces are dependent on the repetition of specific habits – the everyday practices that precisely replicate dualist and absolutist mental structures in social structures. This is the classifying habitus, and its principles of perception are founded on casual, superficial non-comprehension of the social world. A coherent classifying habitus, therefore, requires continual splitting and disavowal to sustain the cognitive structures of misrepresentation that produce and deepen social divides. It is this splitting and disavowal that becomes, over and over, the essence of the paired processes of stereotyping and "archetyping," as the self is never always congruent with the defining criteria of one or another oppositional category. Ideologically constructed identities – unlike human beings – are either competent or incompetent, independent or dependent, knowing or known, helpful or helpless, good or bad, able or disabled, and so on. To the contrary, given increasing mobility and multiple places of home, people are both Canadian and "foreign," settled and unsettled, belonging and out of place, white and "of colour," colonizer and colonized, and oppressor and oppressed. Excluded and included.

Ambiguity may be unbearable in the face of repeated traumas, hardship, or threats to survival. Shame is disdain for the divided self, necessitating the rejection – and often projection – of undesirable parts. Unreconciled ambiguity insists that all perceptions and dispositions must align with material and symbolic profits in the preferred – or most forceful – system of capital, leaving no room for multiple identities and alternative inclinations. Splitting and disavowal entails abandoning one game in favour of another, thereby sacrificing any and all assets and profit potential in the former, and submitting to the assigned starting position and associated rules of exchange and gain of the latter. Compliance and the necessary devaluation of all held assets buy a place – usually among the least – in the new field of play. The appearance of coherence is achieved through self-alienation and the perpetual reinforcement – yet denial – of the internal split. To give in to the market-state system of capital is to engage in the necessary daily dividing practices of all sorts. While official discourse of the market-state – common sense – insists that social inclusion is universally available through full compliance with market rules, particularly that of "earning a wage," the very structure of capital production and exchange is built on processes and outcomes of social exclusion. The market-state social field is organized by a system of capital that protects the value of its resources through enhancing their scarcity and thus ensuring ever wider and deeper social and internal divides. This is social exclusion by design.

Alternatively, incoherence of habitus may be sustained improvisation, which gives authentic expression to an ambiguous self. Self-imposed social exclusion is testimony to a divided, yet integrated, self and habitus. Integrated ambiguity, or conciliation of contraries, functions to preserve a subordinate social field and protect one's assets – particularly one's symbolic power – in that system of capital. A cleft habitus permits the simultaneous occupation of dominant and dominated social positions in conflicting social fields. For example, agents may maintain material and symbolic assets and an upward trajectory in a secondary system of capital while having minimal capacity for accruing capital in the market-state social field. Integrated ambiguity is to see and know different and often contradictory systems of capital and divergent rules of the game all at once, and to be inclined towards practices that preserve a coherent yet ambiguous self.

7. Social Inclusion: Ideas and Practices of Reconciliation

1 I use the term "radical" with intention here – not to be provocative with respect to our heightened sensibilities regarding radicalization of young people who are trained to sacrifice themselves in acts of terrorism, but for its original Latin reference to "the root of things." To turn towards and make room for difference is to subvert the very foundations of the market-state social field and the roots of social exclusion.
2 From Thomas & Woodruff (1999, 3–5).
3 This is an intentional reference to Object Relations Theory. Along with scholars such as S. Clarke (1999), I consider the unconscious psychological processes described by Melanie Klein and others to be consequential at all levels of interpersonal relationships and thus productive in the dynamics of social exclusion.
4 Bourdieu makes quite a lot of the paradox that is integral to my "I." He writes: "From this paradoxical relationship of double inclusion flow all the paradoxes which Pascal assembled under the heading of wretchedness and greatness, and which ought to be meditated on by all those who remain trapped in the scholastic dilemma of determinism and freedom: determined (wretchedness), man can know his determinations (greatness)

and work to overcome them. These paradoxes all find their principle in the privilege of reflexivity: 'Man knows that he is wretched. He is therefore wretched, because he is so; but he is really great because he knows it.' Or again: 'The weakness of man is far more evident in those who know it not than in those who know it.' It is no doubt true that one cannot expect any greatness, at least in matters of thought, except through knowledge of 'wretchedness'" (2000b, 130–1).

5 Lederach & Lederach (2010) relate stories of face-to-face encounters and reconciliation in communities torn by protracted conflict and "unspeakable violence." If such interpersonal engagement between enemies of war is possible, surely it is possible to reach across the divides produced by the slow, structural violences of poverty and social exclusion.

6 This discussion is based on the philosophy and principles of restorative justice and the related practice of circles. I have drawn from a variety restorative justice scholars and practitioners, including Ball, Caldwell, & Pranis (2010), Lederach (2005, 2014), Vaandering (2010, 2014), and Zehr (2005, 2014).

7 Lily Hiebert Rempel, personal communication, 23 January 2014.

8 Kerry Fast, personal communication, 17 January 2014.

References

Adams, H. (1999). *Tortured people: The politics of colonization* (rev. ed.). Penticton, BC: Theytus Books.

Ades, J., Apparicio, P., & Séguin, A.-M. (2012). Are new patterns of low-income distribution emerging in Canadian metropolitan areas? *Canadian Geographer/Géographe canadien, 56*(3), 339–61. http://dx.doi.org/10.1111/j.1541-0064.2012.00438.x

Aliber, M. (2002). Informal finance in the informal economy: Promoting decent work among the working poor. Working Paper on the Informal Economy. Geneva: International Labour Organization.

Anderson, B. (2006). *Imagined communities: Reflections on the origin and spread of nationalism* (rev. ed.). London, New York: Verso.

Anderson, E.K., & Hoy, J.V. (2006). Striving for self-sufficient families: Urban and rural experiences for women in welfare-to-work programs. *Journal of Poverty, 10*(1), 69–91. http://dx.doi.org/10.1300/J134v10n01_04

Armstrong, D., & Coleman, B. (2001). *Health care needs of Mennonite women living in Elgin County.* St Thomas, ON: Elgin-St Thomas Health Unit.

Arribas-Ayllon, M. (2005). Genealogy and the subject of welfare: A question of which techniques? *Critical Psychology, 15*, 8–41.

Aydemir, A., & Skuterud, M. (2005). Explaining the deteriorating entry earnings of Canada's immigrant cohorts, 1966–2000. *Canadian Journal of Economics/Revue canadienne d'économique, 38*(2), 641–72. http://dx.doi.org/10.1111/j.0008-4085.2005.00297.x

Baker Collins, S. (2002). *Vulnerability and assets in urban poverty: Bringing together participatory methods and a sustainable livelihoods framework.* Doctoral thesis. University of Toronto.

Ball, J., Caldwell, W., & Pranis, K. (2010). *Doing democracy with circles: Engaging communities in public planning.* Ann Arbor, MI: Sheridan Books.

Ballingall, A., & Monsebraaten, L. (2016, 1 February). Hundreds of adoption cases on hold as Motherisk probe continues. *Toronto Star*. Retrieved from http://www.thestar.com/news/canada/2016/02/01/hundreds-of-adoption-cases-on-hold-as-motherisk-probe-continues.html

Banerjee, R. (2009). Income growth of new immigrants in Canada: Evidence from the Survey of Labour and Income Dynamics. *Relations industrielles/ Industrial Relations, 64*(3), 466–88. http://dx.doi.org/10.7202/038552ar

Banerjee, R., & Lee, B.Y. (2015). Decreasing the recent immigrant earnings gap: The impact of Canadian credential attainment. *International Migration, 53*(2), 205–18.

Banting, K.G., & Myles, J. (2015). Framing the new inequality: The politics of income redistribution in Canada. In D.A. Green, W.C. Riddell & F. St-Hilaire (Eds), *Income inequality: The Canadian story*. Montreal: McGill-Queen's University Press.

Barkan, E.R. (2006). Introduction: Immigration, incorporation, assimilation, and the limits of transnationalism. *Journal of American Ethnic History, 25*(2/3), 7–32.

Barry, B. (2002). Social exclusion, social isolation, and the distribution of income. In J. Hills, J. Le Grand, & D. Piachaud (Eds), *Understanding social exclusion* (13–29). Oxford: Oxford University Press.

Bateman, D. (2015, 15 June). Health professionals across Canada protest healthcare cuts for refugee claimants, *Toronto Star*. Retrieved from http://www.thestar.com/news/investigations/2015/06/15/should-all-refugee-claimants-health-costs-be-covered-decision-after-election.html

Beck, U. (1992). *The risk society: Towards a new modernity*. Thousand Oaks, CA: Sage.

Benn, M. (2000). New labour and social exclusion. *Political Quarterly, 71*(3), 309–18. http://dx.doi.org/10.1111/1467-923X.00306

Blalock, L.L., Tiller, V.R., & Monroe, P.A. (2004). "They get you out of courage": Persistent deep poverty among former welfare-reliant women. *Family Relations, 53*(2), 127–37. http://dx.doi.org/10.1111/j.0022-2445.2004.00003.x

Blanchfield, M. (2015, 28 April). Auditor General report takes on First Nations health, lacklustre inmate rehabilitation. *Huffington Post*. Retrieved from http://www.huffingtonpost.ca/2015/04/28/auditor-takes-aim-at-firs_n_7160848.html

Blanco, H. (1994). *How to think about social problems: American pragmatism and the idea of planning*. Westport, CT.: Greenwood Press.

Block, F., & Somers, M.R. (2014). *The power of market fundamentalism: Karl Polanyi's critique*. Cambridge, MA: Harvard University Press. http://dx.doi.org/10.4159/harvard.9780674416345

Block, S., & Galabuzi, G.-E. (2011). *Canada's colour-coded labour market: The gap for racialized workers.* Toronto: Canadian Centre for Policy Alternatives.

Block, S., Galabuzi, G.-E., & Weiss, A. (2014). *The colour coded labour market by the numbers.* Toronto: Wellesley Institute.

Bloemraad, I., Korteweg, A., & Yurdakul, G. (2008). Citizenship and immigration: Multiculturalism, assimilation, and challenges to the nation-state. *Annual Review of Sociology, 34,* 153–79.

Boo, K. (2012). *Behind the beautiful forevers: Life, death, and hope in a Mumbai undercity.* New York: Random House.

Bourdieu, P. (1977). *Outline of a theory of practice.* R. Nice (Trans.). Cambridge: Cambridge University Press. http://dx.doi.org/10.1017/CBO9780511812507

Bourdieu, P. (1984). *Distinction: A social critique of the judgement of taste.* Cambridge, MA: Harvard University Press.

Bourdieu, P. (1986). The forms of capital. In J.G. Richardson (Ed.), *Handbook of theory and research for the sociology of education* (241–58). New York: Greenwood Press.

Bourdieu, P. (1989). Social space and symbolic power. *Sociological Theory, 7*(1), 14–25. http://dx.doi.org/10.2307/202060

Bourdieu, P. (1990a). *In other words: Essays towards a reflexive sociology.* M. Adamson (Trans.). Stanford: Stanford University Press.

Bourdieu, P. (1990b). *The logic of practice.* R. Nice (Trans.). Stanford: Stanford University Press.

Bourdieu, P. (1991). The peculiar history of scientific reason. *Sociological Forum, 6*(1), 3–26. http://dx.doi.org/10.1007/BF01112725

Bourdieu, P. (1996). *The state nobility: Elite schools in the field of power.* L.C. Clough (Trans.). Stanford: Stanford University Press.

Bourdieu, P. (1998). *Acts of resistance against the tyranny of the market.* R. Nice (Trans.). New York: The New Press.

Bourdieu, P. (2000a). Making the economic habitus: Algerian workers revisited. *Ethnography, 1*(1), 17–41. http://dx.doi.org/10.1177/14661380022230624

Bourdieu, (2000b). *Pascalian meditations.* R. Nice (Trans.). Stanford: Stanford University Press.

Bourdieu, P. (2003). *Firing back: Against the tyranny of the market (2).* L. Wacquant (Trans.). New York, London: Verso.

Bourdieu, (2004). Gender and symbolic violence. In N. Scheper-Hughes & P.I. Bourgois (Eds), *Violence in war and peace: An anthology* (339–42). Oxford: Blackwell.

Bourdieu, P. (2005). Principles of an economic anthropology. In N.J. Smelser & R. Swedberg (Eds), *The handbook of economic sociology* (75–89). Princeton: Princeton University Press.

Bourdieu, P. (2007). *Sketch for a self-analysis*. R. Nice (Trans.). Cambridge: Polity Press.

Bourdieu, P., & Wacquant, L. (1992). *An invitation to reflexive sociology*. Chicago: University of Chicago Press.

Bourdieu, P., & Wacquant, L. (2000). The organic ethnologist of Algerian migration. *Ethnography, 1*(2), 173–82. http://dx.doi.org/10.1177/14661380022230723

Bourdieu, P., & Wacquant, L. (2004). Symbolic violence. In N. Scheper-Hughes & P.I. Bourgois (Eds), *Violence in war and peace: An anthology* (272–274). Oxford: Blackwell.

Bourdieu, P., et al. (1999). *The weight of the world: Social suffering in contemporary society*. P.P. Ferguson (Trans.). Stanford, CA: Stanford University Press.

Bowker, G.C., & Star, S.L. (2001). Pure, real and rational numbers: The American imaginary of countability. *Social Studies of Science, 31*(3), 422–5. http://dx.doi.org/10.1177/030631201031003006

Brandt, D. (1993). *Wild mother dancing: Maternal narrative in Canadian literature*. Winnipeg: University of Manitoba Press.

Brandt, D. (1996). *Dancing naked: Narrative strategies for writing across centuries*. Stratford, ON: Mercury Press.

Braun, W. (2008, 15 September). Second-class Mennonites. *Canadian Mennonite, 12*.

Braun, W. (2013, July 8). Ministry in a very different world: MCC workers address physical, spiritual hunger in Mexican colonies. *Canadian Mennonite, 17*, 4–9.

Brenner, N., Peck, J., & Theodore, N. (2010). Variegated neoliberalization: Geographies, modalities, pathways. *Global Networks, 10*(2), 182–222. http://dx.doi.org/10.1111/j.1471-0374.2009.00277.x

Brooks, K. (2002). *Elgin-Oxford legal clinic project*. St Thomas, ON: Legal Aid Ontario.

Brown, J.B., & Lichter, D.T. (2004). Poverty, welfare, and the livelihood strategies of nonmetropolitan single mothers. *Rural Sociology, 69*(2), 282–301. http://dx.doi.org/10.1526/003601104323087615

Browne, R. (2015, 18 March). The real target of Taber's new law: Mennonites? *Maclean's*. Retrieved from http://www.macleans.ca/news/canada/tabers-real-target-mennonites/

Burchardt, T., Le Grand, J., & Piachaud, D. (1999). Social exclusion in Britain 1991–1995. *Social Policy and Administration, 33*(3), 227–44. http://dx.doi.org/10.1111/1467-9515.00148

Byrne, D.S. (2005). *Social exclusion* (2nd ed.). Buckingham, UK: Open University Press.

Cañás Bottos, L. (2008a). *Old Colony Mennonites in Argentina and Bolivia: Nation making, religious conflict and imagination of the future.* Leiden, Boston: Brill. http://dx.doi.org/10.1163/ej.9789004160958.i-216

Cañás Bottos, L. (2008b). Transformations of Old Colony Mennonites: The making of a trans-statal community. *Global Networks, 8*(2), 214–31. http://dx.doi.org/10.1111/j.1471-0374.2008.00192.x

Cañás Bottos, L. (2009). Order and dissent among Old Colony Mennonites: A regime of embedded sovereignty. In T.G. Kirsch & B. Turner (Eds), *Permutations of order: Religion and law as contested sovereignties* (107–23). Farnham, UK: Ashgate.

Cannon, S. (2000a, 28 October). The long road home, *The Record*, H1–2.

Cannon, S. (2000b, 27 October). When dreams die, *The Record*, A1, 9.

Caron Malenfant, É., Lebel, A., & Martel, L. (2010). *Projections of the diversity of the Canadian population.* Ottawa: Statistics Canada.

Castro, P. (2004). The 'return' of the Mennonites from the Cuauhtémoc Region to Canada: A perspective from Mexico. *Journal of Mennonite Studies, 22,* 25–38.

CBC (Canadian Broadcasting Corporation). (1992). Mennonite mob [Television series episode]. In *The fifth estate.* Toronto: CBC.

Chambon, A. (2005, June). Personal communication. Comments on first draft of PhD thesis.

Chambon, A. (2012). Disciplinary borders and borrowings: Social work knowledge and its social reach, a historical perspective. *Social Work & Society, 10*(2), 1–12.

Cixous, H., & Calle-Gruber, M. (1997). *Hélène Cixous, rootprints: Memory and life writing.* London, New York: Routledge.

Clarke, J. (1999). Whose business? Social welfare and managerial calculation. In M. Purdy & D. Banks (Eds), *Health and exclusion: Policy and practice in health provision* (45–61). London: Routledge.

Clarke, J. (2003). Turning inside out? Globalization, neo-liberalism and welfare states. *Anthropologica, 45*(2), 201–22. http://dx.doi.org/10.2307/25606141.

Clarke, J., & Newman, J. (1997). *The managerial state: Power, politics and ideology in the remaking of social welfare.* London: Sage.

Clarke, S. (1999). Splitting difference: Psychoanalysis, hatred and exclusion. *Journal for the Theory of Social Behaviour, 29*(1), 21–35. http://dx.doi.org/10.1111/1468-5914.00089

Clements, L. (2005). Winners and losers. *Journal of Law and Society, 32*(1), 34–50. http://dx.doi.org/10.1111/j.1467-6478.2005.313_1.x

Cleveland, G., & Hyatt, D. (2003). Child care subsidies, welfare reforms, and lone mothers. *Industrial Relations, 42*(2), 251–69. http://dx.doi.org/10.1111/1468-232X.00289

Coburn, D. (2000). Income inequality, social cohesion and the health status of populations: The role of neo-liberalism. *Social Science & Medicine, 51*(1), 135–46. http://dx.doi.org/10.1016/S0277-9536(99)00445-1.

Collyer, M., Düvell, F., & de Haas, H. (2012). Critical approaches to transit migration. *Population Space and Place, 18*(4), 407–14. http://dx.doi.org/10.1002/psp.630.

Commins, P. (Ed.). (1993). *Combating exclusion in Ireland: A midway report.* Brussels: Observatory on National Policies to Combat Social Exclusion, European Commission.

Cormack, P., Cosgrave, J.F., & Harling Stalker, L. (2012). Who counts now? Re-making the Canadian citizen. *Canadian Journal of Sociology/Cahiers canadiens de sociologie, 37*(3), 231–52.

Corrigan, P. (1991). Viewpoint: Power/difference. *Sociological Review, 39*(2), 309–34. http://dx.doi.org/10.1111/j.1467-954X.1991.tb02983.x

Cox, C. (2011). The resilient word: Linguistic preservation and innovation among the Old Colony Mennonites in Latin America. Paper presented at the Mennonite Studies Conference on Anti-modern pathways: "Horse and buggy" Mennonites in Canada, Belize and Latin America. University of Winnipeg.

Cranford, C.J., Vosko, L.F., & Zukewich, N. (2003). Precarious employment in the Canadian labour market: A statistical portrait. *Just Labour: A Canadian Journal of Work and Society, 3*, 6–22.

Crocker, W.A. (2013). More than A, B, C: Old Colony Mennonites and the challenges of Ontario public education policy. *Transnational Social Review: A Social Work Journal, 3*(2).

Currie, E. (2004). *The road to whatever: Middle-class culture and the crisis of adolescence.* New York: Metropolitan Books.

D'Ambrosio, A., Tiessen, A., & Simpson, J.R. (2012). Development of a food frequency questionnaire for toddlers of Low-German-speaking Mennonites from Mexico. *Canadian Journal of Dietetic Practice and Research, 73*(1), 40–4. http://dx.doi.org/10.3148/73.1.2012.40

Dangschat, J.S. (2009). Space matters: Marginalization and its places. *International Journal of Urban and Regional Research, 33*(3), 835–840. http://dx.doi.org/10.1111/j.1468-2427.2009.00924.x

Darity, W., Jr, & Hamilton, D. (2012). Bold policies for economic justice. *Review of Black Political Economy, 39*(1), 79–85. http://dx.doi.org/10.1007/s12114-011-9129-8.

Das, N.K. (2009). Identity politics and social exclusion in India's northeast: A critique of nation-building and redistributive justice. *Anthropos, 104*(2), 549–58.

Davies, J.S. (2005). The social exclusion debate: Strategies, controversies and dilemmas. *Policy Studies, 26*(1), 3–27. http://dx.doi.org/10.1080/01442870500041561.

Davis, D. (2004). Manufacturing mammies: The burdens of service work and welfare reform among battered black women. *Anthropologica, 46*(2), 273–88. http://dx.doi.org/10.2307/25606199.

de Haan, A. (1998). 'Social exclusion': An alternative concept for the study of deprivation? *IDS Bulletin, 29*(1), 10–19. http://dx.doi.org/10.1111/j.1759-5436.1998.mp29001002.x.

de Haan, A. (1999). *Social exclusion: Towards a holistic understanding of deprivation*. Villa Borsig Workshop Series: Inclusion, Justice, and Poverty Reduction. Retrieved from eldis website: http://www.eldis.org/assets/Docs/28069.html.

de Haas, H. (2010). Migration transitions: A theoretical and empirical inquiry into the developmental drivers of international migration. Working Paper No. 24. Oxford: International Migration Institute, James Martin 21st Century School, University of Oxford.

de Haas, H. (2012). The migration and development pendulum: A critical view on research and policy. *International Migration (Geneva, Switzerland), 50*(3), 8–25. http://dx.doi.org/10.1111/j.1468-2435.2012.00755.x

deGroot-Maggetti, G. (2002). *A measure of poverty in Canada: A guide to the debate about poverty lines*. Toronto: Public Justice Resource Centre.

DeKeseredy, W.S. (2009). Canadian crime control in the new millennium: The influence of neo-conservative US policies and practices. *Police Practice and Research, 10*(4), 305–16. http://dx.doi.org/10.1080/15614260802586301

DeKeseredy, W.S. (2011). *Contemporary critical criminology*. London, New York: Routledge/Taylor & Francis Group.

Department for International Development. (2005). *Reducing poverty and tackling social exclusion*. DFID Policy Paper. London: DFID.

Doern, G.B., Maslove, A.M., & Prince, M.J. (2013). *Canadian public budgeting in the age of crises: Shifting budget domains and temporal budgeting*. Montreal: McGill-Queen's University Press.

Dominelli, L. (2004). *Social work: Theory and practice for a changing profession*. Cambridge: Polity Press.

Dutcher, V.A. (2004). Writing without the "protection of angels": Notes from the middle voice. *Feminismo/s, 4*, 39–60.

Dyck, A., & Fuller, L. (1989). East Elgin Literacy Assessment Project. *Canadian Women's Studies, 9*(3/4), 50–1.

Dyck, C.J. (Ed.) (1993). *An introduction to Mennonite history: A popular history of the Anabaptists and the Mennonites* (3rd ed.). Scottdale, PA; Waterloo, ON: Herald Press.

Edwards, C. (2009). Regeneration works? Disabled people and area-based urban renewal. *Critical Social Policy, 29*(4), 613–33. http://dx.doi.org/10.1177/0261018309341902

Emerson, E., Honey, A., Madden, R., & Llewellyn, G. (2009). The wellbeing of Australian adolescents and young adults with self-reported long-term conditions, impairments or disabilities: 2001 to 2006. *Australian Journal of Social Issues, 44*(1), 39–54.

ESDC (Employment and Social Development Canada) (2015, 9 January 2015). *Temporary Foreign Workers*. Retrieved 6 February 2015 from http://www.esdc.gc.ca/eng/jobs/foreign_workers/reform/info_emp.shtml

Ens, A. (1994). *Subjects or citizens? The Mennonite experience in Canada, 1870–1925*. Ottawa: University of Ottawa Press.

Epp, F.H. (1974). *Mennonites in Canada, 1786–1920: The history of a separate people*. Toronto: Macmillan.

Epp, F.H. (1982). *Mennonites in Canada, 1920–1940: A people's struggle for survival*. Toronto: Macmillan.

Epp, G. (2013, 27 March). Personal communication.

Epp, M. (2000). *Women without men: Mennonite refugees of the Second World War*. Toronto: University of Toronto Press.

Esping-Andersen, G., Gallie, D., Hemerijck, A., & Myles, J. (2001). A new welfare architecture for Europe? Report submitted to the Belgian Presidency of the European Union.

European Commission. (2012). *Employment and social developments in Europe 2011*. Luxembourg: Publications Office of the European Union.

Eurostat. (2000). *European social statistics: Income, poverty and social exclusion* (2000 ed.). Luxembourg: Office for Official Publications of the European Communities.

Eurostat. (2007). Comparative EU statistics on income and living conditions: Issues and challenges. Paper presented at the EU-SILC Conference, Luxembourg.

Evans, P.M. (2007). (Not) taking account of precarious employment: Workfare policies and lone mothers in Ontario and the UK. *Social Policy and Administration, 41*(1), 29–49. http://dx.doi.org/10.1111/j.1467-9515.2007.00537.x

Faist, T. (2004). Towards a political sociology of transnationalization: The state of the art in migration research. *Archives Européennes de Sociologie, 45*(3), 331–66. http://dx.doi.org/10.1017/S0003975604001481

Faist, T. (2008). Transstate spaces and development: Some critical remarks. In L. Pries (Ed.), *Rethinking transnationalism: The Meso-link of organisations* (63–80). New York: Routledge.

Fast, K. (2004). Religion, pain, and the body: Agency in the life of an Old Colony Mennonite woman. *Journal of Mennonite Studies, 22,* 103–29.

Fast, K. (2011, 18 March). Personal communication.

Fast, K. (2012, 20 July). Personal communication.

Fast, K. (2016, 16 March). Personal communication.

Fausset, R. (2012, 21 August). Amid drug war, Mexico homicide rate up for fourth straight year, *Los Angeles Times.* Retrieved from http://latimesblogs. latimes.com/world_now/2012/08/in-midst-of-drug-war-mexican-homicide-rate-increase-for-fourth-straight-year.html

Fehr Kehler, T. (2004). *A Kanadier Mennonite woman's experience.* Women's Concerns Report No. 172. March-April. Winnipeg, MB: MCC – Committees on Women's Concerns.

Feldberg, G., & Vipond, R. (1999). The virus of consumerism. In D. Drache & T. Sullivan (Eds), *Market limits in health reform: Public success, private failure* (48–61). New York: Routledge.

Figueiredo, J.B. & de Haan, A. (Eds). (1998). *Social exclusion: An ILO Perspective.* Geneva, Switzerland: International Labour Office.

Foner, N., & Simon, P. (2015). Introduction. In N. Foner & P. Simon (Eds), *Fear, anxiety and national identity: Immigration and belonging in North America and Western Europe* (1–30). New York: Russell Sage Foundation.

Fowler, B. (Ed.). (2000). *Reading Bourdieu on society and culture.* Oxford: Blackwell.

Franklin, U. (1992). *The real world of technology.* Concord, ON: Anansi.

Freire, P. (1974). *Education for critical consciousness.* London, New York: Sheed & Ward.

Freire, P. (1998). *Pedagogy of freedom: Ethics, democracy, and civic courage.* Oxford: Rowman & Littlefield.

Frenette, M., & Morissette, R. (2003). *Will they ever converge? Earnings of immigrant and Canadian-born workers over the last two decades.* Analytical Studies Branch research paper series. Ottawa: Statistics Canada.

Friedman, M., and Friedman, R. (1962). *Capitalism and freedom.* Chicago: University of Chicago Press.

Friesen, J.J. (Ed.). (1989). *Mennonites in Russia, 1788–1988: Essays in honour of Gerhard Lohrenz.* Winnipeg, MB: CMBC Publications.

Fromm, E. (1941). *Escape from freedom.* New York: Henry Holt.

Fudge, J., & Vosko, L.F. (2001). By whose standards? Reregulating the Canadian labour market. *Economic and Industrial Democracy, 22*(3), 327–56. http://dx.doi.org/10.1177/0143831X01223002

Gacitua-Mario, E., & Wodon, Q. (2001). *Measurement and meaning: Combining quantitative and qualitative methods for the analysis of poverty and social exclusion in Latin America*. Washington, DC: World Bank.

Gallant, J., & Mendelson, R. (2015, 17 December). Damning review of Motherisk drug testing sparks call for second probe, *Toronto Star*. Retrieved from http://www.thestar.com/news/gta/2015/12/17/review-of-motherisk-drug-testing-sparks-call-for-public-inquiry.html

Gambrill, E. (2013). *Social work practice: A critical thinker's guide* (3rd ed.). Oxford, New York: Oxford University Press.

Gilbert, N.L., Auger, N., Wilkins, R., & Kramer, M.S. (2013). Neighbourhood income and neonatal, postneonatal and Sudden Infant Death Syndrome (SIDS) mortality in Canada, 1991–2005. *Canadian Journal of Public Health, 104*(3), 187–92.

Giroux, H. (2004). *The terror of neoliberalism: Authoritarianism and the eclipse of democracy*. Aurora, ON: Garamond Press.

Gleeson, D. (1992). School attendance and truancy: A socio-historical account. *Sociological Review, 40*(3), 437–90. http://dx.doi.org/10.1111/j.1467-954X.1992.tb00398.x

Goldring, L., & Joly, M.-P. (2014). Immigration, citizenship and racialization at work: Unpacking employment precarity in southwestern Ontario. *Just Labour, 22*, 94–121.

Goldring, L., & Landolt, P. (2011). Caught in the work-citizenship matrix: The lasting effects of precarious legal status on work for Toronto immigrants. *Globalizations, 8*(3).

Gonzalez, E. (2005). *"It's all work to me": Mothering, work and welfare among Black and Chicana women in Los Angeles*. Los Angeles: University of California, Los Angeles.

Good Gingrich, L. (2003a). Social exclusion as an individual kind: A categorical point of view. *Canadian Review of Social Policy/Revue canadienne de politique sociale, 52*(Fall/Winter), 93–115.

Good Gingrich, L. (2003b). Theorizing social exclusion: Determinants, mechanisms, dimensions, forms, and acts of resistance. In W. Shera (Ed.), *Emerging perspectives on anti-oppressive practice* (3–23). Toronto: Canadian Scholar's Press/Women's Press.

Good Gingrich, L. (2006). *Contesting social exclusion: An interrogation of its self-imposed expressions*. PhD thesis, University of Toronto.

Good Gingrich, L. (2008). Social exclusion and double jeopardy: The management of lone mothers in the market-state social field. *Social Policy and Administration, 42*(4), 379–95. http://dx.doi.org/10.1111/j.1467-9515.2008.00610.x

Good Gingrich, L. (2010a). Single mothers, work(fare), and managed precariousness. *Journal of Progressive Human Services, 21*(2), 107–35. http://dx.doi.org/10.1080/10428230903301410

Good Gingrich, L. (2010b). The symbolic economy of trans-border governance: A case study of subjective exclusion and migrant women from Mexico. *Refugee Survey Quarterly, 29*(1), 161–84. http://dx.doi.org/10.1093/rsq/hdq008

Good Gingrich, L., & Lightman, E. (2004). Mediating communities and cultures: A case study of informal helpers in an Old Order Mennonite community. *Families in Society, 85*(4), 511–20. http://dx.doi.org/10.1606/1044-3894.1838

Good Gingrich, L., & Preibisch, K. (2010). Migration as preservation and loss: The paradox of transnational living for Low German Mennonite women. *Journal of Ethnic and Migration Studies, 36*(9), 1499–518. http://dx.doi.org/10.1080/1369183X.2010.494825

Good Gingrich, L., & Snyder, P. (1997). *A mother's garden: Planting seeds of hope. A learning resource.* A peer nutrition workers' training manual. Waterloo, ON: Oracle Design.

Government of Ontario. (2005). *Ministry of Community and Social Services, Social Assistance.* Vol. 2007. Toronto: Queen's Printer for Ontario.

Government of Ontario. (2007). *English Language Learners ESL and ELD Programs and Services. Policies and Procedures for Ontario Elementary and Secondary Schools, Kindergarten to Grade 12.* Toronto: Government of Ontario.

Guenther, B.L. (2004). A road less traveled: The evangelical path of Kanadier Mennonites who returned to Canada. *Journal of Mennonite Studies, 22*, 145–66.

Guenther, T.F. (2000). Theology of migration: The *Ältesten* reflect. *Journal of Mennonite Studies, 18*, 164–76.

Guerrero, J. (2012, 4 February). Mexico drought chokes cattle, crops. *Wall Street Journal.* Retrieved from http://www.wsj.com/articles/SB10001424052970203711104577201043392294110.html.

Gutiérrez, N.C. (2014). *Mexico: Availability and cost of health care – Legal aspects.* Report for US Department of Justice. Washington, DC: The Law Library of Congress, Global Legal Research Center.

Hacking, I. (1999). *The social construction of what?* Cambridge, MA: Harvard University Press.

Hack-Polay, D.D. (2008). Migrant integration: Case for a necessary shift of paradigm. *Journal of Identity and Migration Studies, 2*(1), 37–56.

Hallsworth, S., & Lea, J. (2011). Reconstructing Leviathan: Emerging contours of the security state. *Theoretical Criminology, 15*(2), 141–57. http://dx.doi.org/10.1177/1362480610383451

Harcourt, B.E. (2011). *The illusion of free markets: Punishment and the myth of natural order.* Cambridge, MA: Harvard University Press.

Hay, C. (2004). The normalizing role of rationalist assumptions in the institutional embedding of neoliberalism. *Economy and Society, 33*(4), 500–27. http://dx.doi.org/10.1080/0308514042000285260

Hayward, C., Simpson, L., & Wood, L. (2004). Still left out in the cold: Problematising participatory research and development. *Sociologia Ruralis, 44*(1), 95–108. http://dx.doi.org/10.1111/j.1467-9523.2004.00264.x

Hedberg, A.S. (2007). *Outside the world: Cohesion and deviation among Old Colony Mennonites in Bolivia.* Uppsala: Uppsala Universitet.

Hedges, K. (1996). "Plautdietsch" and "Huuchdietsch" in Chihuahua: Language, literacy and identity among the Old Colony Mennonites in northern Mexico. PhD thesis, Yale University.

Hertz, N. (2001). A plan for the world: Exclusion. *New Statesman (London, England), 14*(629), 22–3.

Hickey, S. (2012). Social exclusion and adverse incorporation. Retrieved 16 August 2012 from http://www.chronicpoverty.org/page/social-exclusion

Hickey, S., & du Toit, A. (2007). Adverse incorporation, social exclusion and chronic poverty. CRPC Working Paper No. 81. Manchester, UK: Chronic Poverty Research Centre. http://dx.doi.org/10.2139/ssrn.1752967

Hills, J., Le Grand, J., & Piachaud, D. (Eds). (2002). *Understanding social exclusion.* Oxford: Oxford University Press.

IOM (International Organization for Migration). (2014). *Global migration trends: An overview.* Paris: IOM – Migration Research Division.

Janzen, W. (1998). *Build up one another: The work of MCCO with the Mennonites from Mexico in Ontario 1977–1997.* Kitchener, ON: Mennonite Central Committee Ontario.

Janzen, W. (2004a). One door to Canadian citizenship will close on August 14, 2004. Memo. Ottawa: Mennonite Central Committee.

Janzen, W. (2004b). Welcoming the returning "Kanadier" Mennonites from Mexico. *Journal of Mennonite Studies, 22*, 11–24.

Johnson, R. (1993). Editor's introduction. Pierre Bourdieu on art, literature and culture. In P. Bourdieu (Ed.), *The field of cultural production: Essays on art and literature* (1–25). New York: Columbia University Press.

Juhnke, J.C. (1989). *Vision, doctrine, war: Mennonite identity and organization in America, 1890–1930* (Vol. 3). Scottdale, PA: Herald Press.

Kasdorf, J. (1995). Work and hope: An Anabaptist Adam. *Mennonite Quarterly Review, 69*(2), 178–204.

Keil, R. (2002). "Common-sense" neoliberalism: Progressive Conservative urbanism in Toronto, Canada. *Antipode, 34*(3), 578–601. http://dx.doi.org/10.1111/1467-8330.00255

Kennedy, P. (2005). Social policy, social exclusion and commodity fetishism. *Capital and Class, 29*(1), 91–114. http://dx.doi.org/10.1177/030981680508500115

Kincheloe, J.L., & McLaren, P. (2011). Rethinking critical theory and qualitative research. In K. Hayes, S.R. Steinberg & K. Tobin (Eds), *Key works in critical pedagogy: Joe L. Kincheloe* (285–326). Rotterdam, Boston: Sense. http://dx.doi.org/10.1007/978-94-6091-397-6_23

Krahn, C., & Sawatzky, H.L. (1990). Old Colony Mennonites. Retrieved 24 July 2012 from http://www.gameo.org/index.php?title=Old%20Colony%20Mennonites.html

Kraybill, D.B. (2001). *The riddle of Amish culture* (rev. ed.). Baltimore: Johns Hopkins University Press.

Kulig, J.C., and Fan, J. (2013). Understanding death and dying among the Low-German-speaking Mennonites: Perspectives from a closed religious group. *Journal of Hospice and Palliative Nursing: JHPN: The Official Journal of the Hospice and Palliative Nurses Association, 15*(1), 52–9. http://dx.doi.org/10.1097/NJH.0b013e3182632e3b

Kulig, J.C., and McCaslin, C. (1998). Health care for Mexican Mennonites in Canada. *Canadian Nurse, 94*(6), 34–9.

Kulig, J.C., Babcock, R., Wall, M., & Hill, S. (2009). Being a woman: Perspectives of Low-German-speaking Mennonite women. *Health Care for Women International, 30*(4), 324–38. http://dx.doi.org/10.1080/07399330802694989

Kulig, J.C., Wall, M., Hill, S., and Babcock, R. (2008). Childbearing beliefs among Low-German-speaking Mennonite women. *International Nursing Review, 55*(4), 420–6. http://dx.doi.org/10.1111/j.1466-7657.2008.00645.x

Le Grand, J. (1998). Possible definition of social exclusion. Discussion paper. Centre for Analysis of Social Exclusion (CASE) meeting, London School of Economics.

Lederach, J.P. (2005). *The moral imagination: The art and soul of building peace.* Oxford, New York: Oxford University Press. http://dx.doi.org/10.1093/0195174542.001.0001

Lederach, J.P. (2014). *Reconcile: Conflict transformation for ordinary Christians.* Harrisonburg, VA: Herald Press.

Lederach, J.P., & Lederach, A.J. (2010). *When blood and bones cry out: Journeys through the soundscape of healing and reconciliation.* Oxford, New York: Oxford University Press.

Lenoir, R. (1974). *Les exclus: Un Français sur dix.* Paris: Seuil.

Levinas, E. (1969). *Totality and infinity: An essay on exteriority.* A. Lingis (Trans.). Pittsburgh, PA: Duquesne University Press.

Levinas, E. (2006). *Entre nous: Thinking-of-the-other*. M.B. Smith, & B. Harshav (trans.). London, New York: Continuum.

Levitt, P., & Glick Schiller, N. (2004). Conceptualizing simultaneity: A transnational social field perspective on society. *International Migration Review, 38*(3), 1002–39. http://dx.doi.org/10.1111/j.1747-7379.2004.tb00227.x

Levitt, P., & Jaworsky, B.N. (2007). Transnational migration studies: Past developments and future trends. *Annual Review of Sociology, 33*(1), 129–56. http://dx.doi.org/10.1146/annurev.soc.33.040406.131816

Lewis, J. (2007). Gender, ageing and the "new social settlement": The importance of developing a holistic approach to care policies. *Current Sociology, 55*(2), 271–86. http://dx.doi.org/10.1177/0011392107073314

Lewis, R., & Jakubec, L. (2004).: *The adequacy, suitability and affordability of Canadian housing*. 2001 Census housing series. Issue 3. Retrieved August 2004 from http://www.cmhc-schl.gc.ca/Research

Lightman, E. (2003). *Social policy in Canada*. Toronto: Oxford University Press.

Lightman, E. (2005, May 9). Personal communication.

Lightman, E., Herd, D., & Mitchell, A. (2006). Exploring the local implementation of Ontario Works. *Studies in Political Economy, 78*, 119–44.

Lightman, E., Herd, D., & Mitchell, A. (2008). Precarious lives: Work, health, hunger among current and former welfare recipients in Toronto. *Journal of Policy Practice, 7*(4), 242–59. http://dx.doi.org/10.1080/15588740802258508

Lightman, E., Mitchell, A., & Herd, D. (2005). Welfare to what? Workfare in Ontario. *International Social Security Review, 58*(4), 95–106. http://dx.doi.org/10.1111/j.1468-246X.2005.00227.x

Lightman, E., Mitchell, A., & Herd, D. (2010). Cycling on and off welfare in Canada. *Journal of Social Policy, 39*(4), 523–42. http://dx.doi.org/10.1017/S0047279410000279

Lightman, E., & Riches, G. (2000). From modest rights to commodification in Canada's welfare state. *European Journal of Social Work, 3*(2), 179–90. http://dx.doi.org/10.1080/714052823

Lightman, E., & Shor, R. (2002). Askanim: Informal helpers and cultural brokers as a bridge to secular helpers for the ultra-Orthodox Jewish communities of Israel and Canada. *Families in Society, 83*(3), 315–24. http://dx.doi.org/10.1606/1044-3894.26

Lightman, N., & Good Gingrich, L. (2012). The intersecting dynamics of social exclusion: Age, gender, race and immigrant status in Canada's labour market. *Canadian Ethnic Studies, 44*(3), 121–45. http://dx.doi.org/10.1353/ces.2013.0010

Loewen, R. (1993). *Family, church, and market: A Mennonite community in the Old and the New Worlds, 1850–1930*. Toronto: University of Toronto Press.

Loewen, R. (2004). Foreword. *Journal of Mennonite Studies, 22,* 7–9.

Loewen, R. (2007). *To the ends of the earth: Low German Mennonites and old order ways in the Americas.* Paper presented at the "Amish in America" Conference, Elizabethtown, PA.

Loewen, R. (2013a, 14 August). Boxing up the Old Colony Mennonites. *Canadian Mennonite, 17*(16). Retrieved from http://www. canadianmennonite.org/articles/boxing-old-colony-mennonites

Loewen, R. (2013b). *Village among nations: "Canadian" Mennonites in a transnational world, 1916–2006.* Toronto: University of Toronto Press.

Lovell, T. (2000). Thinking feminism with and against Bourdieu. In B. Fowler (Ed.), *Reading Bourdieu on society and culture* (27–48). Oxford: Blackwell.

Lugones, M. (2007). Heterosexualism and the colonial/modern gender system. *Hypatia, 22*(1), 186–209.

Lund, B. (1999). "The poor in a loomp is bad": New labour and neighbourhood renewal. *Political Quarterly, 70*(3), 280–4. http://dx.doi. org/10.1111/1467-923X.00230

MacKinnon, D. (2012). Reinventing the state: Neoliberalism, state transformation, and economic governance. In T.J. Barnes, J. Peck, & E. Sheppard (Eds), *The Wiley-Blackwell companion to economic geography* (344–57). Chichester, UK: Blackwell. http://dx.doi.org/10.1002/9781118384497.ch21

Macpherson, C.B. (1962). *The political theory of possessive individualism.* Oxford: Oxford University Press.

Madanipour, A., Cars, G., & Allen, J. (Eds). (2000). *Social exclusion in European cities: Processes, experiences, and responses.* London: The Stationery Office.

Mahrouse, G. (2010). "Reasonable accommodation" in Québec: The limits of participation and dialogue. *Race & Class, 52*(1), 85–96. http://dx.doi. org/10.1177/0306396810371768

Mannila, S., & Reuter, A. (2009). Social exclusion risks and their accumulation among Russian-speaking ethnically Finnish and Estonian immigrants to Finland. *Journal of Ethnic and Migration Studies, 35*(6), 939–56. http://dx.doi. org/10.1080/13691830902957718

Marmur, D. (2002). *Ethical reflections on social inclusion.* Perspectives on social inclusion series. Toronto: Laidlaw Foundation.

Martin, S. (2004). Reconceptualising social exclusion: A critical response to the neoliberal welfare reform agenda and the underclass thesis. *Australian Journal of Social Issues, 39*(1), 79–94.

Martin, S. (2010). Reconceptualising young people's engagement with work and welfare: Considering "choice." Conference paper presented at the XVII International Sociological Association World Congress of Sociology, Gothenburg, Sweden.

McKenzie, B., & Wharf, B. (2010). *Connecting policy to practice in the human services* (3rd ed.). Don Mills, ON: Oxford University Press.

McMenamin, M. (1989). *Employment, education and potential workforce participation of the poor in East Elgin county.* St Thomas, ON: St Thomas/Elgin Unemployed Help Centre.

Mennonite Central Committee (MCC). (2007). Lost citizenship concerns continue to surface. MCC Canada Release, Ottawa, ON.

Mikler, J. 2009. *Greening the car industry: Varieties of capitalism and climate change.* Cheltenham, UK, and Northampton, MA: Edward Elgar.

Mills, M.B. (2003). Gender and inequality in the global labour force. *Annual Review of Anthropology, 32*(1), 41–62. http://dx.doi.org/10.1146/annurev.anthro.32.061002.093107

Mitchell, A., Lightman, E., & Herd, D. (2007). "Work-first" and immigrants in Toronto. *Social Policy and Society, 6*(3), 293–307. http://dx.doi.org/10.1017/S1474746407003636

Mitrovica, A., & Bourette, S. (2004, April). The wages of sin. *Saturday Night,* 28–36.

Montero, M. (2009). Methods for liberation: Critical consciousness in action. In M. Montero & C.C. Sonn (Eds), *Psychology of liberation: Theory and applications* (73–91). New York: Springer. http://dx.doi.org/10.1007/978-0-387-85784-8_4

Moriña Diez, A. (2010). School memories of young people with disabilities: An analysis of barriers and aids to inclusion. *Disability & Society, 25*(2), 163–75. http://dx.doi.org/10.1080/09687590903534346

Morissette, R., and Picot, G. (2005). *Low-paid work and economically vulnerable families over the last two decades.* Ottawa: Statistics Canada.

Morissette, R., & Sultan, R. (2013). *Twenty years in the careers of immigrant and native-born workers.* Ottawa: Statistics Canada.

Mullaly, B. (2007). *The new structural social work* (3rd ed.). Don Mills, ON: Oxford University Press.

Munck, R. (2005). *Globalization and social exclusion: A transformationalist perspective.* Bloomfield, CT: Kumarian Press.

Murphy, B.K. (1999). *Transforming ourselves, transforming the world: An open conspiracy for social change.* London: Zed Books.

Nevile, A. (2007). Amartya K. Sen and social exclusion. *Development in Practice, 17*(2), 249–55. http://dx.doi.org/10.1080/09614520701197200

Noël, A. (2002). *A law against poverty: Quebec's new approach to combating poverty and social exclusion.* Ottawa: Canadian Policy Research Networks.

OECD (Organisation for Economic Co-operation and Development). (1999). *The battle against exclusion: Social assistance in Canada and Switzerland.* Vol. 3. Paris: OECD.

OECD. (2005). Policy brief: Helping workers to navigate in "globalised" labour markets. Paris: OECD. Available online at http://www.oecd.org/dataoecd/44/19/35044139.pdf

OECD. (2008). *Growing unequal? Income distribution and poverty in OECD countries*. Paris: OECD.

OECD. (2014). *Focus on top incomes and taxation in OECD countries: Was the crisis a game changer?* Paris: OECD.

Offe, C. (1985). New social movements: Challenging the boundaries of institutional politics. *Social Research, 52*(4), 817–68.

Parsons, J. (1997). The interface of structure and process in identity: Pierre Bourdieu's contribution. In P. Sachdev (Ed.), *Social work discussion papers: Trends in social work education* (47–59). St John's, NL: Memorial University of Newfoundland, School of Social Work.

Pavis, S., Hubbard, G., & Platt, S. (2001). Young people in rural areas: Socially excluded or not? *Work, Employment and Society, 15*(2), 291–309. http://dx.doi.org/10.1177/09500170122118968

Peck, J. (1999). New labourers? Making a New Deal for the 'workless class'. *Environment and Planning. C, Government & Policy, 17*(3), 345–72. http://dx.doi.org/10.1068/c170345

Peck, J. (2001). *Workfare states*. New York: Guilford Press.

Peck, J., & Tickell, A. (2002). Neoliberalizing space. *Antipode, 34*(3), 380–404. http://dx.doi.org/10.1111/1467-8330.00247

Pekaruk, A. (2004). *Ontario Works payments and review of the controls in the service delivery model technology: Audit report*. Hamilton, ON: City Manager's Office.

Peters, J. (1985). The Waisenamt: A history of Mennonite inheritance custom. MS #0919673953. Mennonite Village Museum, Steinbach, MB.

Peters, J. (1988). Mennonites in Mexico and Paraguay: A comparative analysis of the colony social system. *Journal of Mennonite Studies, 6*, 198–214.

Picot, G., & Hou, F. (2015). Immigration, low income and income inequality in Canada: What's new in the 2000s. Working Paper No. 148. Canadian Labour Market and Skills Researcher Network. January.

Picot, G., & Sweetman, A. (2012). *Making it in Canada: Immigration outcomes and policies*. IRPP Study. Vol. 29. 1–48. Montreal: Institute for Research on Public Policy.

Pisati, M., Whelan, C.T., Lucchini, M., & Maître, B. (2010). Mapping patterns of multiple deprivation using self-organising maps: An application to EU-SILC data for Ireland. *Social Science Research, 39*(3), 405–18. http://dx.doi.org/10.1016/j.ssresearch.2009.11.004

Pleace, N. (1998). Single homelessness as social exclusion: The unique and the extreme. *Social Policy and Administration, 32*(1), 46–59. http://dx.doi.org/10.1111/1467-9515.00085

Popp, S., & Schels, B. (2008). "Do you feel excluded?" The subjective experience of young state benefit recipients in Germany. *Journal of Youth Studies, 11*(2), 165–91. http://dx.doi.org/10.1080/13676260701851111

Price, B.E. (2007). The threat of privatization: The impetus behind government performance. *International Journal of Public Administration, 30*(11), 1141–55. http://dx.doi.org/10.1080/01900690701225325

Prince, M.J. (2001). How social is social policy? Fiscal and market discourse in North American welfare states. *Social Policy and Administration, 35*(1), 2–13. http://dx.doi.org/10.1111/1467-9515.00216

Quiring, D.M. (2003). *The Mennonite Old Colony vision: Under siege in Mexico and the Canadian connection.* Steinbach, MB: Crossway.

Quiring, D.M. (2004). Intervention and resistance: Two Mennonite visions conflict in Mexico. *Journal of Mennonite Studies, 22,* 83–101.

Raphael, D. (2010). *About Canada: Health and illness.* Halifax, NS: Fernwood.

Reay, D., & Lucey, H. (2004). Stigmatised choices: Social class, social exclusion and secondary school markets in the inner city. *Pedagogy, Culture & Society, 12*(1), 35–51. http://dx.doi.org/10.1080/14681360400200188

Redekop, C.W. (1969). *The Old Colony Mennonites: Dilemmas of ethnic minority life.* Baltimore: Johns Hopkins University Press.

Reimer, B. (2004). Social exclusion in a comparative context. *Sociologia Ruralis, 44*(1), 76–94. http://dx.doi.org/10.1111/j.1467-9523.2004.00263.x

Reitz, J.G., Banerjee, R., Phan, M., & Thompson, J. (2009). Race, religion, and the social integration of new immigrant minorities in Canada. *International Migration Review, 43*(4), 695–726. http://dx.doi.org/10.1111/j.1747-7379.2009.00782.x

Reutter, L.I., Stewart, M.J., Veenstra, G., Love, R., Raphael, D., & Makwarimba, E. (2009). "Who do they think we are, anyway?" Perceptions of and responses to poverty stigma. *Qualitative Health Research, 19*(3), 297–311. http://dx.doi.org/10.1177/1049732308330246

Richardson, L., & Le Grand, J. (2002). *Outsider and insider expertise: The response of residents of deprived neighbourhoods to an academic definition of social exclusion.* London: Centre for Analysis of Social Exclusion, London School of Economics.

Riches, G. (2001, 17–20 June). The human right to food: Re-inventing social welfare. Paper presented at the Xth Biennial Conference: Canadian Social Welfare Policy, Calgary, AB.

Richmond, T., and Saloojee, A. (Eds). (2005). *Social inclusion: Canadian perspectives.* Halifax, NS: Fernwood.

Rodgers, G. (1995). What is special about a "social exclusion" approach? In G. Rodgers, C. Gore, & J.B. Figueiredo (Eds), *Social exclusion: Rhetoric, reality, responses* (43–55). Geneva: International Institute for Labour Studies, ILO.

Room, G. (1995). Poverty and social exclusion: The new European agenda for policy and research. In G. Room (Ed.), *Beyond the threshold: The measurement and analysis of social exclusion* (1–9). Bristol: Policy Press.

Rorty, R. (1988). Science as solidarity. In J.S. Nelson, A. Megill, & D.N. McCloskey (Eds), *The rhetoric of the human sciences* (38–52). Madison: University of Wisconsin Press.

Rose, N. (1999). *Powers of freedom: Reframing political thought.* Cambridge: Cambridge University Press. http://dx.doi.org/10.1017/CBO9780511488856

Rosenberg, M., & Torres, N. (2012, 21 March). Stubborn drought expected to tax Mexico for years. *Reuters.* Retrieved from http://www.reuters.com/article/2012/03/21/us-mexico-drought-idUSBRE82K1E520120321

Saloojee, A. (2003). *Social inclusion, anti-racism and democratic citizenship.* Perspectives on social inclusion series. Toronto: Laidlaw Foundation.

Sassen, S. (1998). *Globalization and its discontents: Essays on the new mobility of people and money.* New York: New Press.

Saunders, R. (2005). *Does a rising tide lift all boats? Low paid workers in Canada.* Ottawa: Canadian Policy Research Networks.

Sawatzky, H.L. (1971). *They sought a country: Mennonite colonization in Mexico.* Los Angeles: University of California Press.

Schmidt, K.D., Zimmerman Umble, D., & Reschly, S.D. (2002). Introduction: Insiders and outsiders. In K.D. Schmidt, D. Zimmerman Umble, & S.D. Reschly (Eds), *Strangers at home: Amish and Mennonite women in history* (1–20). Baltimore: Johns Hopkins University Press.

Schneider, F., & Enste, D.H. (2003). *The shadow economy: An international survey.* Cambridge: Cambridge University Press. http://dx.doi.org/10.1017/CBO9780511493591

Scott, E.K., Edin, K., London, A.S., & Kissane, R.J. (2004). Unstable work, unstable income: Implications for family well-being in the era of time-limited welfare. *Journal of Poverty, 8*(1), 61–88. http://dx.doi.org/10.1300/J134v08n01_04

Sen, A. (2000a, 20 July). East and west: The reach of reason. *New York Review of Books, 47*(12), 33–8.

Sen, A. (2000b). *Social exclusion: Concept, application, and scrutiny.* Manila: Asian Development Bank.

Shamir, R. (2008). The age of responsibilization: On market-embedded morality. *Economy and Society, 37*(1), 1–19. http://dx.doi.org/10.1080/03085140701760833

Shields, J., Kelly, P., Park, S., Prier, N., & Fang, T. (2012). Profiling immigrant poverty in Canada: A 2006 Census Statistical portrait. *Canadian Review of Social Policy/Revue canadienne de politique sociale*, (65–6), 92–111.

Shola Orloff, A. (2002). Explaining US welfare reform: Power, gender, race and the US policy legacy. *Critical Social Policy, 22*(1), 96–118. http://dx.doi.org/10.1177/02610183020220010801

Shucksmith, M., & Chapman, P. (1998). Rural development and social exclusion. *Sociologia Ruralis, 38*(2), 225–42. http://dx.doi.org/10.1111/1467-9523.00073

Shucksmith, M., Shucksmith, J., & Watt, J. (2006). Rurality and social inclusion: A case of preschool education. *Social Policy and Administration, 40*(6), 678–91. http://dx.doi.org/10.1111/j.1467-9515.2006.00526.x

Sidhu, N. (2013). *Accessing community programs and services for non-status immigrants in Toronto: Organizational challenges and responses.* Toronto: Social Planning Toronto. http://www.socialplanningtoronto.org/wp-content/uploads/2013/08/Accessing-Community-Programs-and-Services-for-Non-status-Immigrants-in-Toronto-Organizational-Challenges-and-Responses.pdf

Silver, H. (1994). Social exclusion and social solidarity: Three paradigms. *International Labour Review, 133*(5–6), 531–78.

Sim, D. (2000). *A survey of the opinions of Aylmer residents regarding the services provided by the Aylmer police.* London, ON: Aylmer Police Board.

Simon, R.I., & Eppert, C. (1997). Remembering obligation: Pedagogy and the witnessing of testimony of historical trauma. *Canadian Journal of Education, 22*(2), 175–91. http://dx.doi.org/10.2307/1585906

Simon, R.I., Rosenberg, S., & Eppert, C. (2000). Introduction. Between hope and despair: The pedagogical encounter of historical remembrance. In I. Simon Roger, S. Rosenberg, & C. Eppert (Eds), *Between hope and despair: Pedagogy and the remembrance of historical trauma* (1–25). New York: Rowman & Littlefield.

Smith, C.H. (1957). *The story of the Mennonites.* Newton, KS: Mennonite Publication Office.

Smith, D.E. (1999). *Writing the social: Critique, theory, and investigations.* Toronto: University of Toronto Press.

Smith, E. (2005). Faculty of Social Work tackles cyberabuse. 30 March. Retrieved 7 April 2005 from http://www.news.utoronto.ca/bin6/050330-1169.asp

Social Exclusion Unit. (2001). Preventing social exclusion: Report by the Social Exclusion Unit, March. Retrieved from http://www.cabinet-office.gov.uk/seu/index.htm

Social Exclusion Unit. (2006). *Reaching out: An action plan on social exclusion.* London: Social Exclusion Unit.

Standing, G. (2011). *The precariat: The new dangerous class*. London and New York: Bloomsbury Academic.

Stewart, M.J., Reutter, L.I., Makwarimba, E., Veenstra, G., Love, R., & Raphael, D. (2008). Left out: Perspectives on social exclusion and inclusion across income groups. *Health Sociology Review, 17*(1), 78–94. http://dx.doi.org/10.5172/hesr.451.17.1.78

Stiglitz, J.E. (2009). Moving beyond market fundamentalism to a more balanced economy. *Annals of Public and Cooperative Economics, 80*(3), 345–60. http://dx.doi.org/10.1111/j.1467-8292.2009.00389.x

Stiglitz, J.E. (2013). *The price of inequality: How today's divided society endangers our future*. New York: W.W. Norton.

Stiglitz, J.E., Sen, A., & Fitoussi, J.-P. (2009). *Report by the Commission on the Measurement of Economic Performance and Social Progress*. Paris: Commission on the Measurement of Economic Performance and Social Progress (CMEPSP).

Swift, K.J., & Callahan, M. (2009). *At risk: Social justice in child welfare and other human services*. Toronto: University of Toronto Press.

Thiessen, J. (2003). *Mennonite Low German dictionary: Mennonitsch-Plattdeutsches Wörterbuch*. Madison, WI: Max Kade Institute for German-American Studies.

Thomas, R.R., & Woodruff, M.I. (1999). *Building a house for diversity: How a fable about a giraffe and an elephant offers new strategies for today's workforce*. New York: R. Thomas & Associates/American Management Association.

Thompson, E.P. (1967). Time, work-discipline, and industrial capitalism. *Past & Present, 38*(1), 56–97. http://dx.doi.org/10.1093/past/38.1.56

Till, M. (2005). Assessing the housing dimension of social inclusion in six European countries. *Innovation: The European Journal of Social Science Research, 18*(2), 153–81.

Touzin, T., & Thompson, G. (1993). *Research and analysis of the Low German speaking Mennonites from Latin America*. Frogmore, ON: Mennonite Help Centre.

Towell, L. (1999). The road to bountiful. *Canadian Geographic: Through the lens photography annual*, 44–57.

Towell, L. (2000). *The Mennonites*. London: Phaidon.

Treaster, C., Hawley, S.R., Paschal, A.M., Molgaard, C.A., & St Romain, T. (2006). Addressing health disparities in highly specialized minority populations: Case study of Mexican Mennonite farmworkers. *Journal of Community Health, 31*(2), 113–22. http://dx.doi.org/10.1007/s10900-005-9002-4

Tsuda, T. (2012). Whatever happened to simultaneity? Transnational migration theory and dual engagement in sending and receiving countries. *Journal of Ethnic and Migration Studies, 38*(4), 631–49. http://dx.doi.org/10.10 80/1369183X.2012.659126

Tsui, M., & Cheung, F.C.H. (2004). Gone with the wind: The impacts of managerialism on human services. *British Journal of Social Work, 34*(3), 437–42. http://dx.doi.org/10.1093/bjsw/bch046

Turner, Kira. 2014. "Living on the edge: Old Colony Mennonites and digital technology usage." *Journal of Amish and Plain Anabaptist Studies, 2*(2): 165–85.

UNDESA (United Nations Department of Economic and Social Affairs) – Population Division. (2015). *World population prospects: The 2015 revision, key findings and advance tables.* New York: United Nations.

UNDESA (United Nations Department of Economic and Social Affairs). (2016). *International migration report 2015: Highlights.* New York: United Nations.

UNDP (United Nations Development Programme). (2010). Human development report 2010. *The real wealth of nations: Pathways to human development (20th anniversary ed.).* New York: Palgrave Macmillan.

Unger, M. (1991). Mexican Mennonites in Ontario: A cultural study. MSW thesis, Wilfrid Laurier University.

United Nations World Summit for Social Development. (1995). *The Copenhagen Declaration and programme of action.* Vol. 133. New York: United Nations Department of Public Information.

Uppal, S., & LaRochelle-Côté, S. (2015). *Changes in wealth across the income distribution, 1999 to 2012: Insights on Canadian society.* Ottawa: Statistics Canada.

Urry, J. (1999). Of borders and boundaries: Reflections on Mennonite unity and separation in the modern world. *Mennonite Quarterly Review, 73*(3), 503–24.

Urry, J. (2007). *None but saints: The transformation of Mennonite life in Russia, 1789–1889* (2nd ed.). Kitchener, ON: Pandora Press.

Vaandering, D. (2010). The significance of critical theory for restorative justice in education. *Review of Education, Pedagogy & Cultural Studies, 32*(2), 145–76. http://dx.doi.org/10.1080/10714411003799165

Vaandering, D. (2014). Implementing restorative justice practice in schools: What pedagogy reveals. *Journal of Peace Education, 11*(1), 64–80. http://dx.doi.org/10.1080/17400201.2013.794335

van Reenen, J. (2001). The new economy: Reality and policy. *Fiscal Studies, 22*(3), 307–36. http://dx.doi.org/10.1111/j.1475-5890.2001.tb00044.x

Veit-Wilson, J. (1998). *Setting adequacy standards: How governments define minimum incomes*. Bristol, UK: Policy Press.

Vosko, L.F. (2002). Mandatory "marriage" or obligatory waged work: Social assistance and single mothers in Wisconsin and Ontario. In S. Bashevkin (Ed.), *Women's work is never done: Comparative studies in care-giving, employment, and social policy reform* (165–99). New York, London: Routledge.

Vosko, L.F. (2010). *Managing the margins: Gender, citizenship, and the international regulation of precarious employment*. Oxford, New York: Oxford University Press.

Vosko, L.F. (Ed.). (2006). *Precarious employment: Understanding labour market insecurity in Canada*. Montreal: McGill-Queen's University Press.

Vosko, L.F., Preston, V., & Latham, R. (Eds). (2014). *Liberating temporariness? Migration, work, and citizenship in an age of insecurity*. Montreal: McGill-Queen's University Press.

Wacquant, L. (1987). Symbolic violence and the making of the French agriculturalist: An enquiry into Pierre Bourdieu's sociology. *Australian and New Zealand Journal of Sociology, 23*(1), 65–88. http://dx.doi.org/10.1177/144078338702300105

Wacquant, L. (1996). Reading Bourdieu's "capital." *International Journal of Contemporary Sociology, 33*(2), 151–70.

Wacquant, L. (1998a). Negative social capital: State breakdown and social destitution in America's urban core. *Netherlands Journal of Housing and Environmental Research, 13*(1), 25–40. http://dx.doi.org/10.1007/BF02496932

Wacquant, L. (1998b). Pierre Bourdieu. In R. Stones (Ed.), *Key sociological thinkers* (215–29). New York: New York University Press.

Wacquant, L. (2000). Logics of urban polarization: The view from below. In R. Crompton, F. Devine, M. Savage, & J. Scott (Eds), *Renewing class analysis* (107–19). Oxford: Blackwell.

Wacquant, L. (2001). The penalisation of poverty and the rise of neo-liberalism. *European Journal on Criminal Policy and Research, 9*(4), 401–12. http://dx.doi.org/10.1023/A:1013147404519

Wacquant, L. (2004). Following Pierre Bourdieu into the field. *Ethnography, 5*(4), 387–414. http://dx.doi.org/10.1177/1466138104052259

Wacquant, L. (2007). Pierre Bourdieu. In R. Stones (Ed.), *Key sociological thinkers* (2nd ed.). (Vol. 13, 261–77). New York: Palgrave Macmillan.

Wacquant, L. (2009). *Punishing the poor: The neoliberal government of social insecurity*. Durham, NC, London: Duke University Press. http://dx.doi.org/10.1215/9780822392255

Walcott, R. (2014). In this moment: Thoughts on decoloniality, social justice and radical collectivities. Paper presented at the The International Day for the Elimination of Racial Discrimination Annual Lecture, School of Social Work, York University, Toronto.

Wall, S. (2005). Perfectionism, public reason, and religious accommodation. *Social Theory and Practice, 31*(2), 281–304. http://dx.doi.org/10.5840/soctheorpract200531213

Whelan, C.T., & Maître, B. (2008). Social class variation in risk: A comparative analysis of the dynamics of economic vulnerability. *British Journal of Sociology, 59*(4), 637–59. http://dx.doi.org/10.1111/j.1468-4446.2008.00213.x

Wiebe, G. (1981). *Causes and history of the emigration of the Mennonites from Russia to America*. H. Janzen (trans.). Winnipeg: Manitoba Mennonite Historical Society.

Wilson, B., Lightman, E., & Mitchell, A. (2009). *Sick and tired: The compromised health of social assistance recipients and the working poor in Ontario*. Toronto: Community Social Planning Council of Toronto; Wellesley Institute; SANE.

Winslade, J., & Monk, G. (2008). *Practicing narrative mediation: Loosening the grip of conflict*. San Francisco: Jossey-Bass.

Wolff, J. (2005). Ambivalent consequences of social exclusion for real-existing democracy in Latin America: The example of the Argentine crisis. *Journal of International Relations and Development, 8*(1), 58–87. http://dx.doi.org/10.1057/palgrave.jird.1800045

Yalnizyan, A. (2000). *Canada's great divide: The politics of the growing gap between rich and poor in the 1990s*. Toronto: Centre for Social Justice.

Yalnizyan, A. (2013). *Study of income inequality in Canada: What can be done*. Presentation to the House of Commons Standing Committee on Finance. Toronto: Canadian Centre for Policy Alternatives.

Yanes, P. (2008). News from the South: Perspectives on basic income in Mexico and Latin America. Paper presented at the Basic Income Earth Network Congress, Dublin, Ireland.

Zehr, H. (2002). *The little book of restorative justice*. Intercourse, PA: Good Books.

Zehr, H. (2005). *Changing lenses: A new focus for crime and justice* (3rd ed.). Scottdale, PA: Herald Press.

Zehr, H. (2014). *The little book of restorative justice: Revised and updated*. New York: Good Books.

Zhao, J., Xue, L., & Gilkinson, T. (2010). *Health status and social capital of recent immigrants in Canada: Evidence from the Longitudinal Survey of Immigrants to Canada*. Ottawa: Citizenship and Immigration Canada. Retrieved from http://publications.gc.ca/site/archivee-archived.html?url=http://publications.gc.ca/collections/collection_2015/cic/Ci4-139-2010-eng.pdf

Index

www.ingramcontent.com/pod-product-compliance
Lightning Source LLC
Chambersburg PA
CBHW021850020426
42334CB00013B/267